The New Great Game

Oil and Gas Politics in Central Eurasia

Brigadier (retd)
Dr. Muhammad Aslam Khan Niazi (Makni)
Islamabad, Pakistan

Raider Publishing International

New York   London   Swansea

Second Printing

ISBN: 1-934360-56-2

Published By Raider Publishing International

www.RaiderPublishing.com

New York   London   Swansea

Printed in the United States of America and the United Kingdom
By Lightning Source Ltd.

Dedicated...

To the efforts of noble people and organizations striving for peace and prosperity of the mankind.

Table of Contents

The New Great Game

Oil and Gas Politics in Central Eurasia

*Brigadier (retd)
Dr. Muhammad Aslam Khan Niazi (Makni)
Islamabad, Pakistan*

INTRODUCTION

Oil and Gas Politics in Central Eurasia, given an acronym, the 'New Great Game' by eminent scholars in this field, had its roots manifested even in the early 20th Century. The scenario of the mega conflict of World War I is an example when the time clock ticked at July 1917. US Ambassador in London initiated a desperate telegram to Washington, projecting dwindling British stamina to wage the war, saying, "The Germans are succeeding. They have already sunk so many fuel oil ships that this country may very soon be in a perilous condition; even the Great Fleet may not have enough fuel. It is a very grave danger."[1] Such was the impact of a commodity called 'oil', emerging in the backdrop of international conflicts that denial of which could simply bring the war machinery of any power to a grinding halt.

In October 1917, Britain's Secretary of State for Colonies, Mr. Walter Long, warned the House of Commons, "You may have men, ammunition and money, but if you do not have oil, all of your other advantages would be of comparatively little value."[2] Oil shortages were so horrific for Britain that they soon banned pleasure driving. The oil crunch was no less significant in USA also. 'Gasoline-less Sundays' were introduced there. No one except doctors, police and emergency vehicles would escape the restriction; not even President of United States who would walk to the church. Oil, beyond doubt became the linchpin commodity on which the edifice of world powers rested. Capacity of power(s) to deny oil to other power(s) would sound her/ their death knell; a reality of course to reckon now.

9

By October 1918, the German Army had exhausted its reserves and petroleum crisis seemed inevitable. Berlin estimated that its war (oil) stamina would only stretch from six to eight months with limited defensive operations. German High Command estimates were grossly off the mark. Germany surrendered within a month on 11 November 1918, with empty tanks of its war machines. Senator Berenger of France had to glorify the role of oil ten days later, admitting that oil, "the blood of the earth was the blood of victory". Also maintaining that, "oil would be the blood of peace."[3] Farmers and industrialists including civil population shall call for more oil, more oil, and even more oil. Lord Curzon in the same period had said that, "Allied cause had floated to victory upon a wave of oil."[4]

A year later, in 1919 Woodrow Wilson summed up the criticality of possession of oil, though modestly, by saying, "Is there any man, let me say any child that does not know that seed of war in the modern world is industrial and commercial rivalry."[5] Out of the assertion quoted by the Guardian recently, even non-professionals can establish the oil equation conveniently because industry hinges on energy and fossil fuel is the most elaborate source of energy. Any one denied access to oil by any rival power would mean dragging her down from the pinnacle of glory. As a sequel to such struggle, humanity is witnessing a perpetual strife in the international arena, particularly by the powers that be since the beginning of 20th Century, to sustain their might. The demonstrated theme, while pursuing geo-political and geo-strategic aims, might have been rather simplistic but the wizards and political pundits pick up the undercurrents readily. Larger intensity of such undercurrents, as maintained by majority of scholars, passes through hydrocarbon reserves. The historians have recorded mode and severity of oil and gas politics very carefully. There is almost ambiguity-free chronology of events available to the researchers in the context of energy. However, two events have generated the oil activity to a scale, which finds no precedence hitherto fore. First: is the political change in the former USSR and second; the

10

knowledge about impending depletion of known reserves of fossil fuel from the planet on which flourishes the might of some leading powers. The political change in Central Eurasia (Central Asia and Caucasus Region) enabled the West to rush, explore and bid for the host countries' reserves to augment their own or others, already accessible to them across the globe. At the same time, ticking clock of depletion of oil and gas has transformed this commodity-seeking element, as of necessity, to frantic urgency. As a result stir in the international relations, particularly in the domain of diplomacy and geopolitics, has emerged rather clear. Central Eurasia with vast hydrocarbon resources has obviously not escaped the attention of regional as well as extra-regional powers, each maintaining different perception and an exclusive brand of strategies to promote respective national interests. Such an endeavor by the actors in Central Eurasia now bears the label of the 'New Great Game', which emerges through the pattern of conduct of geopolitics, diplomacy and at times, intrusion in the political climate of target states discreetly.

In order to keep a sharpened focus on the purposeful aspect of the 'New Great Game', a qualifying reference to 'oil and gas politics in Central Eurasia' has enabled to manage an enormous stretch of the scope. The chemistry of conflicts, options of conflict resolutions and history of alliances coupled with state exterior maneuvers and actors' military capabilities stand sidelined; brief and tangential references once a while not withstanding. It aims at focusing at a single, well defined 'problem' i.e. establishing the onset of oil and gas politics in Central Eurasia, the 'New Great Game', as remarked by some reputed scholars like Lutz Kleveman, Paul Roberts, George Monbiot and a score of others whose sources have been quoted in the succeeding text. As an imperative thus, following specific questions have been explored:

- What is the historical perspective of Central Eurasia, its geography and significance?
- What are the oil and gas statistics of the region, of the Caspian littorals in particular and other leading

11

economies that cannot escape but to be the manipulating powers in the arena?

- What is the ensuing hydrocarbon and pipeline politics that originates on the logic of combined view of the previous two queries?
- How do the regional and extra regional powers come to join the 'game' to give it geo-strategic dimensions?
- What is the magnitude of regional and extra-regional actors' involvement individually to achieve respective ends by applying vast means?
- What deductions, conclusions or findings become available after above questions are answered? In other words, inferring causation and generalizing the findings stage is reached to conclude the substance.
- When one knows so much after above coverage that marks achieving of the 'book' objectives, logically recommend a possible but brief way-out strategy to cool down the cauldron.

Chapter One opens up with a poetic note of Hsein Pi, indicating Central Eurasian culture that bears deep print of the geography as well as climate and its environment. 'Yurt' is the focal point that symbolizes its civilization. While there had been fine overlap among the cultures of its two main components according to the perception about its broad parameters, there are nonetheless some areas of demarcation too. It is therefore prudent to deal with them separately as Central Asia and Caspian-Caucasus Region. Geography shapes the destinies of the countries and their cultures. Hence, brief coverage was imperative to comprehend Central Eurasian significance through the prism of history that remains always the trustworthy guide. Along with the geographic narratives of these countries, when hydrocarbon factor is played, stratification emerges even clearer among them. Some geopolitical aspects have also been introduced to build upon them the arguments for subsequent clarity of thought process. The history makes an interesting basis to analyze the present behavior of the states with reasonable accuracy to forecast their future. In case of Central Eurasia, there is a unique peculiarity also when the preceding statement, hypothetically meets the merit but in reality, it does not. It is so because Central Eurasia is no longer a 'no go' area. When access possibility to its hinterlands improved on withdrawal of the Soviets, the element of intrigues and introspection became corollary to this development. Consequently, a cobweb-like scenario has emerged, thus making the game not only intense but complicated as well.

Chapter Two deals with the statistics of oil and gas reserves of Central Eurasia. Thanks to some credible sources, which keep record of oil and gas statistics at global level. Central Eurasia no doubt makes one of the important segments in the history as well as in the modern oil scenario. J D Henry was doing brilliant job when he quoted, "in 1829 there were eighty two petroleum pits (in Baku)."[6] The oil gushers had not been found in 1829 and hence simple statistics. The advancement of geological survey capabilities has enabled the man to probe any corner of the planet and embark on exploration probabilities through satellite imagery. It has resulted in maintaining elaborate statistics of oil. In fact, the field has become so vast and diverse that there are considerable differences in the oil and gas statistics among two or more agencies about the same source and site. However, wider generalization and comparative scrutiny helps in reaching the authentic figures. The chapter of statistics, supported by oil and gas tables rather lavishly within the main text, has been given early precedence to cover so that whichever country or actor is discussed in any chapter with reference to their hydrocarbon health, one knows what she holds in her reserves, what it needs to consume locally and what are its export capabilities or import limitations. It thus becomes obvious that a developed country with massive outlay of industry becomes extremely vulnerable if her fate hinges on the smooth inflow of oil and gas from distant and not always friendly locations. It would also indicate why a particular country is compelled to orient her geo-political and diplomatic approaches in a peculiar way, precisely because of the energy restraints. Conversely, backward but oil and gas rich countries sitting on vast hydrocarbon reserves would appear a subject of global blackmail or indigenous ineptitude if they failed to transform the destiny of their societies for the good by reaping Caspian "black gold" bonanza to the tune of US $ 4-6 trillions.

Chapter Three gives elaborate coverage of hydrocarbon politics and pipeline wrangling, which set forth in the wake of massive political change brought about in 1991 in Central Eurasia on Russian withdrawal to its present boundaries of Russian Federation. Based on previous two chapters, the debate relevant to the title of the book starts taking shape from this chapter onward. Erstwhile Central Eurasian states being the Soviets subjects had their door closed but the region saw rush of oil companies from 1991 onwards, which they initially claimed to be the possible substitute of Middle East. Chevron Oil Company (US), BG (British Gas), Eni (Italy) and Lukoil (Russia) were some of the leading companies to bring in massive investment. The region that contains oil and gas mainly comprises the Caspian littorals territories. Caspian Sea Region, a landlocked stretch of territories, had inadequate communication infrastructure to reach drilling sites with ease to explore and extract it using heavy plants. Even this impediment could be handled perhaps but what turned out to be beyond the prowess of investing oil companies was the daunting task of transporting its huge quantities to commercially viable outlets. Pipelines, the traditional means to carry oil cheaply were either non-existent or were deficient in capacity and security considerations like the ones available in the former Soviet era from Azerbaijan, Turkmenistan and Kazakhstan. Major hurdles in transportation emerged when plans to undertake new pipelines construction over vast stretches became contingent upon the political decisions of the regional and extra-regional actors. It led to severe pipeline wrangling.

14

Host states i.e. Azerbaijan, Kazakhstan, and Turkmenistan were subject to multi directional pull from the North (Russia), East (China), South (Iran) and the West, Turkey representing US for Western interests. Of the four directional contenders, 'North', 'West', and very recently, 'East' have been more assertive. The whole episode has not only shaped the intensity of hydrocarbon politics but also the belief that pipeline wrangling would end up nowhere. Pepe Escobar was quick to brand these struggles as pipe dreams, raising the question, "Where is the realm these days of former US security advisor Brent Scowcroft, former White House chief of staff John Sununu and former defense secretary and current invisible man Dick Cheney? They are happily dreaming of, and working for, the establishing of Pipelinistan."[7] However, the opening of Baku-Tbilisi-Ceyhan pipeline, with capacity to deliver a million barrels a day direct to the Mediterranean outlet, has raised hopes that pipe dreams may now be materializing. Yet the complexity of Central Eurasian geo-politics would persist if not aggravate soon as a full-fledged conflict and thus Central Eurasian woes will linger on.

Chapter Four deals with some plausible arguments, how a seemingly simple hydrocarbon and pipeline competition transforms itself to a game of greater dimension, magnitude and order, called, the 'New Great Game'. The emerging geo-strategic dimensions haunt some scholars to the extent that oil adventure in the Middle East and Caspian Region are leading to the talk of World War III. S. Bakhtiari is of the opinion in a chilling article that after 9/11 episode, the new oil age and World War III have already started. Dr. W.H Zeigler has comments to make on Bakhtiari's remarks as an extension of oil thoughts, "The eventual military dominance of production capabilities in the Middle East and the Caspian Area by powerful consumer nation, perhaps with the support of local elites, is a possibility that underlines Bakhtiari's contention."[8] Disregard to the severity of these comments, consensus is emerging fast among scholars that mighty struggle is underway with the hidden agenda of placing these oil resources into 'safe hands' which may be US, Russia, Europe, Private Companies or some friendly Governments in the emerging coalition. The aim of whole exercise would be to control reserves for securing diminishing production until such time hydrocarbon intensive economies are prepared to face inevitable oil and gas shortages. Once one is clear on such possibilities, it becomes worthwhile to focus on the actors' role, their guise and game to reinforce the strategic dimensions of the New Great Game.

Chapter Five, coverage about the actors' role in Central Eurasian game, makes it rather obvious where the contestants are slipping on moral grounds and where they are indulging in double speak. It also makes it abundantly manifest that who suspects whom and the extent of obtaining mistrust among them. In the context of Central Eurasian reserves, one sees blood in the actors' eyes as well as some blood on their sleeves because ongoing instability in Caucasus and total neglect to push Central Asia to workable democratic governments, connoting some semblance of the Western democracy are the ample proof of complicity of the game players in the arena. No doubt, Central Eurasia has to bear the crunch of these developments. The game actors loathe to be tagged with much talked about, the New Great Game. In fact, some scholars have put forth arguments, albeit unsuccessfully, that quest for oil and gas in Central Eurasia is merely an exploratory venture, similar to those of 19th Century and early 20th Century. Therefore, it makes obligatory for an analyst to allow them a margin of doubt for their sake and approach the subject cautiously through scrutiny of behavior of the states and pursued diplomacy, which is an effective instrument as well as a tool of any foreign policy during the time when peace prevails. This chapter also aims to focus on state maneuvers while carrying out assessment of, say, US or Russia's moves of geo-strategic dimensions to seek respective interests and priorities in the region. Does a sort of legitimacy emerge? On the contrary, if it does not stand the logic and by implication exposes its weak areas of unholy motives, then the actors ought to be blamed for the proportionate share of fault, though not quantifiable in empirical terms. Call it diplomacy imperatives or the symptoms of the 'New Great Game', some vocal sources like Senator Sam Brownback, with capability to influence US diplomacy and foreign policy orientation, maintain straightforward questions to assert US role to initiate pro-active policy in Caspian, highlighting what is at stake in this region and what is the take? He, however, soon recedes to a rather simplistically obvious theme of 'helping' Caspian-Caucasus countries to sustain themselves as politically sovereign and economically vibrant states. He could be right but others will not perceive him nonchalantly. He contends, "Our window of opportunity to influence events there is very narrow…If we do not act soon we may find that we are too late to take advantage of a unique opportunity."[9] Fortunately, there is no dearth of scholarship to question native governments or extra-regional actors on the need to ensure legitimacy through diplomacy. Since the arguments in favor of the 'New Great Game' are usually more convincing and congruent, so at a later stage of discussion, the elements seem to support the hypothesis for drawing conclusions. At the end of chapter, one stands clear about the actors' prerogatives, compulsions and their choicest tools to advance diplomacy or prevent objective to the opponent(s) through various machinations: direct intimidation, offering charming economic prospects, abetting dictators, manipulating Caspian Sea legal regime issue, stoking intensity in the insurgency prone regions or for that matter deflating or inflating environments concern.

Chapter Six is a crucial chapter. In the backdrop of preceding discussion, arguments have been made to support the hypotheses that establish the simmering severity of the New Great Game among the actors. The emerging paradigm in the entire episode proves that name and description notwithstanding, the power play of the interests is undeniably there. The West, pioneered by the USA and represented by Turkey has the moral ground to advocate diversity and not hook the Central Eurasian destiny to the good will of only Iran and Russia. At the same time, though Russia does not stand restricted from participation in the energy flow projects, it tends to maintain claim over the resources of its 'backyard' or 'near abroad'. Conversely, Iran's integration to the oil stream would hypothetically give the episode added legitimacy. This would entail a spectacular shift in the US-Iranian foreign policy orientation and hence a challenge to peacetime diplomacy of both the countries that is not in sight yet. Of late, the European Union has emerged as an actor in the arena also. Though its policy initiatives go by the accepted norms of international relations, it may be rather early to speculate its success on forcing an element of sobriety on the 'New Great Game'. On the top of 'worry' list is the regrettable urge by other actors to muster military muscles in the arena under the guise of staying ardent proponents of the peace and prosperity. Conclusions thus hinge on the arguments and substance to prove the ongoing simmering of the 'New Great Game'.

Chapter Seven contains some recommendations that may be pertinent to draw in the light of pursued stance. The design of the 'New Great Game' that is increasingly showing a tendency to lean towards 'muscle' diplomacy rather than reason, is enough to force the 'peace mongers' to look for certain way-out from the impending dilemma. The earlier the world would acknowledge snowballing of threat in Central Eurasia, sooner it would inspire the intellectuals to chart a course for purposeful peace contingencies. The urgency demands that the process can initiate in reverse order as well because conscience and not the myopic interest of states generally push the scholars.

CHAPTER-ONE

HISTORIC PERSPECTIVE, GEOGRAPHY AND SIGNIFICANCE OF CENTRAL EURASIA

"As a great yurt are heavens,
Covering the Steppe in all direction
On the plain of Chihle,
Under the mountains of Yen,
Blue blue is the sky,
Vast vast is the Steppe
Here the grass bends with the breeze
Here are the cattle and sheep."[10]

Hsien-pi

Profiling Central Eurasia

Because of geographical and demographic contrast, there exists clear demarcation of Central Asia and Caucasus Region, which has been dealt with separately including history of Caspian Region where mostly the hydrocarbon reserves are located. In the ongoing debate, any reference made to geography, political climate, demographic order and brief oil and gas index would thus be instantly comprehended in the context of its relevant significance. Incidentally, within the Central Eurasia, the Caspian Region makes its nucleus to focus upon.

Central Asia

It essentially denotes the region in present day perception as the area occupied by Afghanistan, adjacent Chinese Province of Xingjian and newly independent Central Asian Republics (CARs) of Kazakhstan, Uzbekistan, Turkmenistan, Tajikistan, and Kyrgyzstan. For short these are also being referred as '–stans' though Xingjian is an exception which does not taper on '–stan' except when its relatively old label is used, 'Chinese or Eastern Turkistan'. The area is historically vital to the regional as well as non-regional powers. Geographers differ on the views to demarcate its geography using varying terminology. David Siner called it Inner Eurasia.[11] Sir H. J Mackinder with own interpretation referred to it as part of 'heartland' and hence world island to denote its strategic significance. He asserted in his 1904 paper that whosoever commanded the 'world island' shall rule the world'.[12]

David Christian also described it as "Inner Eurasia," adding, what is now called as Post Soviet Space[13]. Arab accounts refer to it as 'Mavra-un-Nahr'. Some historians have also referred to it as 'Trans-Oxiana' and others so simply as 'Turkestan'.[14] Dr Muhammad Anwar Khan is of the view that, "Central Asia is considered as one of the cradle of mankind... the abode of progenitors of the earliest man... Caucasoid and Mongoloid races sprouted from Central Asia."[15] Its ancient civilization flourished on the banks and valleys irrigated by Amu and Syr Darya which were, in the ancient times, part of Caspian Sea and Black Sea ecological system, ultimately extending as far as Mediterranean. Caspian Sea to the west, Hindukush and Pamir Mountain in the south, Tianshan Range, Gobi Desert in the east and Siberia in the north demarcates Central Asia. The Ural Mountain Range is its boundary with the West. It has total area of about 6.2 million sq km and population of approximately 100 million people. Geographers have placed Central Asia at 46°-95° E Longitudes and 30°-55° N Latitudes[16]. Two of the largest deserts in the world lie in the center of the vast landscape of the mountains. One is

KaraKum meaning black desert, over which most of Turkmenistan territory stretches while Kyzlkum meaning red desert, extends from northern Uzbekistan to southern Kazakhstan. Well-irrigated valleys have major urban centers that have developed around the oases. Harsh climate with sparse population traditionally made Central Asia easy to conquer while it was a nightmare for the rulers. "Empires rose and fell periodically throughout its history,"[17] writes Ahmed Rashid.

Persia, India and China historically shared Central Asian culture and political vicissitudes. The pattern of migration in East-West direction since Mesolithic and Neolithic times prove Central Asians' role in the regions. As regards political influence, China essentially remained confined to the adjoining `Turkistan` while Persian Empires of Achaemnides (600-330 BC) and Sassanides rulers (226-691 AD) maintained their hold over large stretches; both in Cis and Trans-Oxiana. Alexander the Great, provoked by the rivalry of Achaemnides finally eliminated their king near the city of Merv, Turkmenistan's present 'Mary' in 330 BC. Thereafter, no worthwhile power could match Greeks who marched eastward and captured Bactria (Balkh) and Parthia (Khurasan).

The Scythians, also known as Sakas, Yueh-Chis and Huns rose from the Central Asian folds. Historians like H.A.R. Gibbs agree that the 2nd Century BC was a period of upheavals in Central Asia[18]. The powerful Hiung-Nu people were dispossessing weaker tribe of their pasturelands and forcing them to migrate westward. Between the beginning and mid of the second century BC, last of the most powerful branch of Yueh-Chi, were also driven down to Sogdiana (present Samarqand). Soon, another group called Kang, took possession of Sogdiana and drove Yueh-Chi to Bactria and Afghanistan mountains. In this area, along with the settled Persian peasantry they came across in fusion with `Tukhari` race, what the Chinese called them Ta-Hia.

Map-1: Eurasia
(Source: URL at http://cacf.tripod.com/map.htm)

Nevertheless, there were some periods of stability in the regions as well. As the people gradually took up the sedentary occupations, Shamanism, Maniism, Hinduism and Zoroastrianism appeared as the folks' religions. Kishanas, who emerged as the branch of their Yueh-Chi ancestors, were to adopt Buddhism and held Afghanistan and Northern India with Peshawar as their capital. King Kanishka was their prominent ruler who ruled from 78-96 AD. Indo-European languages emerged during this period when Sogdian (early Turkish) served as lingua franca[19].

History turns chapter with Arabs arriving on the scene after defeating Sassanian King Yazdgird II in the Battle of Nehawand in 641 AD. Gradually, Arab rule kept expanding even though at the base of Muslim's power, authority shifted from Umayyad Caliphs to Abbasides. Islam penetrated more deeply and after a span of about hundred years, second decisive battle won by Arabs over Chinese at the bank of Talas River in 751 AD, established Islam as the religion to stay. As Adshead puts it, in Central Asia Islam, "failed... as tornado but succeeded as a glacier."[20] Comparatively Abbasides were liberal to their Eastern possession, which stretched across Oxus with

Arabic equivalent called 'Mavra-un-Nahar'. When the caliphs' hold had been fluctuating, Tahiride Dynasty (820-872 AD), Saffaride Dynasty (867-908 AD) and Samanides (874-902 AD) sprung in Khurasan, Sajistan and Trans-Oxiana respectively. These were followed by local dynasties to include Ghaznavides (902-1186 AD), the Qarakhanides (999-1211 AD), the Seljuk's (1037-1109 AD), the Ghorides (1010-1206 AD) and the Khwarzamshahis (1077-1231 AD). Of the above dynasties, first three were of Persian origin while remaining two were Turkish.

Temuchin (Changez Khan) led Mongols, called Tokyu (Turk) initially in 6th Century AD, who rose from southern Mongolia in 1207 and went blustering through Central Asia. Ibn Battuta traveled in Central Asia almost after 100 years since Changez Khan's conquest and wrote about Bukhara, "This city was formerly the capital of the lands beyond the Oxus. It was destroyed by accursed Tinkiz (Changez) the Tatar, the ancestor of the kings of Iraq, and all but a few of its mosques, academies and bazaars are now lying in ruins."[21] At the time of death of Changez Khan in 1227, Mongols had vast empire. Rule of Central Asia went to his son, Chughtai, Caucasus went to the eldest, Juchi, while Oktai possessed Zungaria and Tulai ruled over Mongolia and Persia. In later part of 13th Century, Chughtais and Temurides from Chughtai lineage embraced Islam. Mongols held sway for the next two centuries over continental empire. Juchi's son Batu conquered Central Russia, Poland, Hungary, Bulgaria and Moldova with Sarai as Capital on lower reaches of Volga River. Tulai's son Hilaku captured Baghdad (1258) and went beyond up to Aleppo. His brother Kublai Khan became emperor of China where Mongols ruled for about 150 years. Several dynasties emerged and vanished out of Mongols lineage that kept splitting to weaken their initial four power bases that they had inherited upon the death of great Khan, Changez Khan in 1227.[22]

In 15th Century AD, Russian rulers launched counter attack on the Turkic dynasties in Central Asia,

23

Caucasus and Siberia while they had lived for over two centuries as Mongol's vassal states and principalities. In 1480, they subdued Sarai, Kazan in 1556, Bashkiria in 1574, Siberia in 1581, Derbent, Gilan and Volga Region in 1721, Kyrgyz in 1734, Orenberg in 1740, Northern Caucasus region in 1783 while Southern Caucasus went to Russia in 1829. Kokand fell first in 1866, Bukhara in 1868, Khiva in 1873, Merv in 1882 and Panjdeh was the last to be subdued in 1885.[23] The significant feature in Russian expansion is their marvelous perseverance to achieve their expansion objectives for over four centuries. Thus, the Czarists fully imposed their rule on Central Asia, though it was unique experience for Turkic population. They subjected them to complete 'Russification' in many ways to break their ethno-religious and politico-religious bonds. When Communism replaced Imperial Russia, through 1917 Revolution, they even hardened their stance more and tyrannized the local population thoroughly. As a result, there was chain of uprising, about 250 of them on record, starting from Syed Hussein's struggle in Kazan in 1533. Some prominent resistance movement had been that of Imam Shymile's in Dagestan in 19th Century AD, Basmachi movement in early 20th Century AD and that of Chechen's in 1941-42. Soviets eliminated these anti-Soviet struggles ruthlessly. Large persecution and draconian punishments to the groups as well individuals have stayed fresh on the memory of their afflicted posterity. The Crimean Tatars, Cherkess, Mishkhetians, Turks, Karachais, Bulkars, Chechens, Digors and Avars were deported forcibly to inhospitable Siberia, which then meant issuance of a death warrant.

Russian Empire under the Soviets could not sustain her size and grandeur due to its vastness with incompatible and weak economy. It occupied 1/6 of the Earth's surface with 22 million sq kms area, over half of Europe, 1/3 of Asia and had 11 time zones of the World's 24 zones. Its east-west stretch measured 10,000 kms and north-south 5000 kms. Socialism, a man made ideology ultimately proved utopian. Its last strategic blunder to capture

24

Afghanistan in 1979 sapped her fragile economy, which hastened her downfall. Central Asian Republics won freedom so suddenly in 1991 that an ambivalent phase of 'to be or not to be' gripped them, finally opting to declare independence. The empire, Russian consolidated in 500 years since 1480, beginning with capture of Sarai to 1979 capture of Afghanistan, packed off to her core territory, Russian Federation, just in a few months time by 1991. A phenomenon rightly stunned the whole world because it had no parallel.

The geographers and anthropologists view the emergence and delineation of CARs as highly unrealistic. Initially devised to pre-empt the spread of pan-Islamism through fragmenting homogenous population of particular areas, the permanence given to the CARs boundaries had turned out to be a strange paradox. During the Soviets time, the legacy of division engineered by Joseph Stalin was remarkable success. Political wishes besides, their formation fixed ancient cultural and linguistic distinctions between nomads of Steppe, of deserts, of mountains and sedentary Turkic and Persian population. Nevertheless, conflict prevails. A close look at the borders reveals several points of tension. Some have listed about two dozen of them; if not the high probabilities, these are at least the possibilities of friction in the inter-state relations. The regional leaders, though aware of these anomalies, have down played them.[24] Yet the emerging trends of nationalism present a potent threat to CARs individually as well as collectively. Even Islam, considered as the binding force of all these populations has remained a fragile cohesive force. The governing machinery of these republics bears a deep communist stamp and hence suspects political Islamic forces, which they are striving to hold them in check. The old Muslim leadership and 'darwesh' order (Sufism) concentrated in Tashkent and spread over rural areas during Soviet time is now split into nation-state boundaries.

Conversely, Scott B. MacDonald quoting Oliver Roy, a French authority on Islam, comments on the recent trends, saying, "Political Islam has been stimulated by such things as poverty, uprootedness, crises in values, identities and decay of educational system. These socio-economic realities are alive and well in Central Asia. They have already given birth to radical Islamist group, seeking to over throw old order ... As the West rediscovers Central Asia, it needs to be fully aware of the ground upon which it is walking."[25] At the state-level, there had been attempts however to harmonize their political aspects of affairs as an entity. While in the field of communications, airlines and power generation, there appears some kind of willingness to collaborate but in case of currency, banking and custom regimes, worthwhile consensus has not developed. Common Central Asian Market agreed upon in 1993 and Common Economic Zone between Kazakhstan, Kyrgyzstan and Uzbekistan created in 1994 lack any substance. The fact that in any of the envisaged union of interest, at least one or two of the CARs pursue independent orientation amply highlights the intensity of discord among them. In addition to the psychological stupor maintained by Turkmenistan and Uzbekistan, claiming legitimacy to lead the Turkic race individually, there is yet another potent reason. That is, economies of all CARs compete against rather than complementing each other.[26] Thus, they are likely to remain divisive at the international forum despite their historic homogeneity. Here under follow some specific details about Central Asian countries:-

Kazakhstan occupies the second largest area within the Post-Soviet territories, after Russia, in the region. It borders with China in the east, Russia in the north, Kyrgyzstan, Uzbekistan and Turkmenistan in the south, Russia and the Caspian Sea to the west. Its total population is a little over 17 million. Astana, old Aqmola, is its new capital but Almaty remains its defacto capital, which has 1.2 million population. The Republic occupies a total area of 2.7 million sq kms. Based on geographic identity, the country has four regions. These are, one, the Caspian and Aral Regions, second, the Desert and Semi-Desert Regions, third the Kazak Steppe and fourth the Eastern and Southeastern Highland. Almaty, Ustkamenogorsk, Karaganda, Kyzalorda, Jambol, Chimkent, Uralsk, Atyrau and Aktyubinsk are some of the major urban centers. 41 percent of the total population is Kazak while there are other sizable groups particularly of Russian and German. These later-settled people of Russian and German origin have the trend to shift north and hence Kazaks population ratio is likely to increase further.[27]

Turkmenistan Republic occupies the total area of 0.49 million sq kms and has a population of about 4 million. Its capital is at Ashkhabad whose population is about 0.42 million. Turks being 72 percent of the total population constitute the major segment. It borders the Caspian Sea to the west, Kazakhstan in the north, Uzbekistan in the east and Iran-Afghanistan in the south. Chard Zhou, Tashauz, Mary, Menbashid and Nebi-Dag are some of its important urban centers.[28]

Uzbekistan Republic occupies a total area of 0.45 million sq kms with a population of about 22.1 million people. Having Tashkent as its capital, it has a population of 2.2 million people. Turkmenistan to the west, Kazakhstan to the north and northwest, Kyrgyzstan on the east and Tajikistan/Afghanistan on southeast and south, border Uzbekistan. Uzbeks make 71.4 percent of the total population. It has some other prominent urban centers such as Bukhara, Kokand, Farghana and Khiva. Besides these, Namangan, Andejan, Karshi and Urgench are also important communication centers.[29]

Tajikistan has total area of 0.143 million sq kms and a population of 5.4 million. It has borders with Afghanistan in the south, China to the east, Kyrgyzstan on its north and Uzbekistan to the west and northwest. It has the capital at Dushambe with its population of 0.6 million. Dushanbe and Khujend are the only large towns while Kulyab and Kurgan Tyube have population of 69,000 and 53,000 people respectively. Tajiks make 62.3 percent of the total population[30].

Kyrgyzstan Republic occupies a total area of about 0.2 million sq kms with a population of 4.63 million. Bishkek is its capital having a population 0.65 million. It shares borders with Kazakhstan to the north, China in the east and southeast, Tajikistan in the South and Uzbekistan to the west. Kyrgyz make 52.4 percent of the population. Besides its capital, Bishkek, it has important urban centers like Osh and Przhevalsk[31].

Afghanistan has a total area of about 0.65 million sq kms and population of 24.4 million people. With capital at Kabul, it shares border with Pakistan in the east, Iran in the south and southwest, Turkmenistan in the west and northwest, Uzbekistan and Tajikistan in the north and China in the northeast. Pashtuns are the predominant segment of the society, which are 44 percent of the total population. The figures are however controversial and vary from a source to source. It is completely a landlocked country. Besides Kabul, Kandhahar, Jalalabad and Mazar-e-Sharif are its main urban centers[32].

Xingjian (Sikiang), a predominantly 'Uighars' Autonomous Region, the northwestern province of China, occupies about 1.7 million sq kms with capital at Urumqi. In medieval period, it was known as Kashgharia and Eastern Turkistan. Chinese named it Sikiang meaning 'new territory'. It formed part of Chinese empire during Han Dynasty from 202 BC to 220 AD. China gained and lost the area many times. Kunlun and Karakoram mountains to the south, Tianshan Range in the southwest, Altai in the north and Pamir Range in the west bound this province. Tarim basin occupies its half of the spread. Through Gobi Desert, it opens up to the east into Kansi, to the northeast into Mongolia, Kazakhstan to the northwest, Kyrgyzstan and Badakhshan province of Afghanistan to the west and Pakistan to the south. Its Uighar (Muslim) population is a powerful branch of Turkic-Mongol group, which is striving for freedom since last captured by Chinese in 1877. Out of 15 million Chinese Muslims, about 8 million live in Xingjian. "Chinese Authorities are presently alarmed by the diffusion of pan-Islamism, the resurgence of pan-Turkism and the spread of pan-Kazak sympathies...., it should be stressed that Kazak(Turkish) traditional culture has so far been better preserved in Xingjian than in Kazakhstan."[33]

Caspian-Caucasus Region

It is complex mix of an intertwined mosaic of people, sitting on east-west and north-south routes. The fact that Asiatic and European empires through history had been yearning with equal ferocity to include it as a whole or its slice, suggests how essential role it had been playing in the make up of struggle of domination. Azov Sea and Black Sea to the west, borders with Turkey and Iran to the south, Caspian Sea to the east and horizontal line drawn between Volga and Don Rivers in the north, bound the region. Nicholas Awde is of the opinion, "The Caucasus map of today owes as much to the upheavals and invasions of Byzantium and Ottoman Empire as it does to eighty years of Soviets rule and the pipeline lobby." The Western view, largely based on the Soviets nostalgia about the area, termed it as their, "Jewel in the Crown."[34] However, the scholars also maintain with a tinge of sorrow that it is a land, which no longer would inspire the likes of Tolstoy, Pushkin and Myakovsky and providing idyllic holiday resort for millions of Russians on the Black Sea. Instead, it is now the hotbed of mafias, ethnic strife, Chechnya war and the border clashes. It has been asserted that the Caucasus has become the most militarized area in the world. There are at least 30 major ethnic groups, usually intermingled and overlapped. Azerbaijan, Armenia and Georgia are the major components, which constituted three of the Soviet Republics of USSR. Each of them had large ethnic groups out of the mainstream population which were governed as separate autonomous republic or autonomous province within these three republics. Georgia had autonomous provinces of Abkhazia and South Ossetia, Azerbaijan had Nakhichevan and Nagorno-Karabakh Autonomous Provinces.[35] The region had sort of geographic or ethnic absurdities. For instance, a thin strip of Armenian territory separated Nakhichevan Autonomous Republic from its main political unit, Azerbaijan. Similarly, Nagorno-Karabakh, though part of Azerbaijan, is largely Armenian inhabited region whose population fluctuated from 94% Armenian in 1921 to 76% in 1989 census; the year Supreme Soviet decreed to control it directly from Moscow. Armenia resorted to military solution by occupying the enclave in 1992-1994 war with Azerbaijan including the 'Lachine Strip', which separated it from Armenia. The conflict has however emerged beyond the local connotations. In fact, it has turned out to be more of an ideological confrontation between the Muslims and orthodox Christians.

In Georgia, political turmoil beset Abkhazia against the mainland government of Georgia, which claims suzerainty over it. Similarly, South Ossetians are vying to merge with North Ossetia, which is included in Russian Federation now.[36] The trouble brewing up in the region does not stop here. In fact, Soviets had recognized the need to delegate some sort of administrative control to the remaining minorities of Northern Caucasians. As a result, it led to creation of seven autonomous republics and provinces, which included Adyghei, Karachai, Cherkess autonomous provinces and the Kalmyk, Chechen-Ingush, Kabardino-Balkaria, and North Ossetian-Dagestan autonomous republics. All these seven regions are witnessing separatist movements of varying degree of intensity, Chechnya being on the bloody top. George Joffe is of the view that intra-state perception dichotomy, say, between Azerbaijan and Armenia or Georgia and Russian Federation is not the only hurdle which makes the peace prospect thin but the ethnic animosity within three states turn the scenario impossible to iron out the conflict like situation.[37] It is because while the Caucasian Governments,

Russia included, have recognition at international level, their sub national minorities do not always acknowledge their legitimacy. The other factor that is denying the region to recover from instability is the Russian psychological fix about Caucasian region and states. Some scholars opine that there has never been true Russian state as they find their identity through empire. That explains why, if not for Gorbachev, at least for rest of the Russians, it had been difficult to accept transformation from USSR-status to the present boundaries with further brewing up of separatist movements in North Caucasus to secede from them. This anticlimax, reverses claims of history and phraseology of 'friendship of people' and 'near abroad' simply as a baffling phenomenon.

After having known the internal dynamics of Caucasus Region, it is pertinent to focus on Caspian as vast hydrocarbon resources reside on its periphery and under its bed. In fact, the profiling of Central Asia and Caucasus becomes imperative only for the sake of keeping aligned to the possible discourse about oil export routes and pipeline directions that contribute a lot to the 'New Great Game'. Otherwise, focus on Caspian littorals would have sufficed, referring to it as 'Caspian Region' or 'Caspian' for short.

Caspian Sea and the Littoral States

Caspian Sea derived its name from a Caucasus tribe 'Caspi'. The Arabic states call it Bahr-e-Qazvin (Qazvin Sea) or Caspian, while the Turks, Europeans and other nations refer to it as the Caspian Sea. Meanwhile, varieties of other names, given to the waterway since 500 years ago, have been recorded. The diversity of names recorded with their different pronunciations call for their examination from various dimensions. One of the reasons for the multiplicity of the names of this waterway is its tourist attraction, because of which its coasts have become the habitat of various tribes, cultures and dialects. Besides, many towns and townships have been constructed in the vicinity.[38] Thus, every area near the Caspian coast has been

31

named either after the name of the tribe residing there or that of a nearby town, so that currently 50 ethnic groups with their own particular dialects including Altai Turks, Indo-Europeans and Iber-Caucasians are coexisting along the Caspian coast.

According to the records and maps left behind by European tourists, historians and geographers, they mention at least six names for this northern waterway. In addition, Arabic, Islamic and Iranian sources list around 35 various names. Explanations…. are included in more than 30 books written on various subjects including geography, history, literature, ethics as well as Islamic jurisprudence and interpretation by Iranian and Islamic writers. Various names listed in those books for the waterway …include: the Caspian Sea, Tabarestan, Bahr-e-Qazvin, Jorjan (Gorgan), Abskoun-e Deilam, Bahr-e-A'ajem, Jilan (Gilan), Astarabad, Sari, Shirvan, Mazandaran, Moghan, Badkoubeh, Haji Tarkhan, Gol-o-Galan, Talisan, Kamroud, Zereh Ojestan, Akfoudeh Darya (Darya Akfoudeh), Kharazm, Khorassan, Jili, Bahr-ol-Ajam, Jebal and Bab-ol-Abvab. An Arab geographist, Naviri, called it Faros Bahr or Hoz (Persian Sea)... In Avesta, the Old Persian language, it is also called Vaurukesh and Farakhkart (the big sea).[39] Besides the famous names of Caspian and Hirkanium, the Europeans call it by other names such as Morgan, Philip, William, Jackson and Dern.

As maintained by Moshe Brawer, it is a landlocked large water body, which has assumed the suffix 'Sea' because of its size, magnitude and geological impact (Map-2). It stretches north south for 1200 kms with an average east-west width of 320 kms and a coastal line of 7000 kms. It has surface area of almost 370,000 sq kms. Its surface is approximately 90 feet below sea level. It bears 50 islands of which Chechen, Artam, Kulaly, Tiulinil, Zhiloi and Ogorchinski are prominent. Some of the major gulfs are Kizliar, Kosmolets in the north, Mangyshlak, Konderli,

Map: 2 The Caspian Sea with NASA Image Below

Source:NASA,
http://eol.nasa.gov/newsletter/DynamicEarth-July 2004

Karabogaz Gol and Karanovedsk in the east and Aghakhan and Baku in the west. Rivers Volga, Emba and Ural drain into the Caspian Sea from the north. Rivers Sulak, Samne and Kura from the west while from the Iranian side Gorgan, Aras and Sufed Rivers fall into the Caspian. It is "the largest inland sea in the world. A long sinuous stretch of water, it spans the imaginary divide between Asia and Europe."[40]

The sea has three zones according to its relief and hydrographical configuration. The north, there is Mangyshlak Bank with average depth of 4-8 meters and an area of 80,000 sq kms. The middle zone, Darbent Basin, with depth of 780 meters has an area of 138,000 sq kms. The southern zone with maximum depth of 1025 meters is called Aspheron Bank and is spread over 152,000 sq kms. According to the US Energy Information Administration report, it is the biggest water body, with 386,000 sq km as surface area. Its total volume of water is 78,700 cubic kilometers. Approximately 130 large and small rivers flow into Caspian Sea of which Volga River is the largest, draining 1400,000 sq km area. Of the total inflow, five major rivers that are Volga, Kura, Terek, Ural and Sulak supply 90% of water.[41]

The Caspian region is prime economic asset with large oil and gas reserves, having history that dates back to BC era. In 450 BC, Herodotus spoke of Persian oil and described production of oil and salt from springs and wells. However, records about the eternal fire of Baku are somewhat hazy. When Hercules defeated Parthian and demolished their temples, some of these were burning natural gas.[42] Azerbaijan, Iran, Turkmenistan, Kazakhstan and Russia share the seacoast, and are the Caspian littoral states. However, three other countries, namely Turkey, Georgia and Armenia, though not among littorals, have such geo-strategic location that within the Caspian-Caucasus System, their mention becomes inevitable. Similarly, Kazakhstan and Turkmenistan, earlier discussed in Central Asian setting, will now be viewed from their westward orientation in Caspian littoral perspective. A brief focus on each would therefore be in order.

Azerbaijan. The country is located on the western shore of the Caspian Sea and the southeastern extremity of Caucasus (Map 3). Azeris spell it as 'Azurbaycan'. Also called the land of 'eternal fire', which inspired 'Zaratushtra' so overwhelmingly in about 1000 BC in Baku area that he and his followers worshiped these fires and thus laid the foundation of Zoroastrian religion. The mysterious but

Map-3: Azerbaijan

majestic fires caused by hydrocarbon leaks were certainly incomprehensible in the Zoroastrian era. On top of it, the phenomenon coincidently bore evidence to an episode of Greek mythology, assuming that Prometheus stole fire from heaven for the welfare of humankind. As a punishment, Olympian gods chained him to a rock to expose him to the torture by vultures. Thus, the fire emanating out of the rocks was considered the divine fire.[43] Generally a mountainous country; it has 7 % of arable land out of its total area of 86600 sq km. It has about 8 million populations with Baku as major urban center as well as seaport on the Caspian Sea. Northern Azerbaijan had been known as Caucasian Albania in the ancient time.[44] It was site of various conflicts involving Arabs, Kazars and Turks. After 11th Century AD, Turks dominated it and became eventually a stronghold of Azerbaijanis who were Shiite Muslims and thus adhered to Islamic culture. Russia acquired it from Persia in 1813 through the Treaty of Gulistan and later in 1820 under the Treaty of Turkomanchai. The significance of Azerbaijan with focus on Baku is amply exemplified when we take stock of the situation in the second decade of the 20th Century. In order to turn the tide of WW-I battles into Germany's favor, General Erich Ludendroff, besides the capture of Rumanian oil fields, had set his sight on Baku at the western shore of the Caspian Sea. Collapse of Russian empire in 1917 and then Bolsheviks coming into power boosted Germany's confidence to secure Baku oil supplies to sustain their huge war machine. The Treaty of Brest-Litovsk paved their way to gain access to Baku oil in March 1918. In the meantime, Turks, an ally of Germany and Austria commenced an assault on Baku. In August 1918, Britain intervened to deny crucial oil supplies to the Germans. They held out only for a month at Baku but it happened to be a devastating denial for Germans. On British withdrawal, Turks captured Baku and restored its independence status in May 1918. However, by the time Turks took Baku, "it was too late to do the German and their oil supply any good."[45]

Azerbaijan's declared independence was short-lived as the Soviets captured it again in 1920. In December 1936, Azerbaijan achieved the status of a separate Soviet Socialist Republic (SSR). She declared finally her independence from the Soviets on 30 August 1991. Azerbaijan and Armenia have been at loggerheads since 1988 over the possession of the enclave of Nagorno-Karabakh, which has Armenian majority. Though the uneasy calm prevails since the 1994 cease-fire, the situation in the Caucasus remains tense. The country has large hydrocarbon reserves, which are a source of attraction for foreign investors. Azerbaijan State Oil Company (SOCAR) has signed several billion dollars agreements with international oil companies. Her pro-western stance and vast oil resources have made it a focal point of attention. Recent completion of the Baku-Tbilisi-Ceyhan (BTC) pipeline to deliver one million barrels of oil per day direct to the Mediterranean would further boost the geo-political significance of Baku among the Caspian littorals and her Caucasian neighbors.

In 2003, President Hyeder Aliyev chose his son as the Prime Minister, clearing his way eventually for succession. In October 2003 election, the President's son Ilham Aliyev was elected as President. It has its own currency called 'manat'. Ganja and Sumgait are the next largest cities. Eighty-nine per cent people speak Azerbaijani Turkic. Out of its 8 million populations, 93 percent profess Islam and about 5 percent are Orthodox Christians including Russians and Armenians. After capture of Nagorno-Karabakh, Armenia virtually holds one fifth of Azerbaijan territory.[46]

Iran. It is strategically located between the Persian Gulf and the Arabian Sea in the south and the Caspian Sea to the north. Though contiguous to Caucasus, it is essentially a Middle Eastern country. It borders Iraq, Turkey, Azerbaijan, Armenia, Turkmenistan, Afghanistan and Pakistan. The Elburz Mountains in the north rise up to 18,600 feet at a peak called Mount Damavend. Islamic theocracy rules it since over throw of Pahlavi monarchy on 11 February 1979. Its history dates back to 1500 BC when Medes occupied it until a Persian, King Cyrus the Great, overthrew Medes and established Achaemnide rule from Indus to the Nile in 525 BC. It fell to Alexander in 330-329 BC, to a succession of Seleucids 312-302 BC, to Greek speaking Parthian, 247-226 BC and later to Sassanian until Arab Muslims defeated them in 641 AD. In the beginning of 13th Century, it was invaded by Mongols, which held their sway until Safavid Dynasty emerged in 1501, to last until 1722. Qajars ousted Safavids in 1794. It became an arena of struggle between Imperial Russia and Victorian England during the second half of 19th Century. Iran's neutrality during World War I did not stop the Russian and the British occupying it though it had been reduced to a buffer state already in the beginning of 20th Century.

A coup in 1921 brought Raza Khan to power who proclaimed monarchy and changed his name to Raza Shah Pahlavi.[47] During WW-II, Iran faced again the Anglo-Russian occupation forces for her pro-Axis leaning that deposed the Shah to enthrone his son Muhammad Raza Shah Pahlavi in 1941. The successor's abrupt westernization agenda alienated the clergy as well as the masses, which led to massive demonstrations against the Shah during 1970s. The Shah, along with his family, had to abdicate the throne on 16 January 1979. Ayatollah Ruhollah Khomeini returned from exile to establish Islamic theocracy in Iran. Farid A Khawari, in his well-researched book, "Oil and Islam" differs to this part of hypothesis of alienation of Shah due to his westernization agenda. In his opinion, USA and Britain abetted the revolutionary struggle by the clergy against the Shah. Mr. Carter's administration, under the influence of Mr. Zbigniew Brzezinski's concept of throwing 'green-belt' against Communist Russia happily bought the risk of toppling her age-old ally, Shah of Iran,

Map-4: Iran

hinging hopes that 'mullahs' of Iran would defy the Soviets push to the south better than the Shah. The unfolding events indicate that the West's deduction proved to be totally out of sync. Khomeini not only restored the Islamic culture in the country but also adopted anti-US stance.[48] Hostage taking of US embassy in Tehran on 4th November

1979 by Iranian revolutionaries further precipitated the US-Iran hostility when US deported Iranian students, imposed economic sanctions, seized Iranian assets in US banks worth $8 billion. USA conducted an aborted raid to free its hostages in April 1980 when Iran had turned down a unanimous Security Council Resolution, requiring her to release the hostages. After captivity of 444 days, Iran finally released them on 18 January 1981. Almost whole of the eighties saw the Iran-Iraq war until Ayatollah Khomeini, finally agreed to cease hostilities on 20 August 1989.

Since the election of Hashmi Rafsanjani in 1991 and Muhammad Khatami in 1997, the country is maintaining balance on a tight rope among the conservatives, led by Iranian clergy, the Guardian Council, and the reformists. However, on the international scene, Iran, in the wake of 9/11, cooperated a great deal in arresting and turning over 'Al-Qaeda' suspects. Yet in January 2002, US President George W. Bush labeled Iran as part of 'axis of evil' on the suspicion of Iranian collaboration with the international terror networks. Since the coalition venture into Iraq, the US has aggressively accused Iran of producing a nuclear arsenal while International Atomic Energy Agency (IAEA) is conducting periodic inspections and dialog with little success. The series of sanctions being clamped on Iran by the United Nations Security Council as of early 2007 and the invectives heaped by Iranian President, Mahmoud Ahmadinejad on America, Israel and Britain has complicated the scenario irreparably. World powers suspect Iran to be developing nuclear arsenal under the garb of acquiring peaceful nuclear energy. In a tit-for-tat situation, the region almost sits on the powder keg that may turn into a deplorable conflagration any time, particularly when a conflict already blazes in the neighboring Iraq. Besides, Iran has some other international disputes. Of these, disputes over distribution of river water with Afghanistan, maritime and land boundaries with Iraq, Tunb and Abu Musa Islands with the UAE and division of Caspian Sea, threatening Azerbaijan exploration of hydrocarbon resources in disputed waters; make Iranian tasks difficult while conducting her regional affairs, particularly when Iranian leadership is overtly antagonistic to the sole superpower, the USA.

It has population of about 70 million people with Tehran, Mashad, Isfahan and Tabriz as the largest cities in that order. Iranian 'rial' is her monetary unit. Farsi (Persian), Azari (Turkic), Kurdish and Arabic are the spoken languages. Predominantly Shiite Muslim population (89 percent), it has a sprinkling of Sunni Muslims, which account for only 10 %. Abadan, Ahraz, Bandar Abass, Bander-e-Anzali, Bushehr, Bandar-e-Imam Khomieni, Bandar-e-Lengeh, Bandar-e-Mahshahr, Bandar-e-Torkaman, Chahbahar (Bandar-e-Bahishti), Jazireh-ye-Khark, Jazireh-ye-Lavan, Jazireh-ye-Sirri, Khorramshahr and Nowshahr are its ports in the Arabian Gulf, Caspian and Arabian Sea.[49]

Turkmenistan. It is one of the Caspian Sea littorals, bounded by Caspian Sea in the west, Kazakhstan to the north, Uzbekistan to the east, Afghanistan and Iran to the south. Karakum is one of the largest world deserts, which spreads over 4/5 of Turkmenistan with an area of 360,000 sq kms out of her total area of 488,100 sq kms. It has a population of about 5 million people, Muslims are 89 percent. Turkmen are 85 percent of the total population of ethnic division, Uzbeks 5 percent, Russian and others are 10 percent. It is a one party republic. Ashkhabad is its capital with two other large cities called Chardzhou and Tashauz. Its seaport on Caspian Sea is called Turkmenbashy.

Historically, Turkmenistan was once part of Persian Empire of Cyrus the Great in BC era and later, of Sassanides Empire, which was eliminated by Arab Muslims in mid 7th Century AD. Seljuk Turks ruled its territory in 11th Century and Mongols from the beginning of 13th Century to 15th Century.

Prior to the 19th Century, Turkmenistan, also known as 'Turkmenia' had two divisions, Khanate of Khiva and Khanate of Bukhara. In 1868 when Khanate of Khiva fell to the Russian Empire, the region became known as Trans-Caspian Region of Russian Turkistan. In 1922, the Soviets made it Turkistan Autonomous Soviet Socialist Republic (ASSR), which was upgraded in its autonomous status further on May 13, 1925 as the Turkistan Soviet Socialist Republic (SSR). On the dissolution of USSR, it declared independence in August 1991; and became member of Commonwealth of Independent States (CIS) on 21 December 1991. Ruled in a rather authoritarian way by Supramurat A. Niyazov, also called 'Turkmenbashi', meaning leader of all Turks, he had promoted self-image at the expense of state until his death. His successor, Gurbanguly Derbymukhamedov, on the eve of his installation as the President in March 2007 vowed to continue 'Turkmenbashi's philosophy by symbolically kissing and holding his book 'Ruhnama' above his head.

Turkmenistan exported her gas through the Russian pipeline, fetching $1 billion revenue. However, in 1993, Russia closed this outlet because of a tariff dispute, forcing Turkmenistan to export limited quantities to Central Asian neighbors. It did not relieve her fund depletion stress because her neighbors could not pay in international currencies.[50] As an alternative; she looked towards Iran, considered the most viable option but remained without meaningful success as US influence blocks all such efforts. Largely living on Western loans, her efforts are focused on depicting the historic grandeur through Turkmenbashi's image projection. Export options to Azerbaijan, Kazakhstan, Russia, Iran and Pakistan are open to her and the other actors.

However, each option is riddled with some sort of impediment(s), which would be discussed subsequently. As regards international disputes, her neighbors upstream also share Amu River, which is her main fresh water source. Thus, it remains as sore point. On the Caspian Sea side, it has dispute with Kazakhstan, Iran and Azerbaijan over the mode and extent of the division of Caspian Sea.

Map-5: Turkmenistan

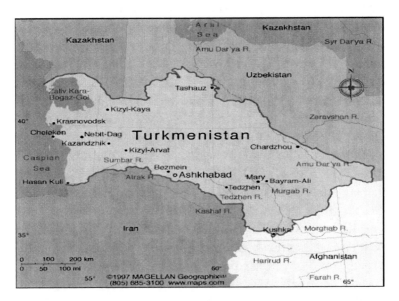

In addition, her land boundary with Kazakhstan remains undemarcated. These potential international disputes make the country vulnerable to external factors.

Kazakhstan. With an area of 2.7 million sq kms, Kazakhstan is bounded by Russian Federation to north, China in the east, Caspian Sea, Russian Federation to the west and Turkmenistan, Kyrgyzstan and Uzbekistan to the south. On the Caspian Sea, it has 1,900 km coastline. Having capital at Astana, it is inhabited by about 17 million people. Almaty, Karaganda, Shymkent, Taraz and Pavlodar are its largest cities in that order. 64 percent people speak 'Qazaq' that is state language while 95 percent speak Russian, which is an official language. Muslims are 47 percent; Russian Orthodox 44 percent and 9 percent are Protestant and others. It has 98 percent literacy ratio. Historically indigenous Kazaks were Turkic nomadic people belonging to different Kazak hordes.[51] They rarely

42

united under a single authority though a chief headed each tribe or group. In 1920, the Soviets made it part of Kyrgyz ASSR while in 1925 it was designated as a Kazak ASSR. In 1927, Soviet forcibly settled Kazaks on farmlands to switch them from nomadic life to sedentary along with Slavs and other Russians who were encouraged to settle in Kazakhstan. Perhaps this is the major cause why minorities, if combined, outnumber the native Kazak majority. During the Soviet era, nuclear testing ground was located in Kazakhstan (Baikanur), which is still operational and thus poses threatening risk to her population. It achieved her independence in 1991 and became member of CIS on December 21, 1991.

Map-6: Kazakhstan

    In 1999, President Nur Sultan Nazarbayev was again elected though widely criticized by opposition, which has been virtually eliminated. An oil and gas rich country otherwise has her 'democracy' prospects eclipsed by the President's authoritarian rule who has harassed independent media and arrested opposition leaders. As regards her international disputes, she has border disputes with China,

Turkmenistan, Uzbekistan and Kyrgyzstan.[52] Preliminaries have been undertaken while complete demarcation is yet to be done. On the Caspian Sea side, Kazakhstan has successfully negotiated division of seabed with Russia and Azerbaijan, yet without reaching any accord over division of the seawater column. Turkmenistan is still to be negotiated with. Syr Darya and Irtysh are its main rivers while Aktau and Atyrau are the seaports that provide her shipping facilities in the Caspian Region.

Russia. The Russian Federation[53] is the largest of the republics of CIS and among Caspian littorals. Occupying most of Eastern Europe and Northern Asia, it stretches from Baltic Sea in the west to the Pacific Ocean in the east, from Arctic Ocean in the north to the Black Sea and Caucasus-Kazakhstan in the south. It has common borders with Norway and Finland in the north-west, Estonia, Latvia, Belarus, Ukraine, Poland and Lithuania in the west, Georgia and Azerbaijan in the south-west, Kazakhstan, Mongolia, China and North Korea in the south and south east. With an area of over 17 million sq km, population of 143 million and capital at Moscow, it is the land of old traditions and history.

The Novograd Dynasty formed by 'Rurik' Vikings, as the tradition goes, set the pace of Russian empire in 862 AD. Christianity took roots in 10th and 11th Century AD when the ruler of Kiev principality assumed the title of Grand Duke. Mongols destroyed Kiev and whole territory divided in princedoms, became their vassal states. In 1480, Duke Ivan-III defeated Mongols and captured Golden Hordes at Sarai. His successor, Ivan-IV, considered the founder of Russian state, also assumed the title of Czar. Westernization undertaken by Peter the Great, from 1698 to 1725 helped Russia to expand significantly. Defeating Sweden in 1709 in the Battle of Poltova, he moved the Russian boundaries to the west. Catherine the Great, 1762-1796, also continued the westernization and expansion pursuit and acquired Crimea, Ukraine and part of Poland. Alexander I, 1801-1825, defied Napoleons attempt to

44

subdue Russia and annexed Finland and Bess Arabia. Alexander II pushed Russian Empire borders to the Pacific and Central Asia from 1855-1881.

Due to monarchical repression and palace intrigues, the Russian Empire as an institution remained prone to decay, visibly and elaborately demonstrated before and during World War I. Humiliating defeat at the hands of Japanese forces at the dawn of 20th Century sapped Russian morale. Disorder, originating from Petrograd (St. Petersburg) soon engulfed whole Russia as a revolutionary movement. On 15 March 1917, Nicholas II abdicated his throne. He was killed along with his family members. Bolsheviks wing of the Social Democratic Labor Party ultimately prevailed. Their war with Germany concluded on signing of humiliating agreement of Brest-Litovsk in March 1918. Losing the war to Poland in 1920, still the Communists managed to regain control of most of their territories. USSR was established on 30 December 1922.

Lenin's death on 21 January 1924 triggered inter-party rivalry when Stalin finally emerged successful after ousting his rival, Trotsky, as commissar of war in 1925, and banished him out of the Soviet Union in 1929. He had him murdered in Mexico City on 21 August 1940. The signing of Soviets-Nazis Friendship Treaty on 24 August 1939 enabled the Soviets to seize a portion of Polish and Finnish territories. Stalin also annexed Bess Arabia and Bukovina from Rumania. Subsequent annexation of Baltic Republics of Estonia, Latvia and Lithuania in June 1940 created 14th, 15th and 16th Soviet Republics (Map 7).[54] Moscow's expansion spree suddenly came to halt when, on 22 June 1941, Hitler launched a massive attack on USSR. Aided by US and British supplies coupled with Russian chivalry and hostile terrain, German offensives were finally blunted. February 1943 happened to be the turning point, culminating in Allied final offensive against Germany in January 1945.

Map-7: Russia

On the Pacific front, seeing the Allied forces nearing victory, in April 1945 the Soviets quickly denounced 'No Aggression Pact of 1941' with Japan and captured Manchuria, Karafuto and Kuril Islands. After the war, dividing defeated Germany into four zones, USSR, USA, UK and France managed one each. At this point of time, intra-Allied antagonism developed to the scale that it came to be described as the 'Cold War', mainly due to the Soviets attempt to pull iron-curtain around her possession in Europe, from Poland to Albania. Nikita Khrushchev succeeded Stalin who died in March 1953. He formalized Eastern European system through Warsaw Pact Treaty Organization that became the main counterweight to NATO.

The Cold War generated tremendous hostility in the military and diplomatic field for 45 years when the world survived mega conflagration between the two powerful blocs twice by a whisker. Once at the time of Berlin Blockade of 1948 and later by Cuban Missile Crisis,[55] planted and later withdrawn by Khrushchev. Aware of the scale of catastrophe, which could be wreaked by WMDs, both sides, the Soviets and the West led by USA maintained dialogue to seek an end of Cold War.

The succession of Mikhail Gorbachev proved an era of reconciliation that ended also the Soviets occupation of Afghanistan and introduced the concepts of 'perestroika' and 'glasnost', which virtually paved the way for dilution of Cold War. Boris Yeltsin emerged even more radical exponent of restructuring (perestroika). However, a coup by hardliners against Gorbachev on 29 August 1991 threatened the whole process. Boris Yeltsin defied the attempt successfully to reinstate Gorbachev who dissolved the Communist Party and proposed formation of Commonwealth of Independent States (CIS) on 21 December 1991. This led formally to the grant of independence along with others to Central Asian and Trans-Caucasian states. Gorbachev resigned on 25 December 1991, leaving Boris Yeltsin in the shaky saddle. Thereafter Russian Federation, under Boris Yeltsin embarked on ambitious agenda to recover Russian economy through shock therapy. In the process, he had to face several reverses, which he attempted to address through sacking of senior government officials. On 31 December 1999, Boris Yeltsin resigned. Vladimir Putin became acting President to win election later on 26 March 2000. Mr. Putin launched a full-scale offensive against Chechens to establish writ of Russian Federation. In 1999, former Russian satellites, Poland, Hungary and Czech Republic joined NATO. Lithuania, Latvia and Estonia followed suit in 2004. Faced with the challenge of economic recovery and switching completely to the free market economy, Russia's domestic milieu has remained plagued with unrest, particularly in north Caucasus.

Besides her crucial role as a powerful nuclear power in the world arena, Russia faces lingering international disputes. China is keen to resolve her disputes over the Amur, Ussuri and Argun Rivers. Similarly, Japan laid claim on Kuril Islands, which is a thorn in relations between Russia and Japan. The border with Georgia is still to be demarcated and OSCE is monitoring volatile areas such as Pankisi Gorge and Argun Gorge. Matters of Caspian Sea surface division are still to be resolved with Azerbaijan, Kazakhstan and other Caspian littorals. Russia has a dispute with Norway over maritime limits in Barents Sea. Border agreement with Estonia concluded in 1996 is yet to be ratified by Russian Federation. Land delimitation with Ukraine is ratified but maritime regime of Sea of Azov and Kerch Strait is still to be resolved. Russia has not ratified 1990 Maritime Boundary Agreement with USA in Bering Sea. Such sores, certainly give enough stock to the Russian leadership whose hands are otherwise full with domestic and international events to conduct power game.

Armenia. A country with an area of 29,800 sq kms and population of about 3 million people has 93 percent Armenian and 7 percent mix of Kurds, Ukrainians and Russians. Located in southern Caucasus and the smallest of the former Soviet republics, (Map 8), Georgia to the north, Azerbaijan to the east, Turkey to the west and Iran to the south bound it. Its land is characterized by rugged mountains and extinct volcanoes. The highest point is that of Mount Aragats (13,435 ft.). It is the same Mount, where according to some expert's interpretation of Biblical reference, rested ark of Noah after the flood. In 6th Century BC, Urartu ruled Armenian Kingdom. However, it was Tigrane the Great, 95 BC-55 BC, who ruled vast stretch of empire from the Caspian Sea to the Mediterranean.

Then on Armenia faced successive invasion by Greeks, Romans, Persian, Byzantines, Mongols, Arabs, Ottoman Turks and finally by Russians.

During Turks rule, its population faced persecution in 1894, 1896 and in April 1915. According to Armenia, the last of the three is termed as the worst horrific genocide of 20th Century when 0.6 to 1.5 million Armenians perished. Turkey denies these figures, accepting only the possible civil war casualties of Armenians.

As Turks were defeated in World War I, independent Republic of Armenia was established on 28

May 1918; soon to be annexed by the Soviet Army on 29 November 1920.

Map-8: Armenia

In March 1922, the Soviets combined Armenia and Georgia to form one republic called Trans-Caucasian SSR. In 1936, Armenia was delinked and made a separate SSR. Armenia has remained locked in dispute over Nagorno-Karabakh enclave since 1988.[56] It declared its independence on 23 September 1991. Armenia resorted to military solution and successfully waged war with Azerbaijan to liberate Armenian majority enclave of Nagorno-Karabakh from 1992-94, accentuating Azerbaijan grievances, which lost 1/5th of territory to Armenia.

The Armenian diaspora historically had been very strong and influential. Out of total 8 million Armenians, 60 percent live worldwide, 1 million each in USA and Russian Federation, the rest in Iran, Syria, Georgia, France, Lebanon, Argentina and Canada. All profess Orthodox Christianity. With capital at Yerevan, its other large cities are Vanadzor, Gyumri, and Abovian. Its monetary unit is called 'dram'.

Georgia. It is a Caucasian country with total area of 69,700 sq km and population of about 4.7 million. Black Sea in the west, Turkey and Armenia to the south, Azerbaijan to the east and Russia to the north bound it. It includes autonomous Republics of Abkhazia, Ajaria and South Ossetia. It proclaimed independence from the Soviets on 6 April 1991. With capital at Tbilisi, Kutaisi, Batumi and Sokhumi are its other large cities (Map 9). Its monetary unit is called 'lari'.

Georgian history dates back to 4 BC and Christianity was introduced in 337 AD. During reign of Queen Tamara, 1184-1213 AD, whole of Trans-Caucasus was under Georgian rule. Mongols captured it in 13th Century. Persians and Turks made it a 'tug of war' in 16th Century, until it became vassal to Russia in 18th Century in exchange of Russian security extended to her against Turks and Persians. In 1918, Georgia pursued anti-Bolshevik stance and declared independence. The Soviets, along with others in Trans-Caucasus annexed Georgian territory in 1922 and thus it became part of Trans-Caucasus SSR. Declared as a separate Georgia SSR in 1936, it gained independence on dissolution of USSR on 6 April 1991.[57]

The government is engaged in armed conflict with Abkhazian since 1992. In 1994 Georgia and Russia signed cooperation treaty that enabled Russia to keep three military bases in Georgia and to train and equip Georgian Army. Similarly, hostilities in South Ossetia and Ajara are simmering ever since. West-leaning Georgians who suspect Russian complicity in Abkhazia and South Ossetian separatist movements express mutual distrust. Similarly, Russia suspects that Georgia helps sheltering rebels in Pankisi Gorge area of Georgian borderland. Edward Shevardnadze elected since 1992 was re-elected with heavy mandate in the 2000 Presidential Elections. Demonstrators swept his government, though leaning to the West and plagued by massive corruption and cronyism, away in 'velvet' revolution. A lawyer and a reformist, Mikhail Saakhashvili, an opponent of Edward Shevardnadze succeeded him in May 2004 after forcing him to resign.

50

Map-9: Georgia

Hosting of the Baku-Tbilisi-Ceyhan (BTC) pipeline through Georgian territory, inaugurated in May 2005, shall give tremendous boost by implication to economy as well as her standing tall with the West. As regards her international disputes, her border with Russia has been delimited but not demarcated in several segments. OSCE observers are monitoring the conflict-prone areas like Pankisi Gorge in Akhmeti Region and Argun Gorge in Abkhazia. Meshkheti Turks scattered throughout former Soviet Union seek return to Georgia while Armenians in Javakheti Region seek greater autonomy and closer links with Armenia.[58] The situation in Georgia would remain a testing ground for the political acumen of its leaders.

Turkey. Republic of Turkey[59] has an area of 0.78 million sq km and total population of about 69 million people. With Ankara as capital, its other largest cities are Istanbul, Izmir, Bursa, Adana and Gaziantep in that order of progression. Turkish 'lira' is its monetary unit. Turkey is located at northeast end of Mediterranean, southeast end of Europe and southwest end of Asia. To its north is Black Sea and Aegean Sea is to the west. Among her neighbors,

51

Greek and Bulgaria are in the west, Ukraine and Russia to the north, Georgia, Armenia, Azerbaijan and Iran to the east while Syria and Iraq are situated to the south.

Map-10: Turkey

The Dardanelle, the Sea of Marmora and the Bosporus divide the country. The European part of Turkey has an area of about 15,000 sq km, equal to Massachusetts, while the Asian portion is stretched over an area of about 770,000 sq km, almost the size of Texas. 99.8 percent of its people are Muslims, including Kurds who make 1/5th of the total population.

On the chapter of international disputes, she has complex maritime, air and territorial disputes with Greece in the Aegean Sea and Cyprus question those remain unresolved with Greece. Syria and Iraq challenge Turkish regulation of water of upper Euphrates and Turkey curtly rebuffs any Syrian claim over her Hatay province. Its border has also remained closed with Armenia as Turkey supports Azerbaijan on Nagorno-Karabakh issue. Kurds, who make 20 percent of its total population are claiming at least autonomous region to which Turkey is not inclined to oblige. About 35,000 people have perished in the Kurds' struggle against Turkey. The recently inaugurated BTC pipeline has enhanced Turkey's economic prospects by implication while it has the capacity to deliver one million barrels of oil a day direct to her Mediterranean Seaport of Ceyhan. Its geo-strategic location makes it extremely important ally of the West as it sits on Bosporus, a solitary choke point for whole of the Black Sea.

CHAPTER – TWO

OIL AND GAS POTENTIALS
(A Comparative View)

History of Oil

The narrative so far amply highlights the significance Central Eurasia has in general and the Caspian Region in particular. History bears testimony that all kings and emperors who ventured into this region underlined its geo-strategic strengths as well as vulnerabilities through an act of aggression or subjugation of masses. Incidentally, 'hydrocarbon' shade of this region also emerges clear since Herodotus times when he wrote about the temples in Baku area, known to be using oil products in the BC era. An eminent writer, J.D. Henry also remarked about Baku, "commercially and ethnographically the Johannesburg of Russia.... the modern, stone built palaces of the oil kings, the new technical school, erected on the best European model and more conspicuous than the ancient landmarks of the city... and the thousands of small shops in which sad-eyed Asiatic sell the famous goods, 'slop' clothing and all kind of ancient weapons."[60] The quote presents an interesting dichotomy. On one side it talks of majestic buildings and palaces of oil kings and on the other side, it portrays Asiatic as sad-eyed and deeply worried. The contrast persists, no wonder even at the dawn of the 21st Century, exactly 100 years later from when J.D. Henry wrote it in 1905. To debate the causes and implications of the dripping poverty, observed by the sides of majestic buildings, though valid but would be a contextual deviation and hence avoided here.

The objective to highlight this aspect here has been to authenticate a phenomenon that the presence of oil, which made the region envy of any power, what sat under it in form of fossil fuel was not known to any of them in present scale and magnitude. Precisely for this reason the figures and statistics of oil and gas started emerging effectively only at the time when 20th Century was well high on the horizon.

Thence mobility certainly improved in the region as well as among the Caspian littorals on land and Caspian Sea that boosted trade of other commodities including caviar, which was then the most precious one. The onset of the Industrial Revolution triggered by the marvelous invention of Internal Combustion Engine accentuated the thirst of machines for the oil, and of the nations who dug deeper and wider, improving in the process hordes of relevant technologies in quest of such a magnificent source of energy. Otherwise, until 1905, the companies or their governments seldom publicized the statistics if maintained at all. It is for this reason that oil experts until 19th Century in Baku area referred to its 82 oil pits and not in term of million of barrels. However, the USA was exception that first struck oil gusher in 1859 and soon it was being stored in barrels, though of non-standard size and shape.

Oil statistics and history of standardization of barrels go side by side. Although pipelines, ship containers, railway bogies and oil tankers carry the oil over long distances, the barrel remains its basic unit. In fact, the oil workers could not contain the flow of first oil gusher in 1859 when the management of Pennsylvania oil well ran out of all types of containers. While collecting beer and wine barrels from anywhere it could lay hands upon, they felt the need to produce 'barrels' exclusively for oil. Thus, the barrel emerged as standard unit, which contained 42 gallons of crude oil.

Interestingly, in Europe, oil is measured in metric tons and in Japan in kiloliters. It was the USA and Canada, first to adopt this barrel as a standard; but why a 42 gallon barrel? History has it that the size was borrowed from England where King Edward IV fixed 42 gallon capacity of a barrel to obviate 'diver's deceit' in the packing of fish. At the time of the Pennsylvania oil well, in the North Sea, herring fishing was a prolific business. Almost a decade before Col Drake drilled his well in 1859, "Pennsylvania producers confirmed 42 gallon barrel as their standard as opposed to say, 31 ½ gallon wine barrel or the 32 gallon London ale barrel, or the 36 gallon London beer barrel.... for the 42-gallon barrel is still used as the standard measurement...in the biggest business in the North Sea, which today, of course is not herring, but oil."[61] It thus explains why reference to the oil quantities in its statistics, would generally be to 'barrels' and not metric tons or kiloliters. Where inevitable, 'factor' has been indicated to convert to barrels.

Caspian Shift and the Oil Scene

Similarly, about the history of product, when Caspian caviar was more alluring than Caspian oil, yet not affecting the world scene since the region was blanket-wrapped by the Soviets; Central Eurasia remained sadly out of the sight until almost end of the 20th Century. However, on the international scene, momentum of the statistics of oil and gas had been building up faster than expected. In 1950s, the Middle East overtook the USA. In the view of a geologist, there the situation was getting as chronic as it was in USA in the earliest days of oil industry that is when the problem became market rather than the production. The increase in world crude oil production from 8.7 million barrels per day in 1948 to 42 million barrels per day in 1972 marked its growth almost five times. On the contrary, US production merely doubled from its 5.5 million barrels per day for the same duration. The shift of these statistics had materialized due to shift of production from one million barrels per day to 18 million barrels per day in Middle East.[62] Until dissolution of USSR, exclusive focus did not aim at the Caspian Region statistics as it was done on becoming the three Caspian littorals, Azerbaijan, Turkmenistan and Kazakhstan, independent in 1991.

Oil and Gas Potentials--A Geologist's View

Geology sets the pace for statistics and Allah shapes the hydrocarbon geology. That is why Middle East, USA, Central Eurasia and some other African and Asian regions float over oil and not the Western Europe, China or the Sub Continent. Its significance thus stands highlighted. For the Caspian Region, geologists like Abram and Narimanov claim that a Russian Engineer, F.N Semyenov drilled the first oil well in 1848 in Bibi-Eibet area of Aspheron Peninsula of Azerbaijan. They also claimed that the first off shore well was also drilled in 1924 near Baku coast. Azerbaijan played a prominent role in oil production during the Soviet era.[63] Similarly during mid eighties discovery of two elephants[64] such as Tengiz and Karachaganak in Kazakhstan proved that despite extracting oil from this region for over 150 years, Central Eurasia (Caspian Basin) still had credible oil potentials.

From a geological point of view, the Caspian Sea belongs to two different basins, the North Caspian, also known as Pricaspian Basin and the South Caspian Basin (Map-11). There are three other basins, which have to be understood since all of it makes a geological system. These are the North Usturt Basin, Mangyshlak Basin and Amu Darya Basin. The North Usturt Basin occupies the territory between the northern part of the Caspian Sea and the southern tip of the Ural mountain belt. Mangyshlak Basin is located directly east of Caspian Sea and south of North Usturt. Amu River Basin occupies eastern Turkmenistan, western Uzbekistan and northern Afghanistan. In the light of a credible study by Manik Talwani, Andrei Belopolsky and Dianne Berry, these four basins will be covered one by one, which constitute the major concentration of hydrocarbon resources in Central Eurasia.[65] It would also indicate how the groundwork for elaborate statistics is laid out merely by scientific survey with forecasts so close to the reality. Like arithmetic, geology has standard terminology and hence recourse to the geologist's text has been made.

South Caspian Basin. This geological basin contains the largest proven oil and gas resources in the Central Asian and Caucasian countries of the Caspian Region. Three Caspian littorals' territories, Azerbaijan, Kazakhstan, and Turkmenistan, lie in the South Caspian Basin. It is 400 km across in the northwest to southeast direction and is 900 m deep. Two main folding ranges, the great Caucasus and the lesser Caucasus-Talesh-Elburz arc surround the basin. Apsheron-Balkanian sill makes its northern boundary. "Low geothermal gradient, about 1.5 C per 100 m provides favorable conditions for the preservation of hydrocarbons at significant depths up to 10 km. Drilling on the South Caspian shelf in Azerbaijan and Turkmenistan revealed that thick 2,500-3,000 meters shallow-water sediments accumulated from the late Jurassic to the early Pliocene, as Alikhanov asserts in his study."[66] Clark is of the view that the oil-bearing suite is made of sandstone and siltstone that are probably deltaic deposits of the Paleo-Volga River. The buried Paleo-Volga valley has been disclosed by seismic surveys in the central part of the Caspian.[67] Geologists have identified Pereriva Suite as one of the most important producing intervals in the subsurface. It is particularly important in the Azeri, Chiragh, and Guneshli fields, where it is up to 110 m. "The main reservoirs of the fields located on the Apsheron Peninsula that is a major producing interval offshore has been designated as Balakhany Suite."[68]

North Caspian (Pricaspian) Basin. The limits of this basin have been identified as the southeastern margin of the Russian platform and extending to the northern coast of the Caspian Sea. The topographic elevations are below sea level and can be as low as 24m. Two Caspian littorals i.e. Russia and Kazakhstan claim the territory within the North

Caspian Basin. A large part of the Russian Caspian shelf (southern part of the basin), however, is off limits for exploration because it is a sturgeon spawning ground. Two super giant fields Tengiz and Karachaganak and a large number of smaller fields are located in this basin.[69] The northern, western and southwestern parts of the depression are gas prone, while the east and southeast are oil prone.[70]

Map-11: Caspian Region's Geological Basins
Source: US Energy Information Administration: www.eia.doe.gov January 2004

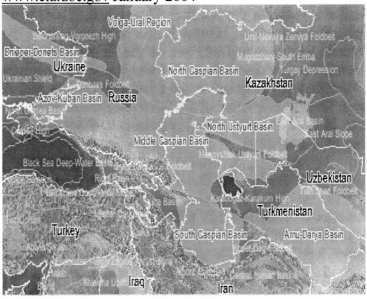

North Usturt Basin. The Basin spreads over an area of 240,000 sq km. To the north lie the North Caspian Basin, the Mugodzar and Chelkar down warps to the northeast, the Aral-Kyzlkum zone of highs on the east, and on the south lays the Mangyshlak-Central Usturt system of highs. The basin opens into the Caspian Sea on the West. The distribution of reserves among the plays follows a pattern i.e. Middle-Upper Jurassic rocks contain over 60 percent of the oil and gas, Triassic rocks, 10 percent; the Lower Cretaceous section, 21 percent; and Eocene rocks, 8 percent.[71]

Mangyshlak Basin. The basin is located on the western part of Turan platform. Central Mangyshlak rift formed in Early Paleozoic time. Oil and Gas exploration activity since 1990 has been targeting the middle part of the basin. Other areas of the basin, such as the eastern Mangyshlak, the Uchkuduk depression, Buzuchi Peninsula, and the continuation of the Mangyshlak basin off the Caspian shore, have yet not been explored for oil and gas. Geological evidence suggests that the Uchkuduk depression contains Middle and Upper Triassic oil and gas reservoirs similar to those in the southern Mangyshlak. There is an increasing amount of interest in the northern part of the Buzuchi Peninsula and offshore on the Caspian Sea shelf. Seismic surveys demonstrate that many onshore structures on the Buzuchi Peninsula extend into the Caspian Sea. A large, favorable structure of the Jurassic-Cretaceous age has been identified north of the Kalamkas anticlinal zone and west of Karazhanbas.[72]

Amu River Basin. The Basin is spread over an area of 370,000 sq km of eastern Turkmenistan and western Uzbekistan; while about 57,000 sq kms extend to northern Afghanistan. Its southwestern border lies at the base of the Kopet Dag. The Amu Darya Basin lies within the Turanian plate, a feature that extends into the Caspian Sea and farther west into Europe as the Scythian platform. On the north, the basin is connected with the West Siberian platform through the Turgay depression. The Amu Darya Basin has a complex tectonic structure. The Merv[73]-Serakh zone of highs and the Uch-Adzhi arch are separated by the Bayram-Ali arch. These three structural elements are sometimes united into the Mary-Uch-Adzhi monocline, which dips southward and forms the north flank of the Murghab depression. Over 130 gas, gas-condensate and oil fields are located in the Amu Darya Basin. Uzbekistan shares 60 percent to 40 percent with Turkmenistan. The Amu Darya Basin is gas prone. Oil is found only as small pools in the Chardzhou and Bukhara gas-oil regions. Of the total assessed hydrocarbon resources in the basin, 4 percent is oil, and 96 percent is gas. The Yashlag area in the central part of the Murghab region is the most promising area for oil and gas exploration. O Connor and Sonnenberg assess the undiscovered resources of this area at 120 tcf of gas, 7 billion barrels of condensate, and 3-4 Gb of oil.[74]

Geological Epitomization. By now, it is clear that the Caspian-Caucasus geology based oil and gas potentials estimates are very bright. Central Eurasian Region includes a number of petroleum basins that are different in their geological development, reservoir types, hydrocarbon types, quantity and nature of resources. Azerbaijan territory includes part of the South Caspian basin. Kazakhstan's territory contains a part of the South Caspian and whole of the North Caspian, Mangyshlak, and North Usturt basins. Turkmenistan is spread over the South Caspian and Amu Darya basin. Uzbekistan also has the major chunk of the Amu Darya basin. However, large known oil and gas fields are in the Caspian offshore Guneshli, Chiragh, and Azeri areas in Azerbaijan territory but are disputed by Turkmenistan and Iran.

Presently, most of the Turkmenistan Caspian shelf, with more than 40 untested structures, remains relatively unexplored. Turkmenistan is also disputing the Kyapaz field, discovered by Azerbaijan. Turkmenistan undiscovered reserves on its Caspian shelf are assessed at 22 Gb of oil and 168 tcf of gas. The Northern Caspian and northwestern Kazakhstan harbor large amounts of proven reserves and high potential for new discoveries.

Kazakhstan reserves mainly lie in two super giant fields, the Tengiz (oil) and Karachaganak (gas). The recoverable reserves of Tengiz have been recently upgraded to 12 Gb of oil with an estimated 25 Gb of oil in place. The North Usturt and Amu Darya basins have some potential in oil and gas exploration. Amu Darya Basin contains mainly gas reserves with a minor amount of oil. Kazakhstan is a leader among the Central Asian countries in the amount of proven reserves and the potential for new discoveries.[75] It has 10 to 22 Gb of proven crude reserves and 53 to 83 tcf of gas. Turkmenistan also has large gas reserves to the tune of 95 to 155 tcf of gas. Uzbekistan does not have a significant amount of oil but contains large amounts of gas measuring 70 to 105 tcf. It also has a large territory that has not been well explored for oil and gas. The total proven oil reserves of the Central Eurasian countries were estimated by the geologists as ranging from 15 to 31 Gb, while proven gas reserves estimates vary from 230 to 360 tcf of gas. Central Eurasian reserves represent approximately 3-4 percent of the world total proven oil reserves[76]and 6-7 percent of the world gas reserves.

General Review of Oil and Gas Statistics

The Caspian Sea region, also highlighted through geological view, comprises the sea and five littoral states. The region has tremendous significance for the world oil and gas market because of the potential hydrocarbon resources, which stand relatively shadowed by certain geographical and geopolitical constraints that would be discussed in the relevant chapters. Here the focus is on statistics of oil and gas by quoting various sources. Based on the empirical values of oil and gas reserves, some pertinent questions need to be answered. These are:

- What are the proven and prospective reserves of the Caspian Region states?
- What quantities these littoral states are producing, consuming themselves and able to export what is left with them?
- Where does the region stand in comparative view against rest of the world?
- What are production, consumption, export or import potential of leading producers and consumers? Because industrial countries when faced with menace of dwindling production and/or supplies in certain point of time would naturally shudder to see the impending demise of their power-status.

Thus, out of these figures, a logical discussion will ensue for highlighting the struggle, now commonly referred to as the 'New Great Game'. The game in simple phraseology is nothing but the effort by some industrialized countries to avert oil shock to their leading economies by means, which may not meet the transparency standards in the domain of international relations. Before dealing with the oil and gas inventory, some comments on the reserve definition and terminology may be pertinent to enumerate since these are frequently referred but infrequently understood.

'Estimates' are made using the sophisticated seismic survey instruments with a combination of computing techniques; the most common is called as Monte Carlo Simulation to award the reserve various ranking probabilities. Low case is graded as P95 and the high case as P5, which is the 'best estimate' to equate with the 'mean estimates'. Thus, the values related to these two are 'probable reserve' in low case or high case. 'Proved Reserves' are defined generally as those quantities, which, the geological and engineering information indicates with reasonable certainty, can be recovered from a known reservoir under existing economic and operating conditions. Similarly, a 'giant' field has internationally been defined as the one having the potential of more than 500 million barrels of ultimate recovery. However Matt Simon differs and calls it a 'giant field' if it produces 100,000 barrels per day.[77]

The Caspian Region defined to include Azerbaijan, Iran, Turkmenistan, Kazakhstan, Russia, the five sea littorals, also includes Uzbekistan, which though, not a littoral state, but is part of its hydrocarbon system. The geological view also supports this assumption when Uzbekistan has most of Amu Darya Basin along with Turkmenistan.

As seen from the geological count, the region has sizable oil and gas reserves, which have been placed now as 3 percent to 4 percent of the world total.[78] The analysts are optimistic about the proven oil and gas reserves' improved statistics, casting favorable and visible impact on the regional economies by year 2010. The proven oil reserves range between 17-33 Gb that are comparable to Qatar on low end and US on high end. In 2002, regional oil production was recorded as 1.6 million bbl/day, comparable to South American second largest producer, Brazil. By 2010, Caspian Region countries are likely to produce 3.0 to 4.7 million bbl/day.

Table-1 shows that Caspian Region's leading upstream foreign investment projects that enabled Azerbaijan and Kazakhstan to become main oil producers of the region as of 2004 with potentials to grow further by year 2005. Tengiz oil elephant of Kazakhstan and ACG (Azeri, Chiragh and Guneshli) oil elephants of Azerbaijan combined produced 434,000 bbl/day in 2004, which was 1/4th of the region's total production. Their production is likely to touch 2.7 million bbl/day by 2010. Viewing individual score of both the states from these projects only, Azerbaijan alone will touch one million bbl/d mark by 2009 while Kazakhistan would also show significant production for the same period, 1.7 million bbl/d. Thus, Kazakhstan, with the discovery of new giant in 2002 at 'Kashagan', estimated to contain 7-9 Gb of oil, having potential for upward revision to 9-13 Gb, is likely to outclass Azerbaijan and become the lead producer.[79] Conversely, Turkmenistan and Uzbekistan have comparatively smaller role in the field of oil because of their weak oil potential. Thus, the investment and exploratory effort by the Oil Companies is obviously directed towards Azerbaijan and Kazakhstan.

On the other hand, littoral status of Russia and Iran, because of their small share of oil and gas production in the Caspian Region does not emerge prominent.[80]

Table-1: Proven Reserves, Production 2004 and Projections 2005(Source: US Department of Energy Administration: www.eia.doe.gov)

Table 1	The Caspian Sea Region's Leading Upstream Foreign Investment Projects by Country			
Country	Project	Proven Reserves	2004 Production	Projection
Azerbaijan	ACG Mega-Structure (BP et al)	5.4 Billion Barrels	144,000 bbl/d	2005: 460,000 bbl/d 2008-9: 1 million bbl/d
	Shah Deniz (BP et al.)	2.5 Billion barrels 14 Trillion Cubic Feet	not producing	2006: 296 Bcf
Kazakhstan	Tengiz (ChevronTexaco et al.)	6-9 Billion Barrels	290,000 bbl/d	2006: 450,000 bbl/d 2010: 700,000 bbl/d
	Karachaganak (BG, Agip, et al.)	2.4 Billion Barrels	210,000 bbl/d	2008: 240,000 bbl/d
	Kashagan (ENI-Agip, BG, et al.)	7-9 Billion Barrels	not producing	2008: 75,000 bbl/d
Turkmenistan	Cheleken (Dragon Oil)	0.6 Billion Barrels	10,000 bbl/d	2003: 11,000 bbl/d
	Nebit Dag (Burren Energy)	0.1 Billion Barrels	10,000 bbl/d	2003: 12,000 bbl/d
Uzbekistan	Central Ustyurt and Southwest Gissar (Trinity Energy)	Being Developed		2006: 2,600 bbl/d 71 Bcf

Yet another source, International Energy Agency, gives the oil and gas statistics as of 2004, showing the proven and possible quantities of all the littorals including Russia and Iran. It places the region's proven reserves at 15.6 Gb and possible reserves at 163 Gb, also showing the

65

gas proven reserves at 8.3 tcm and possible gas reserves at 9.3 tcm.

Within the Caspian Region perspective, Russia's total share of oil, proven as well as possible reserves, is merely 5 Gb while that of Iran's total share is just about 12 Gb. In term of percentages therefore, Russia and Iran possess barely about 2.8 percent and 6.6 percent of total Caspian Region oil respectively. For the gas reserves, Russian share is negligible. However, Iran has 0.3 tcm of the total Caspian Region proven reserves that are 17.6 tcm. In other words, Iran has 1.7 percent of Caspian's total gas reserves. Table 2 quoted by Ariel Cohen only supports the IAE statistics. Recall that while consulting ensuing tables, showing tcm/bcm of gas and Mt of oil, multiplying the given values with '35.3' and '7.3' will give tcf/bcf of gas and million bbl of oil respectively.

Table 3 is the latest update on Caspian littorals statistics of 2005 vintage. According to this source while it reflects the individual countries score, the region proven reserve in low case have been placed at 17.246 Gb and at 44.194 Gb in high case. The estimates of possible oil reserves, according to this table, stand at 186 Gb. Thus, total oil reserves of the region in low case are 167 Gb and in high case, these are over 194 Gb of oil. A brief arithmetic check suggests that the latter two figures appear to have some discrepancy in the table because the correct total of both, proven as well possible oil reserves comes to 203 Gb in low case and 230 Gb in high case. The region production in 1992 was 0.927 million bbl/day when it soared to 1.336 million bbl/ day in year 2000 and 1.952 million bbl/day in 2004. The scene appears further encouraging when oil productions in 2010 will touch the mark of 2.437 million bbl/day on low side and 5.890 million bbl/day on high side. On the natural gas side, its proven reserves are placed at 232 tcf, and possible reserves at 328 tcf. Thus, the total gas reserves potential of the region stand at 560 tcf mark. It produced 4.10 tcf in 1992, 4.39 tcf in 2000, 4.94 tcf in 2004 and is projected to produce 9.61 tcf per year in 2010.

Table-2

Estimates of Recoverable Oil and Gas Resources in the Caspian Region

	Proven Oil (Billion Barrels)	Possible Oil (Billion Barrels)	Total	Proven Gas (Trillion Cubic Meters)	Possible Gas (Trillion Cubic Meters)
Azerbaijan	3.6	27.0	31.0	0.3	1.0
Kazakstan	10.0	85.0	95.0	1.5	2.5
Turkmenistan	1.5	32.0	33.5	4.4	4.5
Uzbekistan	0.2	1.0	1.2	2.1	1.0
Russia	0.2	5.0	5.0	NA	NA
Iran	NA	12.0	12.0	0	0.3
Total	15.6	163.0	178.0	8.3	9.3

Note: Totals may not add up due to rounding.
Source: U.S. Department of State, Caspian Region Energy Development Report (As Required by HR 3610), undated report attached to letter from Barbara Larkin, Assistant Secretary for Legislative Affairs, to Senator Robert Byrd, April 15, 1997, p. 3.

In the natural gas sector, the Caspian Region emerges more prominent than oil because of its significant gas reserves; estimated to be 232 tcf, comparable to those in Saudi Arabia. As is evident from the graph at Figure-1, Uzbekistan, Azerbaijan and Kazakhstan have seen gradual but modest increase in this field since 1991. Turkmenistan growth moved in an inverse direction on independence and gradually recovered from 1998 onwards. The reasons may be two. One, but not very significant, was the lack of foreign investors interest in the country with poor infrastructure while they were eager to clinch oil deals in other states which were far less investment-intensive.

Second, and perhaps the major reason, was that Turkmenistan emerged as a competitor to Gazprom, a Russian State Gas Company, which had monopoly over the prices and pipeline, affording access to Turkmenistan gas to the world market. Gazprom was inclined to earn more and give less to the producer country.

Table-3: Caspian Sea Region, Oil and Gas Statistics (2010 Projections)

Caspian Sea Region: Survey of Key Oil and Gas Statistics and Forecasts

August 2005

The following table is a survey of oil and gas statistics and forecasts and is not meant to represent official EIA statistics, please see specific sources in the notes below.

OIL

The Caspian Sea Region contains proven oil reserves estimated to be between 17 and 44 billion barrels, comparable to Qatar on the low end and the United States on the high end.

Reserves (Billion Barrels)

Country	Proven Oil Reserves[1] Low	High	Possible[2]	Total Low	High
Azerbaijan	7	12.5	32	39	44.5
Iran		0.1	15		15.1
Kazakhstan	9	29	92	41	61
Russia*		0.3	7		7.3
Turkmenistan	0.546	1.7	38	32.546	33.7
Uzbekistan	0.3	0.594	2	32.3	32.594
Total Caspian Sea Region	17.246	44.194	186	167.246	194.194

Production (Thousand barrels per day)

In 2004, regional oil production reached roughly 1.9 million barrels per day, comparable to South America's second largest oil producer, Brazil. By 2010, production is forecast to reach 3.1 million barrels in the IEO reference case.

Country	1992	2000	2004	Low 2010	High
Azerbaijan	222	309	319	789	1290
Iran				N/A	
Kazakhstan	529	718	1,221	748	2400
Russia*	0	0	0	200	
Turkmenistan	110	157	260	475	1000
Uzbekistan	66	152	150	225	1000
Total Caspian Sea Region*	927.3	1,335.9	1,950.2	2,437	5,890

GAS

The Caspian Sea Region's proven natural gas reserves are estimated at 232 trillion cubic feet, comparable to Saudi Arabia.

Reserves (tcf)

Country	Proven Reserves	Possible Reserves	Total Reserves
Azerbaijan	30	35	65
Iran	0	11	11
Kazakhstan	65	88	153
Russia*	N/A	N/A	N/A
Turkmenistan	71	159	230
Uzbekistan	66.2	35	101
Total Caspian Sea Region	232	328	560

Production (tcf/y)

Regional production reached approximately 4.9 tcf in 2004, comparable to the combined production of S. America, Central America, and Mexico. In 2010, the governments of the Caspian Sea region expect their countries to produce a total of 9.61 Tcf, more than the 2004 production from the entire Middle East

Country	1992	2000	2004	2010	
Azerbaijan	0.28	0.20	0.19	0.8	
Iran					
Kazakhstan	0.29	0.31	0.58	1.24	
Russia*					
Turkmenistan	2.02	1.89	2.07	4.24	
Uzbekistan	1.51	1.99	2.12	3.53	
Total Caspian Sea Region	4.10	4.39	4.94	9.61	

1. Proven reserves are defined by the EIA as those volumes of oil and gas that geological and egineering data show with reasonable certainty to be economically recoverable under existing economic and operating conditions.
2. Possible reserves are less precisely quantified and are defined here to include other reserves found through extensions, divisions, and new discoveries
3 Other estimates (EIA/IEO 2004): 3.2 million bbl/d (Ref. Case, not including Russia), (World Oil, 10 March 2004): 3 million bbl/d
*Only Caspian area oil and gas production
**Source: Reserves: OGJ; Production: EIA; Forecasts: Interfax, EIA, IEA, CERA, SKRIN, APS Review

It left Turkmenistan with little incentive to produce more gas. Turkmenistan output thus dropped from 2.02 tcf in 1992 to just 466 bcf in 1998 when she remained locked with Russia in severe price dispute.

Consequent to new agreements in 1999 and 2003, the productions increased significantly as does the Figure-1 register the upsurge.[81] Uzbekistan, by contrast, is the third largest producer in CIS and one of the top ten natural gas producers in the world.[82] It has enhanced production by 50 percent in 1992-2001 span of time from 1.51 tcf to 2.3 tcf. While the general view about these states sets the thought process in motion, it will be worthwhile to focus on their capacities of proven oil and gas reserves, production and consumption. It would enable to find out what all is left by each of them to export to the world market, a factor that would obviously make the difference.

Caspian Region Oil and Gas Export Potentials

The statistics in Table-1 and Figure-1 show generally, what type and quantity of fossil fuel is held and produced by Caspian Region countries. The real impact on the international market would emerge when each of them is found letting maximum oil and gas reach the world market. In fact, this part is related with the New Great Game. In other words, equation between domestic demands and exports becomes the vital area of statistics. In this context, because of prediction variation in GDP growth of these countries, International Energy Agency takes two sets of scenarios; one characterized by low case and other by high case. Table 4 and Table 5 (Appendix-1) cover the oil aspects of low and high case respectively while Table 6 and 7 (Appendix-1) deal with the gas statistics of low and high.[83] The figures have been quoted in million tonnes (Mt) for oil and billion cubic meters (Bcm) for gas. The tables also indicate relevant 'factors' in case oil and gas quantities are to be viewed in 'million barrels' of oil or 'bcf' of gas. The gap between low and high case has also forced a limitation due to uncertainties of completion of large exploratory and transmission projects, contemplated in Azerbaijan and Kazakhstan. Thus, the experts opine that

69

Azerbaijan oil exports high case forecast would be at 55 Mt in 2010 and 94 Mt in 2020. Similarly, in low case, these are to stay at 30 Mt in 2010 and 68 Mt in 2020 (Table 4 and table 5). Her gas exports figure out only from 2005 onward, which are likely to soar to 5-11 Bcm (Table 6 and Table 7).[84]

Since Azerbaijan has the highest GDP growth rate out of the countries, her economy is likely to recover speedily by registering 7 percent GDP growth up to 2010 in high case and 5.7 percent in low case. At present, her energy sector contribution to GDP is the highest at around 15 percent among the four countries. By 2010, the share is projected to rise 27 percent. In case of Kazakhstan, the tables show that volume of oil and gas production will be higher than Azerbaijan but given the size of large and energy-intensive Kazak economy, it would export less than Azerbaijan. In high case, her exports will be 55 Mt in 2010 and 76 Mt in 2020. In low case, these would remain at 43 Mt and 78 Mt respectively for the both time scales, 2010 and 2020. Because domestic energy consumption is greater in Kazakhstan than Azerbaijan, energy sector share to GDP growth is likely to remain comparatively small. Her GDP growth in first decade (2010) in low and high case would be around 3.5 percent and 5 percent respectively. During the second decade (2020), low and high case GDP growth is likely to remain around 3.8 percent and 5 percent annually. In gas sector, Kazakhstan has no gas export potentials, both in low as well as in high case scenario until 2020. Turkmenistan gas reserves, generally untapped so far, have larger export potential, which are 90 percent of all other regional countries. In the high case scenario, it may be 72 Bcm in 2010 and 111 Bcm in 2020. In the low case forecast, her exports may be 64 Bcm in 2010 and 102 Bcm in 2020. High case scenario for oil being meager may exist at 5 Mt in 2010 and 6 Mt in 2020. As regards Uzbekistan, she is the only country among the four whose economy is not likely to be driven by the energy sector. Her oil exports in high case scenario are expected to be only 2 Mt both in 2010 and 2020. Gas exports in high case may drop to zero and may become negative in 2020. In low case, her exports may be 5 Bcm in 2010 and 6 Bcm in 2020. Her economy is forecast to grow at 3 percent in low case and 4.5 percent in high case.

Caspian Region and the World Hydrocarbon Scene

Having known the exclusive potentials of the Caspian Countries, what they produce or consume and what they can export, it is imperative to focus on how the regional statistics are framed in the global statistics. Some tables have been placed that give figures of the world regions of oil and gas, which would contain the Caspian countries account as well. The comparative scrutiny would make the facts sheet distinctly clear. It would also fetch the answer, why Caspian bonanza, though not comparable to the Middle East, is still very lucrative for the region as well as for the world. Why turning the oil and gas orientation to the west, north, east or to the south is crystallizing a flurry of effort, labeled as the New Great Game on the analogy of the Great Game of the 19th Century between Imperial Russia and Victorian England? In the context of oil and gas, the stakes are enormous.

Table -8 shows the top 25 countries' reserves in two packets, the top ten and next top fifteen. Statistics of two sources, Oil and Gas Journal and World Oil have been given very meticulously.[85] The quantities are in million barrels of oil and billion cubic feet (Bcf) of natural gas. In the oil ranking of top ten, Saudi Arabia leads having 261,900 million barrels (261.9 Gb) out of total world oil 1,265,812 million barrels (1,265.8 Gb). In the natural gas sector, Russia with 1,880,000 Bcf (1,880 tcf) leads the world out of total 6,076,494 Bcf (6,076.494 tcf). In other words, according to Oil & Gas Journal, Saudi Arabian oil reserves are 1/5th of the world and Russia has over 1/3 of the world gas reserves. Similarly the statistics of other possible game actors like Iran, USA, China, Caspian littorals, Canada and India have also been given.

Table- 8: Top 25 Oil and Gas Producing Countries

		Oil (million barrels)				Natural Gas (billion cubic feet)	
Rank[a]	Country	Oil & Gas Journal	World Oil	Rank[b]	Country	Oil & Gas Journal	World Oil
1	Saudi Arabia[c]	[d]261,900	[d]259,400	1	Russia	1,680,000	2,340,500
2	Iran[c]	125,800	105,000	2	Iran[c]	940,000	955,000
3	Iraq[c]	115,000	115,000	3	Qatar[c]	910,000	915,992
4	Kuwait[c]	[d]99,000	[d]99,375	4	Saudi Arabia[c]	[d]231,000	[d]238,500
5	Canada[e]	178,893	4,957	5	United Arab Emirates[c]	212,100	204,050
6	United Arab Emirates[c]	97,800	66,230	6	United States	186,946	186,946
7	Venezuela[c]	77,800	52,450	7	Nigeria[c]	159,000	178,500
8	Russia	60,000	65,393	8	Algeria[c]	160,000	171,500
9	Libya[c]	36,000	30,500	9	Venezuela[c]	148,000	149,210
10	Nigeria[c]	25,000	33,000	10	Iraq[c]	110,000	112,600
	Top 10 Total	**1,077,193**	**831,305**		**Top 10 Total**	**4,737,046**	**5,452,348**
11	United States	22,677	22,677	11	Australia	90,000	142,900
12	Qatar[c]	15,207	27,352	12	Indonesia[c]	90,300	67,650
13	China	18,250	15,509	13	Norway	74,800	74,733
14	Mexico	15,674	14,597	14	Turkmenistan	71,000	-
15	Algeria[c]	11,314	14,000	15	Malaysia	75,000	57,608
16	Norway	10,447	9,395	16	Uzbekistan	66,200	-
17	Brazil	8,500	10,602	17	Kazakhstan	65,000	-
18	Kazakhstan	9,000	-	18	Egypt	58,500	71,250
19	Angola	5,412	8,800	19	Canada	59,069	59,069
20	Azerbaijan	7,000	-	20	Netherlands	62,000	55,100
21	Oman	5,506	5,700	21	Kuwait[c]	[d]55,500	[d]56,600
22	Indonesia[c]	4,700	5,500	22	China	53,325	47,911
23	Ecuador	4,630	4,950	23	Libya[c]	46,400	46,000
24	India	5,371	4,002	24	Ukraine	39,600	-
25	United Kingdom	4,665	4,300	25	Oman	29,280	31,000
	Top 25 Total	**1,225,546**	**978,689**		**Top 25 Total**	**5,673,020**	**6,162,169**
	OPEC Total	**869,521**	**807,807**		**OPEC Total**	**3,062,400**	**3,095,602**
	World Total	**1,265,812**	**1,051,477**		**World Total**	**6,076,494**	**6,803,282**

[a]Rank is based on an average of oil reserves reported by Oil & Gas Journal and World Oil.
[b]Rank is based on an average of natural gas reserves reported by Oil & Gas Journal and World Oil.
[c]Member of the Organization of Petroleum Exporting Countries (OPEC).
[d]Includes one-half of the reserves in the Neutral Zone.
[e]Oil and Gas Journal Canadian oil reserves include heavy (low gravity) oil.

Note: The Energy Information Administration does not certify these international reserves data, but reproduces the information as a matter of convenience for the reader.

Sources: PennWell Publishing Company, Oil and Gas Journal, December 22, 2003, pp. 46-47. Gulf Publishing Company, World Oil, September, 2004, p 63.

For the Central Eurasians, heartening aspect is that with full capacities of oil and gas still to develop, Azerbaijan and Kazakhstan rank among the top 25 oil and gas producers in the world. With considerable variation in cumulative effect, World Oil also quotes these statistics in the same fashion. The difference between the two sources at the "world total" level is huge i.e. over 214 Gb of oil and over 727 tcf of gas. 'World Oil' estimates are modest compared to 'Oil and Gas Journal.' The table also shows another fact based on empirical values that OPEC possesses exclusively more than 70-72 percent of the World total oil and 47-50 percent of the World total gas reserves.

Incidentally, the majority of the OPEC happens to comprise of the Muslim countries. OPEC ability as an organization to manipulate oil as a 'weapon' is a daunting specter to be dreaded by some actors of leading economies. Thus, its effect on the 'New Great Game' will not go unnoticed and would find due elaboration.

By comparison, another significantly authentic source that is maintaining its credibility over the years, beside the US Sources, is that of British Petroleum (BP). It serves 13 million customers across the six continents. Tables 9 to 20 at Appendix-2 are based on the relevant oil and gas tables of BP Statistical Review of World Energy-2005.[86] As these tables will remain the discussion material through out the book text, only the aspects that have direct bearing on our theme would be highlighted here. Table 9 indicates the proven oil reserves on the planet, which has been divided into six main regions:

- North America; includes USA, Canada and Mexico.
- South and Central America includes Argentina, Brazil, Colombia, Ecuador, Peru, Trinidad, Venezuela and others.
- Europe and Eurasia, includes Azerbaijan, Denmark, Italy, Kazakhstan, Norway, Romania, Russian Federation, Turkmenistan, UK, Uzbekistan and others not prominent for oil or gas.
- Middle East; includes Iran, Iraq, Kuwait, Oman, Qatar, Saudi Arabia, Syria, UAE, Yemen and others.
- Africa; includes Algeria, Angola, Chad, Congo, Egypt, E. Guinea, Gabon, Nigeria, Sudan, Tunisia and others.
- Asia Pacific; includes Australia, Brunei, China, India, Indonesia, Malaysia, Thailand, Vietnam and others.

To comprehend the table, it is imperative to focus on their proven oil reserve in the value of percentages. Being concerned with Caspian Region, it emerges that

Caspian Region states reserve share in the world totals almost 4 percent, which is greater than whole of the Asia Pacific Region (3.5%), almost half of south and Central American Region (8.5%), 1/3 of Europe Eurasian Region (11.7%), little less than half of Africa (9.4%) and 1/15th of Middle East (61.7%).

The scrutiny of percentage shares makes amply clear why the Caspian Region, mainly comprising Azerbaijan, Kazakhstan and Uzbekistan is vital area of interest. Thus, the Caspian Region's oil plausibility is established through total production (Table 10, Appendix-2) of the world oil in which it has 2.5 percent of the total world production as of year 2004. The interesting feature is while several countries production is on decline as compared to year 2003 like USA (-2.5 %), Argentina (-5.9 %), Australia (-13.9 %), the Caspian Region production in 2004 surged by 10 percent compared to 2003 even after having taken Uzbekistan decline (-7.8 %) into account. Viewing the production growth of Kazakhstan and Azerbaijan combined it stands above 17 percent.

Table-11, Appendix-2 gives the world oil statistics for consumption with particular focus on change between 2003 and 2004 figures. USA consumes 24.9 percent of total world oil while her consumption reached over 20 million barrels per day in 2004, registering an increase of 2.8 percent over 2003. Similarly, China consumes about 9 percent of total world oil and has registered about 16 percent increase in consumption over 2003.[87] This shade of statistics amply highlights which are the countries that would be eclipsed by the dwindling world oil resources. On the contrary, the booming economies of some countries would force corresponding consumption surge in oil, which may not come infinitely, as oil stocks are also finite. The scenario becomes vivid to comprehend why the stir in hydrocarbon rich area is visible, particularly in third world countries. The rising percentage in consumption in that order of intensity would make prediction clear about leading economic giants who are left with no choice but to be the part of the New Great Game. Careful scrutiny of the consumption magnitude of the regions suggests that in daily consumption North America, Asia Pacific and Europe Eurasia lead among the world regions.

Table 12, Appendix-2 gives the world statistics of the oil products consumption by regions. Of the regional total consumption of oil, North American Region's gasoline consumption is 44.3 percent of it. USA gasoline consumption share is 46.3 percent, registering an increase of 1.7 percent over year 2003. Asia Pacific Region consumption of gasoline is 27.8 percent of the region's total oil consumption while China consumes 25.2 percent and Japan consumes 34.0 percent of its share. Japan gasoline consumption has marginally increased over 2003 by only 0.4 percent. China has registered an increase of 17.1 percent and in the category of middle distillates by 23.4 percent. Japan's consumption of middle distillates equals to that of China but has declined by 2.3 percent as compared to 2003. Europe consumed 23.5 percent gasoline, a decline of 1.5 percent from 2003.

If the oil was boon in 20th Century, Pundits opine that 21st Century is the century of gas. The oil tables highlight that oil reserves or production of some key countries are on decline while consumption is surging.[88] Present proven reserves of 6,337 tcf of gas on the planet (Table 13, Appendix-2) afford a great relief to the present and projected booming economies. The total world statistics[89] for gas proven reserves are shared by some leading gas rich countries like USA having 187 Tcf or 2.9 percent of the world, Russian Federation having 1,694 Tcf or 26 percent of the world, Iran having 970 Tcf or 15.3 percent of the world, and Qatar having 910 Tcf or 14.4 percent of the world. The Caspian Region's share in the world total is over 5 percent which is larger than North America, South and Central America, 1/7th of Europe and Eurasia, 1/8th of Middle East, 3/4th of Africa and Asia Pacific. It thus establishes that Caspian Region has also the potential to become a gas-giant because geologists agree that like oil, its several gas-rich geological blocks are yet to be tapped. It may be coincidence that oil equivalent of

6,337.4 Tcf (179.53Tcm) of total world gas come to 1,134,000 million barrels or 1,134 Gb while total of world oil reserves also stand at 1,188 to 1,265 Gb. In the world total gas reserves, China has barely 1.4 percent share, Japan has no ranking and India has meager share of 0.5 percent. A small exercise through Table 13 contents also help to conclude that over the last several years, Middle East gas reserves have expanded all along while North America's gradually shrunk. South and Central America pattern is 'expanded to shrunk' in 2004 and Europe Eurasian reserves declined in 2004.

Similarly, Table 14, Appendix-2 shows the production statistics of the world natural gas. The USA produces 20.2 percent of the world total but is on decline with decrease of 1.2 percent compared to 2003. Russian Federation is slightly above USA in production (21.9 %), registering an increase of 1.8 percent over 2003. China's share of world total is merely 1.5 percent with significant increase over 2003 by 18.5 percent. India has only 1.1 percent share of the world total and declined in production by 1.7 percent over 2003. The Caspian Region from the production status also emerges prominent because it has about 5 percent share of the world total gas, which is larger than South and Central America (4.8 %), a little less than $1/5^{th}$ of North America, $1/7^{th}$ of Europe Eurasia, half of Middle East, equals Africa and little less than half of Asia Pacific.[90] At the world level, gas production increased by 2.8 percent as compared to 2003 statistics. Thus, the emerging figures confirm that gas pattern is also poised to be equally affecting the leading economies of the world notably USA, China, Japan, Western Europe, Canada and a potential bidder, India with 1.1 percent of the world gas total that is almost at level with Pakistan having 0.9 percent production share of the world.

Table 15, Appedix-2 gives the consumption figures, which are 2,688.3 Bcm for 2004 of world total as compared to 2003 when consumption was 2,603.5 Bcm. Thus, an increase at global level by 3.3 percent has been sighted. Out of the total gas consumed, almost every fourth cubic meter is consumed by USA (24%) and every seventh cubic meter of world gas by Russia (15%). China's consumption (1.5%) has increased by 19 percent while Japan consumption (2.7%) has decreased by 5.7 percent over 2003. Caspian region consumption has been almost half of their production share of world total, 2.7 percent. A detailed analysis of the regions' score suggests that Europe-Eurasia, North America and Asia Pacific lead in the given order. Becoming thus clear about oil and gas proven reserves, production and consumption; the information is also available on the increase and decrease trends of some leading countries who would emerge 'actors' in the New Great Game. Comparing the production to consumption ratio, at the international level, demand has outmaneuvered the production that might explain why the natural gas has become most sought for commodity in 2004. It might have been one of the trigger factors of oil products volatile market indirectly, though oil production had been marginally more than the oil consumption in 2004 (Table 10, 11 for Oil and 14, 15 for Gas, Appendix-2).

Other Energy Sources Statistics

Coal is another hydrocarbon energy source though, not discussed in the context of Central Eurasia being insignificant from geo-political angle. Nevertheless, at international level, it has an impact as an energy source, being 22 percent of the world total energy generation. It is therefore imperative that for advancing an argument, the total energy opportunities at global level should remain on the spectrum as second layer forces to play their role. It would need separate study to visualize the impact of making recourse to these sources of energy like coal, nuclear energy, hydroelectricity and thermal power but suffice to say here that oil and gas had been the most potent sources from feasibility of extraction, storage, transportation and consumption point of view. The fact that whole world was focused during a span of over 100 years in 19th and 20th Centuries and is still craving for the two ingredients of hydrocarbon, oil and gas, proves the logic of their preference over other means. However, now when the world community is being urged by the circumstances to gear up efforts for impending challenges, the coal, hydroelectricity and nuclear energy are receiving renewed attention but not without constraints.

Coal is an ancient commodity and in term of its million tons equivalent (Table-16, Appendix-2) out of world 909,064 Mt of proven reserves, North America share is 28 percent, South/Central America has 2.2 percent, Europe/Eurasia has 31.6 percent, Africa/ Middle East has 5.6 percent while Asia Pacific has 32.7 percent. Asia Pacific leads in the proven reserves of coal. In the world total USA share is 27.1 percent, Russia has 17.3 percent, South Africa has 5.4 percent, China and India have 12.6 percent and 10.2 percent respectively.

On the production side of Coal (Table 17, Appendix-2), at the end of 2004, it stood at 2,732 Mt of oil equivalent as it grew by 7.2 percent over 2003. US produced 20.8 percent of the world production,[91] which grew by 3.3 percent over 2003. China registered an increase of 13.3 percent while producing 36.2 percent of the world total. Indonesia has a share of 3 percent, with increased production by 17.3 percent over 2003. Vietnam had been more ambitious to register growth of 38.6 percent, having 0.5 percent share of the world total. Australia had 7.3 percent share with an increase of 5.2 percent. Europe Eurasia is the only region where production declined collectively by 0.1 percent. Out of the group of 15 countries of the region, France reduced her production by 63.9 percent.

Table 18, Appendix-2 gives the consumption figure of coal in million tons of oil equivalents. Total world consumption figures of million tones equivalent oil of coal by the end of 2004 stood at 2,778 Mt, registering an increase of 6.3 percent over 2003. If this figure is taken as 100%, USA share was 20.3 %, Russia's 3.8 %, China had 34.4 %, India's consumption doubled to 7.4 %, Japan with 4.3 % share increased consumption by 7.7 % while

Australia share was registered as 2.0 % with an increase of 6.9 % over 2003 statistics. The ratio proportion aspects of statistics afford the basis of making certain viable deductions about some countries, which would emerge as 'actors' in the context of Central Eurasian 'New Great Game'.

Nuclear Energy is another source of energy, which is non-hydrocarbon. In simple narrative, hydrocarbon sources are not renewable while others like thermal, nuclear and solar energy sources are renewable. The world, at the end of 2004, produced 624 Mt equivalent of oil energy through nuclear mode. Table 19, Appendix-2 shows that out of the six regions, Europe Eurasia leads with 46.0 percent of the world total, North America with 33.7 percent, Asia Pacific has a 19 percent share. Average increase over 2003 at the world level had been 4.4 percent, which proves that move is underway to lessen their dependence over hydrocarbon resources.

Yet another renewable energy resource is hydroelectricity. That was registered at the end of 2004 as 634.4 Mt of oil equivalent, with an increase of 5.0 percent over 2003. The countries and region share is given in Table 20, Appendix-2. In the production inventory of hydroelectricity, Europe leads with 29.1 percent; North America's share in the production is 22.4 percent while South and Central America closely follow with a 20.8 percent share. Asia Pacific Region has 24.0 percent share. South Africa and Middle East make the lowest dent with negligible share of 3.1 percent and 0.6 percent respectively. Having taken stock of the whole lot of the energy categories, at least from the point of view of demand and desirability, the basis of logic becomes clear to deduce direct and indirect facts. Therefore, reference to combination of various statistics being empirical values would remain frequent while discussing multifaceted aspects subsequently.

CHAPTER-THREE

HYDROCARBON AND PIPELINE POLITICS

Beverly Hillbillies Syndrome

The description of Caspian Region milieu and the fact sheet about the world energy and Caspian 'riches' earlier amply highlight the region's vulnerabilities to be the core subject of regional and extra regional dimensions of geopolitics. Dieter Farwick rightly remarked that geography sets the pace for geopolitics. "Geography determines the destiny of individual human beings and countries. ...Individuals can escape geography but countries cannot.... Geography determines living conditions through location on the globe.... as well as possession of strategic raw material."[92] Oil and gas of the Caspian Region beyond doubt have been the strategic assets and in the limelight since the dawn of 20th Century. An analytical look already cast at their significance and possessions would serve an effective pointer to the fact that regional harmony among the Caspian littorals and geographically crucial neighbors like Georgia, Armenia and Afghanistan shall remain challenging phenomena. The Caspian-Caucasus geopolitical environment bears testimony to this assumption.

What leads to the play of politics or geopolitics in the region? The answer to the query hinges on the chemistry of interstate relationship obtaining in Central Eurasia, in the wake of power vacuum in hydrocarbon rich area, created on withdrawal of Soviets to their present borders called Russian Federation. Militarily weak regional states sitting over vast oil and gas reserves are likely to provoke 'interference' if not an all out aggression by the prosperous but hydrocarbon-scant nations. The 'Beverly Hillbillies' syndrome, which now haunts the world through serious perception it generated in the backdrop of a comedy may be yet another revealing phenomenon. The Beverly Hillbillies was instantaneous hit of 1962 airwaves when millions watched the Clampettes, an Ozark family of Hooterville in America, it nonetheless raised crucial questions about the, "reliability of the petroleum flow and the risk involved in it."[93] Hydrocarbon man in 60s had plenty of it, yet with futuristic approaches, appeared mired by these questions about 'reliability' and the 'risks'. The effort put in by the scholars, corporate bodies and their governments eventually surfaced as an oil politics. Any account while dealing with the past chapters of history in this context emerges as the history of oil.

Paradigm Shift

In Churchill's words, "Mastery itself was the prize of the venture."[94] He emphatically quelled the opponent's criticism as the First Lord of Admiralty before World War I on an issue, whether Royal Navy should shift to oil from coal. The decision was to have strategic connotations, allowing the British fleet move faster on the high seas. Thus, Churchill never blinked to grab such a cutting edge to gain 'mastery' as a reward of shifting the navy from coal to oil. Modern history of oil begins in the late 19th Century, but this vital commodity called 'oil' transformed the world scene particularly in 20th Century. The historians have recorded in particular, three paradigm shifts in this context.[95]

- First, it acted as a remarkable catalyst in the booming business the world over, supporting the capitalist societies to dominate weaker or non-capitalist contenders. The Industrial Revolution,

81

energized by oil in 20th Century resulted in massive scientific advances, which changed face of the globe. Throughout this history of oil, the companies grew larger and massive in their influence. Corporatism virtually engulfed the whole world. As one looks toward 21st Century, the only ingredient that perhaps shares the role in maintaining mastery along with the oil is computer chip. Unfortunately, the computer chip, seen in isolation becomes redundant in effect. In other words, oil nourishes its roots as well.

- Second paradigm shift is visible in evolving national strategies and power politics driven by oil (energy). Japanese incentives to attack Pearl Harbor are open secrets now, which aimed at securing her Pacific northern flank to secure East Indies oil in the south, to sustain her might. Hitler's offensive to capture Caucasus oil fields was another gamble of similar strategy, which stalled again due to her oil thirsty war machine. Suez Crisis of 1956 was nothing but an oil driven piece of geopolitics.[96] USA oil sanctions in part over her ally, Britain, were prompted by Eisenhower's bid to mend the crumbling fence with the Middle East, particularly the Kingdom of Saudi Arabia. Saddam Hussein's Kuwait gamble is also being interpreted as his endeavor to become the leading producer of oil after usurping Kuwaiti oil while the West still had the memory fresh when predominantly Arabs used the oil as a weapon, "engineered from OPEC platform in October 1973."[97] Obviously, the West had no choice but to deny such a superior strategic orientation to Saddam Hussein and evict Iraqi forces from Kuwait.
- Third paradigm shift, which the history of oil exposes, suggests that the world has emerged as a hydrocarbon society and Homosapiens could rightly be labeled as hydrocarbon man. The oil in 20th Century penetrated every shade of human activity

and now, at the dawn of 21st Century, a stage has been reached that by some design if oil and gas were made to disappear, the civilization would reach its last gasps. While the 'dependence' limitation of hydrocarbon man threatens the very existence of human civilization, yet 'man' is not prepared to bid adieu to an addiction of oil and gas guzzling. There are people of vision who see the approaching menace. "The steady decline of world oil production after peak oil....makes for a somber scenario....How we adjust as a global community to the challenge, can only be a great concern to us all."[98] The result is that turmoil at the global scene is snowballing. Modern man is not inclined to relent on energy guzzling because that would deprive him the luxury of comfort or an upper hand in the arena of global power politics. In the meantime, some subjects of fierce debate have been launched inevitably about the environmental concerns, dilemma of energy security and the necessity to maintain balance between economic growth and crystallizing clashing chemistry of the actors that ultimately may tilt the balance of power. With passing of each day, humanity is thus destined to walk on a razor's edge. In such a desperate scenario, a common person would naturally long for miracles to happen, but it is also the law of nature that miracles seldom happen. These are the contexts that expose the oil vulnerabilities, necessitating maneuvers of all sorts, called hydrocarbon politics.

Regional Perception Inequities

Immense diversities characterize the Caspian-Caucasus Region. As an exclusive focus on each country of the region earlier suggests that, it had been a crossroad and meeting points of not only different people but also of different cultures, religions and races. Thus, its convergence of several socio-political and socio-economic forces was a strong plus character on one hand but the clash and collision had also been the logical consequence on the other hand. The convergence is denoted by the fact that there are several dozens of groups that inhabit the Caspian-Caucasus Region but at the same time from its history to present, it had been the arena of catastrophes and political upheavals that go on until to date. For instance, Azerbaijan appears to have irreconcilable grievances due to fall of her territory of Nagorno-Karabakh to Armenia. Similarly, Armenia still mourns persecution of Armenians by Turks in April 1915. As Azerbaijanis have Turkic origin, mutually they stand torn apart with Armenians, both being the casualty of the past as well as present one by one.

Iran-Azerbaijan relations are sore and finger pointing goes on incessantly. Beside territorial disputes, Iran accuses Azerbaijan of instigating Azeri population of Iranian border province for encouraging liberation movements, which has larger Azeri population than that of Azerbaijan. Conversely, Azerbaijan's woes against Iran once she did not support her over Nagorno-Karabakh Issue against Armenia are accumulating, with passing of each day.

Deep rooted hatred; embedded in the inter-ethnic clash has precluded chances of any reconciliation. From Baku, oil exit to the West is ideally through the shortest and relatively inexpensive stretch of territory of Armenia to which Armenia would not agree. Russia makes the best out of this situation on the merit of being an old traditional ally of Armenia as a guarantor of her security. In other words, Russia gets the snipe. Oil, if not through north shall not trickle through west (Armenia) as well. Turkey obviously supports her kins (Azerbaijan) and is accused by Armenia for closing her borders to force a sort of economic blockade.[99]

Georgia after the 'Velvet Revolution' is distinctly pro-West. Russia and Georgia view each other as 'suspects' for their role in the insurgency prone areas of Chechnya, Dagestan against Russia, South Ossetia and Abkhazia against Georgia. Chechnya is another factor, which weakens the Russian case being extremely volatile and a direct threat to oil industry. Thus, Russian efforts to promote pipelines through this area have remained inconclusive despite her unleashing of full might against Chechen separatists. Some analysts believe that Russia's central motivation in pursuing a military option against Chechnya was the former's interest in an oil pipeline to carry Baku oil through Chechnya,[100] because Grozny District had been traditional hub of oil production and refineries.

Kazakhstan and Turkmenistan harbor multi-directional diverse orientation among each other over the regional issues. Afghanistan stumbles to achieve a semblance of stability, which appears yet a far cry. Agreed international borders but not delimitated or demarcated over large chunks of territory between Kazakhstan and Russia, Turkmenistan and Kazakhstan, Uzbekistan and Kazakhstan, Uzbekistan and Turkmenistan and ethno-geographical dichotomy of division of Farghana valley are some other areas of discord which can add fuel to the inter-states simmering fury. In the aftermath of 9/11, as Brill Olcott dwells on, there really was an opportunity to reshape the trajectory of development in this part of the world. But neither the Central Asian states nor the international community has made good use of this 'second chance'.[101] Uzbekistan's unilateral act to sever gas supplies to Kyrgyzstan in the winter 2001 briefly flashes the ugly side of politics to the east of Caspian Sea. Kyrgyzstan and Tajikistan, being upstream, possess more water than their needs while the western Central Asian states have enough energy to satiate the neighbor's thirst for oil and gas. Gregory Gleason opines, ".... they may be able to enter into larger Central Asian market on a monetized basis, leading to rational trade offs between water and power on region-wise basis."[102]

The Caspian Region, being landlocked, forces a compulsion on each of its oil and gas rich littorals to bank heavily on the good will of their neighbors for achieving smooth access routes to the international market. On the contrary, with active conflict flash points and dichotomy in individual approaches throughout Caspian-Caucasus Region, a space is created for the conduct of regional as well as extra regional politics, which has made these littoral states an easy subject of manipulation. To pull the rug from the feet of others', the animosity in international relations has augmented a dispute called Caspian Sea Legal Regime. It thwarts, partially if not wholly, the 'well-wishes' of Frank Vivian about this region who wrote, "the region's wells will shower unimaginable wealth on people whose annual per capita GDP today hovers between $400 and $600; building, a new El Dorado in nations where camels still out-numbered automobiles in 1998."[103]

Caspian Legal Regime Issue

The historian, people of intellect and integrity are always encumbered by the burden of their conscience to record stark truth and nothing but truth."[104] Writes Arundhati Roy, though in different context but supporting such assumption that the historians have also viewed Caspian Legal Regime issue in the same spirit. The dispute had existed between the Soviet and Iranian Governments who had been signing pacts and treaties to resolve the issue, the first one in 1921 and the second in 1940. These agreements, essentially stipulated Iranian and Russian right over Caspian Sea exclusively, denying thus the right of navigation to any third party during the Soviet era. For exploration purpose, 10 NM belt was reserved along each country's shoreline. However, both countries had the lien over the entire remaining seabed for fishery and other commercial purposes but Caspian riches were to be shared through 50/50 formula. Soviets were eager to apply same status to the Black Sea as well because these agreements were trumpeted internationally as a solid platform of argument of success among the neighbors on maritime issues. Indirectly both targeted Turkey, which tilted predominantly to the West since conclusion of World War

I. Later the intricacies emerged when the number of littoral states increased from two (Russia and Iran) to the present five on gaining independence of Azerbaijan, Turkmenistan and Kazakhstan in 1991.

One would note with some degree of relief that the simmering dispute has impeded the development of harmonious views relevant to the Caspian Sea division but it did not stop the oil and gas exploration, minor bickering among the littorals not withstanding. The distribution or division formula of the Caspian Sea is the major cause of disagreement under which lay oil and gas riches. The dispute drew international attention when in July 2001; Iranian gunboats whisked away an Azeri research ship, claiming that it was within the territorial waters of Iran. The episode though did not escalate into a conflict situation but certainly raised possibilities of horrific specter; what if the Caspian Sea was also militarized by the Caspian littorals? It rightly drew their attention to discuss three emerging aspects, commencing in 1991. One, did the Soviet-Iran bilateral treaties of 1921 and 1940 still apply to the Caspian as valid? Two, the need to address the ecological and environmental issues to contain the fall out of fast developing oil and gas extraction and transportation. Three, to agree whether Caspian water body was a sea or a lake and UN Convention on Law of Seas (UNCLOS) was applicable to it or not. If the answer was 'Yes', by implication it meant that every littoral could claim 12 miles from its shore as territorial water and 200 miles exclusive economic zone (EEZ) beyond 12 miles. Any part of the sea out of EEZ was to be considered as the common property of the world nations.[105] Conversely, if answer was 'No' then Caspian resources were to be developed jointly. It is also called as 'condominium' approach.

The Russian Government in the meantime came up with aggressive approach. In October 1994, Russia circulated a paper at the UN, warning that Moscow, "reserved the right to take appropriate measures against Caspian states that unilaterally begin exploring the Caspian

Map 12: Caspian Sea Division Option by Median Line Method

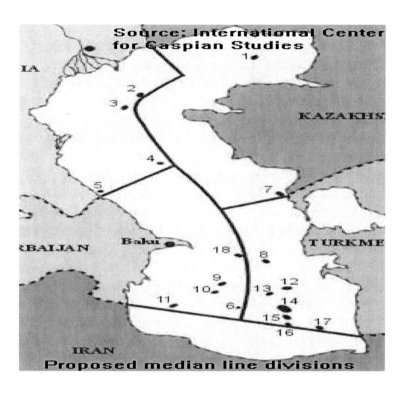

seabed."[106] The failure of the working group, formulated to resolve the issue, to come up with an agreed formula in its second meeting in 1998, led to its suspension for affording more time to individual countries to prepare grounds for consensus. Indirectly, it was face saving effort and admission of failure. However, bilateral engagements paved the way to continue exploring and extracting oil from the Caspian Sea. In July 1998, Kazakhstan agreement with Russia was concluded to divide North Caspian Sea along the Median Line option of the Soviet era and water remaining under joint ownership; with proviso that Iran-Soviet era agreements be deemed valid until a consensus agreement among all Caspian littorals was reached. The agreement at least settled a sore point among them i.e. dispute over oil extraction from Kurmanghazy structure located in Kazakhstan and disputed by Russia and Khyalynskaya field located in Russian Severny Block and disputed by Kazakhstan. According to an agreed formula, access to oil companies of both the counties was permitted to both the sites, with possession right remaining with the native country.

In January 2001, Azerbaijan and Russian presidents issued a joint communiqué, agreeing to divide the seabed but acknowledging navigation rights of each other over the entire sea surface. In other words, it was an agreement over 'divided sea bed and common surface waters'. In November 2001, Kazakhstan and Azerbaijan also signed a bilateral agreement, defining sea sectors among them. Generally, Russia, Azerbaijan and Kazakhstan agree on 'principles and methods' to divide the seabed and the mineral resources under Median Line formula. Turkmenistan agreed to the principles but not the methods.[107] For example in February 1998, Azerbaijan and Turkmenistan, in a joint statement, agreed to divide the sea by 'Median Line' method but disagreement cropped up on the method, where to draw the line from because both claim an oil field called 'Kyapaz' by Azerbaijan and 'Serdar' by Turkmenistan.

Iran agrees to none of these approaches; sticking to her demand of equal distribution of Caspian Sea assets, while Iran shoreline is only 13 % of the whole; as opposed to Kazakhstan 29 %, Turkmenistan 18 %, Azerbaijan 21 % and Russia 19 %.[108] Simple majority on the other side perhaps reinforces their percepts legitimacy against Iran. Charles Coe, commenting on the failure of Caspian littorals leaders summit held on 23-24 April 2002 at Ashkhabad (Turkmenistan) wrote, "Rather than getting down to business, the five opted to dance around the issue and toss an occasional stone, thereby highlighting the fact that major differences still exist between some of the littoral countries and that the debate is likely to drag on for years to come."[109]

Some facts emerge from the pattern of politics of Caspian Sea division, Russia has limited oil and gas stakes in the North Caspian Sea Basin and thus can afford to remain flexible in her options to agree to any favorite formula prescribing 'Condominium'; 'Median Line Method', or 'Divided Sea Bed and Common Water Surface' approaches. In fact, the bilateral agreements to apply until conclusion of comprehensive consensus spell out such option in case of Russia, Kazakhstan and Azerbaijan. Iran's insistence that other four states should assume 1921 and 1940 agreement still valid is not tenable but her discord affords her a pivot of maneuver to muddy water with any state under any of the pretext, including laying her claims over Azeri fields. The Caspian Sea issue has therefore been transformed by each state as an effective geo-political tool to gain space for conducting exterior maneuvers of the kind that plague adversary and suits her own interests. Oil and gas politics is not the limit. With Russia maintaining naval supremacy since the Soviet era and keeping her naval presence in tact at Astrakhan, there is likelihood that Caspian littorals, particularly Russia, may opt to remilitarize the Caspian to maintain traditional influence. It could thus be reckoned as the most dangerous side of the hydrocarbon political platform under the pretext and claims over the Caspian booty.

Politics of Environment

Comparing the violent attack on the World Trade Center and human aggression on environment, Andrew Mckillop writes, "...but few compare this violence to mankind's attack on, and destabilization of the earth's climate through the alteration of its chemical make up."[110] Similarly, with the surge of tremendous Caspian Sea borne activity, the specter of environmental degradation has emerged as a monster. The sea is a home to myriad ecological systems. Caspian coast has several shallow saline pools, which attract over 400 species of migratory birds. The native sturgeon is famous and the region produces 90 % of the world's best 'caviar'.

The discovery of oil and gas reserves may be a point of relief for the littorals' economies but not without headache. In Apsheron peninsula, the waste discharged by Azerbaijan's petroleum industry into the sea, discharges and spill of oil and gas from the sea borne platforms, untreated waste from Volga River into which half of the Russian population and its heavy industry drain their pollution, have made it a legitimate issue of severe environmental degradation (Map-13).[111] Thousands of seals that lived in the Caspian have died since 2000. There exists no workable system to enforce environmental laws and regulation in the region. Similarly, the transportation lines of oil and gas over or through the Caspian Sea are being questioned with striking similarity to Bosporus choke point where Turkey is resenting the increasing oil tankers traffic.

All aspects considered, some experts opine that the environmental degradation, a global issue, does merit attention but the clamor is somewhat exaggerated and largely political. For instance, Georgia targeted Baku-Tbilisi-Ceyhan (BTC) pipeline initially, expressing pollution worries in her Borjomi Valley to extract major concessions.[112] Any plan to connect Turkmenistan or Kazakhstan shore to Baku through subsurface pipelines is instantly resented by Iran and Russia with reference to non-environment friendly development; nonetheless, the card of environment is frequently played by the littorals to advance their political motives without mustering the will to address the basic environmental issues.

International Element of Politics

The statistics show that various sources place Caspian Region oil proved reserve at 48 Gb (BP statistics refer) that are a little over 4 % of the world total of 1,188 Gb of proved reserves. Similarly, the possible oil reserves range up to 163 Gb. On the natural gas account, the region has proven reserves of about 317 Tcf of gas, which makes over 5 % of world proven gas reserve of 6,337 Tcf. When this is the potential of a market and relative power vacuum exists, international factor is bound to creep in the regional hydrocarbon politics. Dick Cheney was frank to admit US interest saying, "the good Lord did not see fit to put oil and gas only where there are democratically elected regimes... But, we go where the business is."[113]

For the US, there may be two distinguishable interests, political and economic. Politically there appears an obvious spurt of activities to gain influence in Central Eurasia. Russia feels obliged to be reckoned a factor in her 'near abroad'. Turkey puts her claim as a progeny of all Turkic races while Iran had been the historic mother country of the large chunk of Central Eurasia since Cyrus the great empire of BC era. To the east, Pakistan, China and India emerge as important, former as potential exit route for the Caspian oil and gas and the latter two as the big future consumer markets to satiate their oil and gas fledgling needs for booming economy. Within the last ten years if the world consumption in certain estimates has increased by, say 100 %, China alone took huge chunk, consuming 50 % out of it. USA, still the largest energy consumer, keeping Turkey in forefront has three political objectives to achieve, to contain Islamic fundamentalism stoked by Iran in the region; to impede nuclear technology and weapons from Central Asian Republics reaching Iran, a factor long neutralized by Russo-Iranian active collaboration in this field, and finally preventing domination or return of Russia to her backyard.

Rosemarie Forsyth makes a fine assessment, "Caspian oil is tied to, and will affect, issues central to current and developing international relations. These include: the political and economic future of Russia... the political and economics future of Turkey, Iran's position in the region...the strategic consequences of greater dependence on the Persian Gulf oil, tension between Pakistan and India, China's future policy towards its neighbors, and potential spread of Islam in the region."[114] Dr. Svante Cornell is of opinion that Caspian-Caucasus Region had to emerge prominent even if oil and gas were not there.

Map-13: Caspian Sea Environments and Installations, Source: (US Energy Information Administration: www.eia.doe.gov) January 2004

It is the geo-political importance of the region that makes it a natural bridge between the East and the West while located between the regional powers i.e. Russia, Turkey, Iran and China.[115] Therefore, Turkey and Caucasus become the priority area for the western influence. EU sponsored project called TRACECA is the manifestation of the developed world interest which is so keen to re-enliven the historic Silk Road. The argument has the weight but obviously, it cannot preclude the factor of Caspian riches, which are drawing particular attention at the dawn of new millennium. In the backdrop of transport corridor

TRACECA, NATO's expansion to Baltic-Black Sea direction by implication turns Russia into a sort of fortress, invested on the periphery by NATO.[116] In other words, the only major Eurasian power, Russia, is also on the Western agenda to neutralize her influence but not her ability to emerge as, what the West would wish, a truly pluralistic state with free market economy. In the context of region's socio-economic scenario and the transitional orientation, rivalry is intensifying among different powers, which are locked on the Caspian oil and gas riches. As the world increasingly views Central Asia as critical to the War on Terror and for oil reserves, Olcott highlights the deep contradiction running through USA policy toward Central Asia, where partnerships with antidemocratic regimes create long-term security risks, and faults the international community for its complicity and lack of effective engagement in the region...recent events in Uzbekistan and Kyrgyzstan demonstrate, tensions in the region lie close to the surface if we are to prevent these states from descending into chaos, the international community must identify solutions to economic, political, and social challenges confronting them.[117]

Noticing perhaps such intricacies, Timothy Thomas grades it as complicated region where 'bloc politics' is rampant, particularly since last quarter of 19th Century pertaining to the Rockefellers, Nobels and Rothschild era. On dilution of USSR, scramble to exploit Caspian oil was witnessed, "Political and economic blocs eventually evolved to vie for influence in the Caspian Sea Region. On the one side, there is loose and unofficial alliance between the US, Turkey and Azerbaijan... On the other side there is an understanding or mutual interest pact among Russia, Armenia and Iran."[118] He also resorts to tiering of states; claiming first category, which exploits and protects oil and gas; the second tier through which oil and gas would traverse and third category states are those, which provide final port-facilities for the access to international market. It is logical to assume that all three tiers have to be in unison though at present these clatter with politics. The test case for any level of success or failure would thus be the direction in which oil and gas would flow ultimately. In other words the hydrocarbon politics on the wheels of political and economic floats has been transformed into yet another kind of struggle called pipeline wrangling.

Oil Companies Competition

The oil is money as well as power; the fact recognized straightaway by oil companies and their supportive governments. Certainly, wheels of booming economies move on the greased axles served by oil and gas. As of August 2004, 373 oil and gas companies operated across the globe. Over 30 companies of different category and capacity were seen active in Central Eurasia alone in addition to the native companies.[119] Of these, British Petroleum (BP), British Gas (BG Group), AGIPs' ENI, Action Hydrocarbon (Australia) Avery Resources (Canada), Burren Company (London), Chevron Texaco (USA), CNPC (China), Exxon Mobile (USA), Gazprom (Russia), Japex (Japan), LUKOIL (Russia), ONGC (India), Rompetrol (Romania), Rosneft (Russia), Tatneft (Russia), Unocal (USA), and YUKOS (Russia), were the most significant to be operating in Caspian-Caucasian Region. In other words, the region is receiving about 10% of the world total exploratory effort that is stupendous in the calculus of hydrocarbon man.

The race to Central Eurasia by the foreign oil companies commenced on emergence of the three additional Caspian littorals and other Caucasus and Central Asian states. In 1993, Chevron Oil Company struck partnership with Kazakhstan and constituted Tengiz-Chevron with projected investment of $20 billion, securing 40 years concession and soon incorporating the oil field of Karachaganak. BG and ENI were also awarded rights to develop the field. In 1997, BG and ENI, in partnership with Texaco (USA) and Lukoil (Russia) concluded a production sharing agreement, PSA, for the same field. In the same year, PSA with North Caspian Consortium was concluded.

In July 1997, Offshore Kazakhstan International Operating Company, OKIOC, struck a giant oil field at Kashagan. Located 75 kms south of Atyrau; it has the potential to become the largest oil field in the world. On Azerbaijan front, in 1994, Azerbaijan International Operating Company/Consortium, AIOC, was raised out of the components like State Oil Company of Azerbaijan Republic, SOCAR, European, US, Russian, Turkish, Japanese and Saudi Arabian partners. In 1995, deal was struck by signing PSA to develop ACG complex of oil fields. The same year PSA was signed between the conglomerates, which constituted Caspian International Petroleum Company. It comprised SOCAR, Lukoil, Agip and Pennzoil for oil prospecting of Karabakh that did not materialize.

In June 1996, deal to prospect and develop Shah Deniz field was concluded. The field located south of Baku was believed to have 250-500 Gb of oil and 2-4 tcf of gas. In this deal SOCAR, BP, State Oil, Lukoil, and TPAO (Turkish National Oil Company) as well as Naftiran Intertrade Company of Iran were partners. Exploration of oil did not always mean success in Azerbaijan[120] but the Azerbaijani authorities suspect the oil companies' failure as 'politicking'. For instance, an oil well drilled by one of the most successful of the companies (Exxon Mobil) at Nakhichevan was an utter disappointment, which was not far from ACG complex in geological terms. Declaring prompt failure by the company is intriguing and reinforces the Azeri view that it may be part of the politics, either to scare off other companies or extract concessions from Azeri Govt to acquire cheap prospecting rights. The same episode was a repeat play while drilling at Oguz in Azerbaijan. If this aspect of politics is kept in mind, it makes sense to relate some companies winding up from an 'elephant' called Kashagan in Kazakhstan initially which later turned to be a giant of all oil fields in Central Eurasia. Yet by year 2000, spurt of PSAs was seen and as many as twenty of them were signed.

Comparatively Turkmenistan attracted lesser intensity of oil giants' activity because of limited oil prospects and logistic constraints. However, a Malaysian Company, Petronas concluded PSA with Turkmenistan government in 1996. Similarly, in 1998, Mobil and a UK based Oil and Gas Company concluded an agreement for exploring Garashsyzlyk area but an oil field already located there was not included. These activities from mid to late nineties qualified nothing less than to be called as oil companies' scramble. Sizeable reserves were struck but early nineties clamor about Caspian Region, grading it the second Middle East soon settled down which was of course an exaggeration. Conversely, pessimism rumored through the region, as a shade of politics or straight factual talk that would not be able to undermine its significance of being a largely untapped region, yet to be explored. Oil companies vied against each other when dozens of PSAs were signed between several foreign companies.

At that moment, unprecedented degree of politics on winning maximum share was seen with covert effort to exclude some and include others. However, a sensitive issue was to crop up now because exploration was one aspect while transportation of oil and gas was another. It was equally lucrative for upstream, midstream and downstream countries as well as for the companies. Who should carry oil and gas to international market and in which direction since the landlocked Caspian Region did not have only inhospitable climate but the terrain characterized by rugged mountains and large deserts as well? After experiencing depth location and high pressure of oil and gas at Tengiz, Mr. Price remarked about, "The oil industry equivalent of alligator wrestling... a geologists' dream but petroleum engineers' nightmare."[121] The foreign investors on the contrary appeared determined to quash 'engineers' nightmare and their accomplishment could be acknowledged after Baku-Tbilisi-Ceyhan pipe dream was transformed into a reality in May 2005. It also led to diversify the export options, which earlier presented no choice but going through Soviet era export infrastructure.

Former Soviet Union routes to the north would have obviously amounted for them risking everything on one endeavor, for which an investor worth the class would never be prepared. Incidentally, this investment related fear with a mix of politics precisely coincided with the geopolitical objectives of their parent countries that would find elaborate exposition subsequently. It obviously led to conduct of various kinds of pull strategies, most favorable to respective national interests of the regional powers, mainly Russia that almost single handedly owned the Caspian assets in the past. Thus, the blueprint for the New Great Game was laid.

Pipeline Routes Configuration

The global hydrocarbon scene indicates proven reserve of oil as 1,188-1,265 Gb.[122] Out of this Caspian share of Azerbaijan, Kazakhstan, Turkmenistan and Uzbekistan accounts for about 47 Gb. In the domain of natural gas, out of about 180 tcm (6,354 tcf) of world total, Caspian region has about 322 tcf of gas. Having such significant level of reserves, the world market would naturally yearn to benefit from these riches, which would bring a great economic boom to the region as well. The geo-political and geo-strategic environments prevailing in Caucasus-Central Asia dictate that any particular brand of exit strategy for these hydrocarbon riches will be contested fiercely among the proponents. While the scrutiny in this domain would follow, it would be pertinent to see the existing and future configuration of export infrastructure of some important pipelines and hence summary narrative of the whole cluster would be given for ready references, coming up at any stage of discussion. Before the dissolution of USSR, the Caspian Region was connected to North-South axis of the Soviet era, having obsolete infrastructure of pipelines with limited capacity and threatened by possibilities of extensive sabotage. At the close of 20th Century, multiple choices emerged at the behest of their contestants on directional basis i.e. East, West, South/ Southwest, and North/ Northwest.

The Western Option makes East-West axis, a deviation at right angle from the previous North-South axis. Thus, pipeline orientation and flow has shifted towards Europe through Turkey. Region's three biggest pipelines leading to the West, include one; Caspian Pipeline Consortium Project (CPC project), two; BTC Pipeline and third, South Caucasus Pipeline (SCP).[123] CPC Project (Map-14) connects Kazakhstan oil to the Russian Port of Novorossiysk on Black Sea. It is 1,568 km long pipeline, which has been restructured from the existing portions. The newly constructed segment of the pipeline is from Komsomolskaya, straight westward to Novorossiysk. The pipeline has afforded Kazakhstan an alternative to the aging infrastructure as well as an export option, which earlier meant only Atyrau-(Kazakhstan) Samara (Russia) exit dominated by Russia. The pipeline was commissioned on 27 November 2001, officially though an oil tanker carrying CPC crude oil had sailed from Novorossiysk earlier on 15 October 2001. It had initial capacity of oil as 560,000 bbl/d with plan to expand its capacity to 1.45 million bbl/d by 2008. By October 2004, after achieving an increase of 33 % to the previous 'through put' oil in CPC, Kazakhstan managed its near capacity utilization to 533,000 bbl/d. In CPC there are 11 stakeholders. These are KazMunailGaz/BP 1.75 %, Shell 1.75 %, Eni 2 %, Omani Govt 7 %, Rosneft-Shell 7.50 %, Exxon Mobil 7.5 %, LukArco 12.50 %, Chevron Texaco 15 %, Kazak Govt 19 %, Russian Govt 24 % and BG Group 2 %.

The second pipeline, BTC pipeline that remained controversial from feasibility point of view was finally completed and inaugurated on 25 May 2005 (Map-15). BTC has added yet another chapter to western resolve, mainly USA, to diversify the export routes for oil and gas.

Map-14: CPC Project (Source: British Petroleum, June 2005 www.bp.com/statisticalreview)

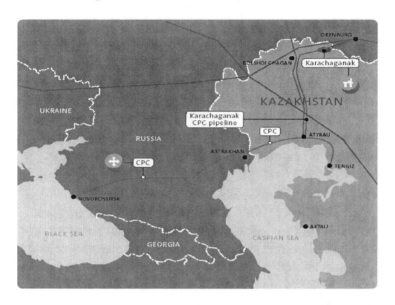

The pipeline will deliver one million barrels of Azeri oil a day from Baku to Turkish Mediterranean seaport of Ceyhan. As Azeri oil production capacity (million bbl/d) to charge it to full capacity from ACG complex (Map-16) is not likely to be achieved before 2009. Plans are afoot that Kazakhstan oil may be integrated by initiating a segment of extended pipeline from Kazak's oil fields to Baku through a project being called Trans-Caspian Oil Pipeline (TCOP, Map-17), subject to overcoming of certain political constraints. Such projects, however, are usually prone to inevitable delays and glitches. Pending completion of TCOP, Kazakhstan will sign a long-awaited inter-governmental agreement with Azerbaijan in October 2005 for the supply of up to 600,000 bbl/d of crude oil to the BTC pipeline. The oil would be delivered from Kuryk, roughly 60 miles south of the major oil port of Aktau, and would then be shipped by tankers across the Caspian Sea to the port of Sangachal, the starting point of BTC in Azerbaijan. The pipeline infrastructure is yet to be built to the southern port, and cost estimates will not be released until the agreement is signed. Kazakhstan officials have said that much of the new oil would come from the Kashagan field.

Map-15: Caspian Region Pipelines Network
Source: (US Energy Information Administration: www.eia.doe.gov) January 2004.

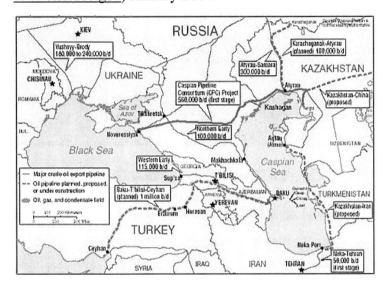

Kazakhstan also announced that it has begun building a new class of Caspian tankers to replace the existing vessels that currently carry much of the region's maritime oil trade. In other words, TCOP shall supplement BTC, which is 1,760 km long pipeline with initial expenditure estimates as $2.9 billion, having 13 stakeholders.[124] The plus point, other than the one that it has provided westward alternative is that it completely bypasses Black Sea and hence that much relief to the Bosporus choke point. During its completion, the project remained marred with rumors of its being 'unfeasible'. Now when cutting edge of Western technology has rendered those fears unfounded, a large number of NGOs are criticizing it on environmental grounds. BTC pipeline means victory for some in the face of others, vanquished.

Map-16: ACG Complex
Source: (US Energy Information Administration:
www.eia.doe.gov) January 2004. (Ignore Map-1 in the
picture)

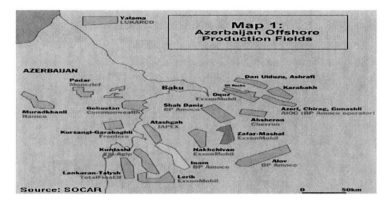

Map-17: Caspian Region Oil Pipelines Orientation
Source :(US Energy Information Administration:
www.eia.doe.gov) January 2004.

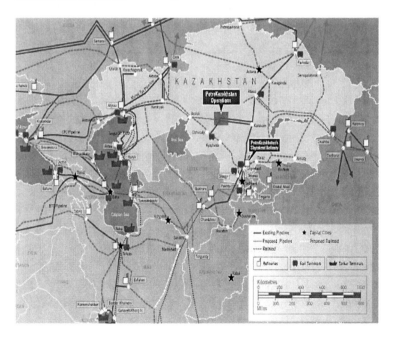

Frederic Starr has labeled it as a feat of engineering and draws its parallel to Suez Canal construction with accompanying geo-strategic implications. The third pipeline (gas) planned for the region through western corridor is the South Caucasus Pipeline (SCP), which has also been referred to by some as Baku-Tbillisi-Erzurum (BTE) pipeline (Map-18). The pipeline, about 900 km long shall originate from Baku, traverse through Tbilisi and onto Turkish town of Erzurum (a smaller but closer town is 'Horasan') where Turkey has a large network of gas installations. Planned at the cost of one billion dollars, the pipeline would deliver 1.5 bcf of gas daily from Azeri gas field called Shah Deniz. It was scheduled to be completed by August 2006 and would have the inherent design to expand its delivery at Erzurum to 0.3 bcf. In order to allow Turkmenistan gas find an alternative exit thorough Western Option and prompt Turkmenistan to look west rather than south or north, USA has lobbied Trans-Caspian Gas Pipeline at 750,000 dollars cost of feasibility study. It would extend through Caspian Sea from Turkmenbashi seaport to connect with SCP at Baku.

Of the prominent oil pipelines, the Baku-Suspsa Pipeline (BSP) is considered a pioneer project of the Western Option when other projects were yet on the board. Consequent to an agreement between Georgian President Edward Shevardnadze and Azerbaijani President Heyder Aliyae on 8 March 1996, Baku oil was to be pumped through an existing but renovated and upgraded 825 km long pipeline to Supsa (Map-15 ante). It led to construction of an oil terminal at Suspsa at the cost of $565 million. The system is also connected with Georgian Seaport of Batumi, located approximately 200 km to the south. It became operational in April 1999 with original design capacity to deliver 100,000 bbl/d. However, recent upgrades in 'throughput' have meant addition to 220,000 bbl/d and 140,000-bbl/d capacities for Supsa and Batumi respectively. Although the design permits to enhance the capacity but Azerbaijan appears keener to charge up its BTC pipeline.

Map-18: Caspian Region Natural Gas Pipelines
Source: (US Energy Information Administration: www.eia.doe.gov) January 2004.

In January 2003, the BSP was shut down for two days due to an explosion near Sveneti, a Georgian village, 60 km from Tbilisi. Georgian separatists were accused for this sabotage. Some see the oil politics play to force Baku to relegate BSP priority in favor of BTC pipeline.[125] Sabotage could be considered as soothing the western camp but the finger could also point to Russian camp for gaining political mileage through such sabotage to prove that BTC also faced high security risk while traversing through Georgia. In certain accounts, BSP is also referred to as 'Western Early Oil Route'.

Eastern Option is wide open and purely driven by 'market' capitalization. The demand in European market, through efficient energy management, would grow barely by a little more than one million bbl/d for Caspian oil during next 10-15 years. Conversely, the Asian market growth is deemed to grow rapidly during the same period by 10 million bbl/d. Therefore, Eastern Option to China and possibly Japan fits in the scheme of things. Besides, it also remains in harmony with Western agenda to diversify the pipeline orientation though West has expressed mute reservations for this project under various sets of pretext like feasibility, cost prohibitive factor and its security over long distances. Thus, Kazakhstan-China Pipeline (KCP) has come up as an answer (Map-19). Its first segment that stretched from Aktobe, also called Aktybinsk, oil field region to Atyrau was completed in 2003. Reportedly, the second phase, scheduled for completion at the cost of $850 million by December 2005 from Atasu to Altawa Pass in Chinese Xingjian Region, has also been successfully completed. With initial capacity of 200,000 bbl/d, it is to be expanded to 400,000 bbl/day. Later Kazakhstan-China Gas Pipeline (KCGP) is likely to become one of the world's longest pipelines with total stretch of about 2,900 km (1,800 miles) and subsequent dream of its extension to the Pacific Ocean would mean its length as 6,400 km with $10 billions tag of expenditure.[126] The pipeline is only at 'feasibility study stage' by Exxon Mobil, CNPC and Mitsubishi. There are constraints being confronted, which may become serious impediments to realize this dream being in clash with economic interests of some actors in the arena.

South and Southeast Options offer an alternative to fulfill Asian market demand most economically through Iran in the south and Afghanistan in the southeast. The one referred to as TAP, once three countries agreed over Turkmenistan-Afghanistan-Pakistan or Trans-Afghanistan Pipeline (TAP) for gas in a tri-lateral agreement signed in

December 2002 while Taliban Gov't fell in December 2001 (Map-20).

Map-19   : Kazakhstan-China Pipeline (KCP)
Source: (US   Energy   Information   Administration: www.eia.doe.gov) January 2004

TAPs' point of origin is Daulat Abad. In some accounts, it has also been named as CentGas (Central Asian Gas) pipeline that would have originated from Kazakhstan.

The construction cost of about 1,400 km long pipeline is estimated to be $2.5 to 3.5 billions. In the process of enlisting investors, a key partner, Asian Development Bank, called for additional feasibility studies, thus delaying the project. However, Afghan imbroglio presents itself as a major deterrent to the investors.

In response to a query, Dr Azmat Hayat Khan, Director Area Study Center, University of Peshawar, Pakistan confirmed that during a Pakistan-Turkmen official's conference in Ashkhabad in early September 2006, the TAP plan had been shelved. Though no official

Map-20: TAP Originating From Turkmenistan (Daulat Abad). Source: (US Energy Information Administration: www.eia.doe.gov) January 2004

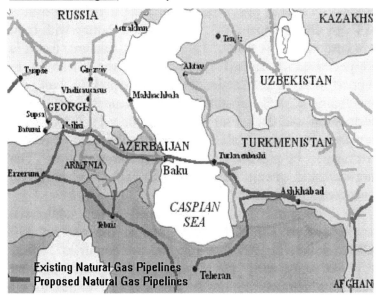

word is available, the Director, being a participant to the conference has left no margin for any authentication. The TAP gas pipeline would have had a flexible element to allow India to join by extending a segment from Sui or Multan (Pakistan) gas installations complex to the nearest Indian border city. Should Turkmenistan gas fail to reach Indian market, it is still possible to access international market through Pakistani seaport of Gwadar. Considering a vast market to the East for Turkmenistan's gas through Pakistan, it is unlikely that this project would be shelved forever, particularly when it will receive favorable view from the Western camp as well. Russia. China and Iran's response would oscillate from cold to negative.

Second option through Iran in the south is geographically more feasible but in power politics, USA and Europe are least inclined to support this option. In fact ILSA[127] (Iran, Libya Sanctions Act of 1996, now no longer applicable to Libya) emerges main binding on international

107

and US oil companies and US for not doing oil and gas business with Iran. Its renewal for another five years in 2001 would mean it would stay in force till 2006 while end of US-Iran hostile posturing is not in sight yet. The details of ILSA are at Appendix-1. As regards to policy with Iran, it is hard hitting. It reads, "The Congress, declares that it is the policy of the United States to deny Iran the ability to support acts of international terrorism and to fund the development and acquisition of weapons of mass destruction and the means to deliver them by limiting the development of Iran's ability to explore for, extract, refine, or transport by pipeline, petroleum resources of Iran." The motives and manipulation of this situation shall be discussed subsequently.

However, Turkmenistan and Iran completed Korpezhe-Kurt Kui (KKK) Pipeline at the cost of 190 million dollars in 1997 that links the two countries. In fact, it is the only early gas export pipeline from Caspian Region, which does not run through Russia. Besides, for oil Turkmenistan and Iran have swap arrangement that became possible only after Iran upgraded domestic distribution system in early 2004. This way transaction of 50,000 bbl/d was to materialize initially and later expanded to 170,000 bbl/d. Swap arrangements are cumbersome as compared to pipelines yet Turkmenistan gets a touch of flexibility by looking south and additional revenues while Iran manages to offset her positional disadvantage. Iranian oil and gas sources are predominantly in the south but it needs colossal amount in the north to cope up with her energy needs. Thus, she has to pump 700,000 barrels of crude oil to the refineries located in the north and 40 Bcm of gas every day.[128] Should the Turkmen and Iranian swap system work amicably, Iran would benefit as a market and save huge shuttling cost of her oil and gas quantities on daily basis to the north. However, by late 2004, differences about the price differential of 'sweet' and 'sour' crude happened to be a snag in the whole arrangement when 'swap' decreased by 75 %, to 75,000 bbl/d.

North and Northwestern Options are propounded mainly by Russia. Soon after independence of the three Caspian littorals, two pipelines were constructed; known as the Northern Early Oil Pipeline (Baku-Novorossiysk) and Western Early Oil Pipeline (Baku-Supsa) with combined capacity of 245,000 bbl/d. From the Western Option orientation point of view only, both pipelines now fall in this corridor. However since they terminate at Novorossiysk and are Russian supported, hence given the northerly label. Conversely, CPC Pipeline, built predominantly by Western investors is put in Western Option though it is more northerly than the above two. The only existing pipeline that is truly northerly is Atyrau (Kazakhstan) - Samara (Russia) Pipeline (ASP) that has been upgraded. With the construction of CPC pipeline, its relevance has decreased due to political and security questions while Caspian littorals are also inclined to diversify their export option and are not poised to hinge on Russia only. The description so far deals with the hardcore structure of the pipelines in the Caspian Region that remains under scrutiny due to diverse political incentives of the contenders. Out of these, BTC, being most contested and controversial, yet completed,[129] will make an apt model to focus upon. Thus, it would enable us what different perception prevailed about this gigantic project.

Politics amidst BTC Euphoria

The completion of BTC has generated success euphoria in the Western camp. Those opposed to this project, on the contrary have been moored psychologically. The composition of the CPC stakeholders indicates conglomerate of the eleven companies, including Russian, who pioneered this venture. Conversely, a close look at BTC shows that none of the Russian or Iranian companies co-joined. While Iran's prospects of participation were obviously blocked by ILSA (Appendix-3), there was no bar on Russian companies who were eager to avail a profitable situation. This was one of the few projects where Russian

Govt. and their companies maintained conflicting approach when the government, to stay away from the project, stopped them.

An eminent scholar Fredrick Starr[130] has looked at BTC from a different angle after its completion, labeling it as one, which represents School of Modernity. He appears inclined to condone in some manner the Jacobian brutalities of French Revolution when in the backlash, Commte Henrie de St. Simon had made a visionary statement that henceforth engineers and not the politicians would change the world. As already said he also draws parallels between BTC and Suez Canal designed and built by French engineer Ferdinand de Lessups[131].

The Russian politicians observed no qualm in criticizing the project vehemently because it amounted to the curtailment of their natural rights in South Caucasus. The critics, some within Turkey, US and Europe, expressed serious reservations about the cost and ability of Caspian littorals to 'through put' required quantities of oil in BTC. Thus, it complicated the politics further. Environment concern and demographic upheavals were the tools available to the opponents who were well equipped with such statistics. They maintained and rightly that the project would uproot 300 villages in backward region of Anatolia in Turkey. Yet the desire to reach the free market through the BTC, sponsors' and the investors' steadfastness prevailed ultimately. However, projected completion is one marvel for the consortium, as ensuing ramifications once the BTC has become operational since December 2005 there are bound to arise some fledging irritants on transmission, price and sharing revenues. The security fear would remain, though a separate protection force to patrol along BTC has been constituted. The recipients of oil revenues i.e. Azerbaijan, Georgia, Turkey, and the crop harvesters of oil, USA, Europe, can certainly muse at their achievement but those deprived and bitter critics of the yesteryears would find it hard to absorb the gripe.

Russia, Armenia and Iran appear humbled to the proportionate grade because US politics through ILSA has

110

worked which Iran had brushed aside, assuming it would not and the West had no choice but to adopt the South (best) or North (preferable) exit routes for the Caspian bonanza. Iran will certainly still wish and possibly act to make BTC ineffective. Russia enjoys hold on some quarters in insurgency prone Georgia as well as Armenia to whom Azerbaijan has lost $1/5^{th}$ of territory of Nagorno–Karabakh. When greater number of petrodollars would reach Azerbaijan coffers, her priorities at least in one context are predictable and that is to build military muscle and retrieve the lost territory. In other words, the imbalance thus created may intensify the hostile politics.

Russia has traditionally stood beside Armenia. In the domain of 'politicking' at least, Iran will obviously extend moral support to Armenia at the cost of added frenzy to Azerbaijan's woes with sole intention to undermine the Western interest. Turkey being the point man of the Western camp shall gain added antagonism against Iran that is historically so easy to inflate. The pattern of politics suggests that convergence of views on the orientation of Caspian Region pipelines is almost perfect as of necessity among Russia, Iran and Armenia thereby giving shape to their 'nexus'. The completion of BTC guarantees the economic interests of the Caspian beneficiaries and their sovereignty. Nevertheless, there are certain thorny questions, which shall not find answer at this stage. Would Russia dab her intensity of coercing the Caspian-Caucasus Region into compliance? In spring 1996, her unilateral act of curtailing Kazak oil flow through CPC for delivery at Russian seaport of Novorossiysk sent a chilling message through the Chevron spine, which now operated Tengiz oil field along with Kazak Oil Company. Reason cited by Russia that Kazak crude was damaging the pipeline being high on sulfur content, could not hold the ground because same crude had been running through the Russian pipeline for many years when Russia operated the oil field.[132]

Similarly, will Iran recognize the value of politically and economically stable governments of

Azerbaijan, Turkmenistan and Kazakhstan once the latter two would opt to accept the Western Option in executing TCGP and TCOP projects respectively remains a big question? The hope glimmers though but it is likely to fade away because taking reconciliatory approach and recognizing the ground realities are diametrically opposed to the 'nexus' pursued interests. If TCOP and TCGP were to become reality in certain frame of time after BTC, that would mean blow to Russian economy which at the moment monopolizes on Turkmenistan as well as Kazakhstan oil and gas market, though slipping fast from her grip. Thus, any attempt to downgrade BTC role would buy them US and European disapproval that may retaliate against the 'nexus', Russia being most vulnerable to the West's economic counter moves.

For these reasons, the opponents of BTC, TCOP and TCGP would perhaps have no choice but to see, on one hand, BTC as a necessary evil to tolerate as a compromise solution and on the other hand to vigorously interdict the efforts of extending Western Option to the east of the Caspian, connecting Kazak-Turkmenistan oil and gas to Baku through Caspian Sea. Incidentally, the pivots of politics, discussed earlier, are readily available to them. In the short term, Azeri–Turkmen bickering over Azeri 'Kyapaz' oil field that is claimed by Turkmenistan makes the TCGP prospects murky. Discovery of gas at Azeri 'Shah Deniz' field has improved Azerbaijan status from a net gas importer to a gas exporter.[133] This aspect will have dampening effect on their mutual discord. The West, led by USA, considers these geopolitical developments an opportunity to create situation in the Southern Caucasus conducive to the world peace through achieving economic and political stability out of erstwhile authoritarian states. The success in Georgia to an extent triggers such hopes, which stand to, consequently, neutralizing Russian coercive diplomacy in the region with no particular flare for democratization process. Turkey being an important ally and Azerbaijan now leaning to the West, NATO has, by implication, become an instrument of stability with its professed war on terrorism. The West, mainly USA and Turkey, perceives that their casting of shadow on the Caspian politics is nothing but a necessity for the region in particular and the world in general. This way the West not only augments security scenario in the region but also the security of hydrocarbon resources, which have become so vital assets for the world at the dawn of third millennium. General John J Sheehan's comments cannot be brushed aside, that he made in September 1997 when he led a contingent of 82nd Airborne Division to conduct an airdrop in Kazakhstan. He said, "The message, I guess is, that there is no nation on earth that we can not get to."[134] While the general may have been overestimating US capabilities as a traditional military self-glorification, yet the neighbors including Russia took solace in toned down comments that it was merely the US's force projection exercise. The defense analysts are left with little doubt, what the 'General' meant.

Broadening Spectrum of the Politics

Most scholars opine that China has expanded her role in the region that remained largely unnoticed so far. Jumping in the Central Eurasian arena has become her necessity because of burgeoning economy, which has been forecast to grow about 8 %. On the contrary, her indigenous oil and gas inventory is terribly short to support massive growth of its economy. As seen in the previous statistics tables for oil and gas, some figures set the record right. China has scant oil reserves of 17.1 Gb that make her share barely as 1.4% of the world total. Similarly, her oil production is by compulsion, modest but comparatively larger than her reserve ratio that is figured as 4.5% or 3.5 million bbl per day of the world total. When her inventory of consumption is seen, it tells all. With meager indigenous reserves and production, her consumption has surged to 6.68 million bbl per day or 8.2% of the world total, registering an increase of 15.8% over 2003.

Similarly, in natural gas her production is 40.8 Bcm or 1.5% of the world total per year, registering an increase of 18.5% over 2003. However, Chinese economy consumes 39 Bcm each year or 1.5 % of the world total, registering an increase by 19 % over 2003. The statistics prove that in order to allow her economy boom, China is left with no choice but to squeeze every ounce of oil and gas. Her rapidly expanding economy shall also consume inevitably the huge stocks of energy as well. While her gas production is keeping pace with her consumption, the yearly surge in 2004 over 2003 had been a colossal 19 %. In other words, her proven gas reserves estimated to be of 2.23 tcm that make only 1.2 % of the world total proven gas reserves shall deplete fast because of ever-increasing consumption.

Assuming that energy efficient measures enable China to steady her current rate of consumption, which at the moment appears a hypothesis though, her gas reserves shall last for only two years time. Her daily consumption of petroleum products is second largest in the world; 5.5 million barrels per day, which is projected to reach 12.8 million barrels per day by 2025. The most significant deal China struck with Kazakhstan was the mutual agreement on KCP, which was scheduled to be completed by late 2005. She is also likely to become Azerbaijan partner in oil and gas. March 2005 visit to China by Ilham Aliyeav marked the priority, both the countries accord to each other. Obviously, Beijing is most interested in Azerbaijan oil. After signing some PSAs between the two Governments, SOCAR has permitted a Chinese oil company to work at Garachukhur oil field. China is thus, placed in a profitable situation.

Having contiguous borders with three of the five Central Asian states, her energy stalking is naturally camouflaged by growth of massive bilateral trade. Chinese trade volumes have doubled with Kazakhstan, grew by 127 % with Uzbekistan while Kyrgyzstan has become third largest trading partner with Xingjian.[135] Thus, it affords her a platform from trade and ethnicity commonalities point of view that she may not be trampling the Central Eurasian

114

sensibilities with which her relationship is expanding no less. Still the same advantage in part has become a Damocles sword for China, charting a course for her to tread it very meticulously. Otherwise, the conspiracy theorists, at an opportune moment may ignite the ethnic turmoil, which has brewed in Xingjian over the past centuries, shattering her dreams to exploit the riches of her Central Asian province.

In this scenario, China would stand bracketed with Russia, Georgia, Azerbaijan, Iran and Armenia who sit on one kind of flash point or the other in Central Eurasia that would be gravely ominous for her economy. Her political rivals would gloat over the situation.

The EU has emerged yet another ingredient of the Central Eurasian politics. The Union's perception of 'wider Europe' stands served when Georgia and Azerbaijan have been integrated through BTC. The perception to revive old 'Silk Road' by proposing TRACECA and INOGATE hinges on such dreams like BTC success that has laboriously emerged as reality from the 'pipe dream' status. BTC is thus a vital ingredient of European energy security as well. When stakes would be high, EU focus on Caspian politics would obviously be a foregone conclusion.

India, of late, has emerged as extremely needy for hydrocarbon energy though by the scale of her indigenous resources, she ranks almost insignificant in oil and gas scenario. Her economy has tremendous potential to grow; it grew 4 % in 2002, surged to 8.2 % in 2003 and is projected to grow by 6.2 % in 2005. Her dependence over oil for the total energy consumed is 30% with imports of 1.4 million bbl per day, which is likely to soar to 2.8 million bbl per day by 2010. Her natural gas consumption has registered rapid increase. From only 0.6 Tcf per year in 1995, her consumption is projected to increase to 1.2 Tcf by 2010 and 1.6 Tcf by 2015 annually. India has shown interest to import Caspian Region oil and gas for which it is a lucrative market.[136] TAP pipeline plan if executed ever, beside the one she is negotiating with Iran, is a possibility for her to join as a very economical alternative. However, her deep-rooted reservations about this option being faced with an adversary of the past prevent her to join the cause though Pakistan is inclined to offer all possible sureties for uninterrupted gas supplies.

In Central Eurasian context, of late the giants have had clashing posturing. India and China were seen biding for the same oil company when China won the deal. It nevertheless marks the frenzy with which India is now poised to commit herself in the game. Jyoti Malhotra rightly remarked, "The Sino-Indian competition over control of Petro-Kazakhstan has been in the news recently, with India's Oil and Natural Gas Corporation (ONGC), having lost out to China National Petroleum Corporation (CNPC) in a dramatic cloak-and-dagger maneuver a couple of weeks ago. Turns out that when the weekend ended (around the India's Independence Day on August 15), India ONGC had been on top with a $3.9 billion bid for company control. But when Monday morning dawned in Almaty, CNPC had come in from the cold with a $4.18 billion offer that Kazakhstan could not possibly refuse."[137] India appears in an aggressive stance to seek extra oil that could guarantee her economic growth for years to come. The politics of purchasing oil and gas giant companies may give a momentary relief to the winner but in the end, the emerging economies may find with certain amount of bad taste that strategic partnership would have been better option than the play of politics to unseat each other. Central Eurasian assets are naturally contiguous to China and at close quarters to India. It is thus possible that both would be vying to benefit from each other's follies if not gains through wisdom. Nonetheless, they have found an interesting battlefield of politics, from NEFA (a sector on Indo-China border) to Central Eurasia, geographic variations not withstanding.

China on her part has not made any concerted effort to veil her designs. Her bid of $20 billion to acquire Unocal was spurned only at the last moment when US nationalism or patriotism personified by Chevron interceded to prevent Unocal going into the Sino baggage. While all goes on,

China's ingress in adjoining Central Eurasia would remain a rocky passage. Chevron's ambush to the Chinese bid cannot be taken in simple business chemistry. It only indicates how determined was USG to keep Chinese influence at the scale that it does not run counter to the US interests. Similarly, Russia's allergy to the build up of foreign influence is no longer a secret. As regards China, despite that, Russia now has peaceful borders with her, she would carefully watch China's moves lest China attempt in cashing her economic influence, backed by her nuclear force projection and ethnic infiltration. In the same context, Russia maintains series of 'first principles' with external and internal connotations.

Externally Russia, "has sought to demonstrate to the world is that Central Asia has remained exclusively in the sphere of Russian interests and that it will not allow any rival power to emerge in the region. Internally these principles have sought to convince the newly independent states of Central Asia as well as the public in Russia that there is an external threat from other regional powers and that Russia is only capable of protecting them against absorption of these powers."[138] Though not spelled out with same clarity and ferocity, by implication, Russia at least on her part still suffers from her 'imperial' stupor as regards to the Caucasus Region as well. Relating these perceptions to the rush for energy, hydrocarbon factors amply manifest that energy stampede shall occur and so shall the Caspian Region remain a favorite rendezvous to contest oil politics. The coverage so far has been restricted to the regional politics that cannot be isolated from the transnational element of geo-strategy. In other words, extended debate becomes imperative in the backdrop of geo-strategic dimensions of the New Great Game and the actors' role to support exclusive exterior maneuvers of their own under the garb of apparently benign, friendly and peaceful diplomacy. No surprise if it turns out to be malignant, 'fiend-ly' and 'piece-full.'

CHAPTER-FOUR

GEO-STRATEGIC DIMENSIONS OF THE NEW GREAT GAME

Geo-politics and Geo-strategy

Academics, theorists and practitioners of geopolitics have varied perceptions of the term 'geo-strategy'. Nonetheless they tend to be in harmony on perceiving it as a sub-field of 'geo-politics', yet more vibrant than the mother subject is. Geo-strategy is concerned with "matching means to ends;"[139] and relevant to our 'book' theme, it would mean matching of country's resources with its geo-political objectives. The hint placed about its being vibrant is further augmented when geo-strategists, in contrast to geo-politicians advance proactive strategies and approaches to the geopolitics in the backdrop of nationalist approaches. Geo-strategy has also remained close to geography in myriad kinds such as human geography, political geography, economic geography, cultural geography, military geography and 'strategic geography'. Of all, geo-strategy is much closer to the strategic geography. Its consensus definition put forth by geo-strategists emphasizes the merger of strategic considerations with geopolitical factors. While geopolitics is apparently a neutral instrument to examine the political and geographic features of different regions, geo-strategy involves comprehensive planning, assigning means for achieving national goals or securing assets of military and political significance. The term 'strategy' is the major component of the term geo-strategy. In modern days, 'strategy' projects extended boundaries with tactics at one end of the spectrum and 'national policy' on the other. Its viable definition reads like this, "A dynamic, logical and conceptual process, pitted against an opposing mindset or resistance, applying a whole gamut or range of 'means' available to attain the stipulated 'end' in the most cost effective way(s)."[140]

Interestingly, geo-strategy has history like any contemporary phenomenon, playing role in the field of international relations. Herodotus talked about the Greek plan to gain the empire of sea. During the golden age of Europe (1890-1919), an era of geo-strategists' paradise, the great powers rose and fell. For them there were no frontiers any longer to explore or colonize. Struggle of a state thus intensified against state(s). After WW-II, geopolitics fell into disrepute because of its suspected association with an exclusive Nazi's brand of 'geo-politics'. However, a famous German geo-strategist, General Karl Haushofar was an ardent exponent of 'geo-strategy', who despite being questioned for war crimes, was recommended to be exonerated after WW-II.

During the Cold War era, N.J. Spykman and George F Kennan charted the course of US foreign policy that would dominate the Western geo-strategic thoughts for the next forty years. Alfred T Mahan, H.J. Mackinder and Fredrick Ratzel are other prominent geo-strategists who could not be ignored. In fact, Fredrick Ratzel was pioneer of the concept of 'raum' (lebensraum) and organic-state theory. He theorized that states were organic and the borders were only temporary. Such propositions were taken by Nazis like 'faith' articles with ambition to sweep the whole world. Conversely, N.J. Spykman and George F. Kennan generally agreed to Mackinder's Theory of Heartland,[141] yet disagreeing in some minor details.

The latest in the series to impact on geo-strategic orientation of the world powers during and after the culmination of the Cold War, are reputed names of Henry Kissinger and Zbigniew Brzezinski. Others who had insight influence are Brook Adams (US), Alexander Dugin (Russia), and Homer Lea (US). Eurasian geo-strategy has remained a favorite subject to ponder about in all ages; precisely because out of the 64 places described by the geo-strategists as the strategic areas the world over, 20 lie in Central Eurasia that have enduring strategic value.[142] Going by simple average proportion yard stick, Central Eurasia draws significance to have almost every third strategic place located in it. Yet more if those on its periphery are also taken into account, the score would gain further in the strategic locations. The argument thus consolidates its strategic significance.

Geo-strategic Dimensions of Central Eurasia
A View in Perspective.

Preceding chapters indicate the geo-strategic significance of the land mass called 'Eurasia'. In a pursuit to remain relevant, Central Eurasia would be focused upon which is reckoned to comprise Central Asia and Caucasus. The readers may well recall that within the stretch of Central Eurasia, a nucleus of the highest interests in the context of oil and gas deposits, was recognized and termed as Caspian Region or Caspian. Thus out of the two segments, history of South Caucasus i.e. Georgia, Armenia and Azerbaijan, is more relevant and thus already covered in the preceding chapters.

Since Central Asia had been traditionally the field of two world powers in 19th and 20th Century to play, what Rudyard Kipling had publicized it as the 'Great Game', it may fit well to recapitulate its salient points. It was played between Imperial Russia and Victorian England between 1813 and 1907 while attempting to engage each other in the strategically important Central Eurasia. The Great Game acronym, according to a statement by Dr Muhammad Anwar Khan, ex Vice Chancellor University of Peshawar and an authority on Central Asian history, "is believed to

120

have been coined first by Captain Arthur Connolly who was executed in Bukhara on espionage charges." Also in his very well researched book, "England, Russia and Central Asia: A Study in Diplomacy," the Great Game chronological account without reference to this acronym has been extensively covered wherein John Wyllie appears to have coined another famous term for British attitude, "Masterly Inactivity." The words 'Great Game' appear once at page 23 of the book only with reference to Palmerston Papers. In the parlance of Russian scholars, the 'Great Game' had been termed as the, "Tournament of Shadows." The expansionist venture far away from the power base of the world powers may now appear encroaching on the subject's rights put under subjugation but in the history of warfare, it had been considered or assumed as a privilege of civilized nations to civilize the barbarians. The moral equivalent had thus been found to dominate the wealth sources of the targeted continents. As remarked by an eminent scholar, "Human nature is innovative and it erected most beau monde around itself. It is inlaid grab in man that made most in history…The word imperialist (imperialism) coined in 19th Century France can appropriately be noticed in extraterrestrial Assyrian, Phoenician, Persian, Greek and Roman leaps beyond their known borders"[143]

The British, predominantly a sea power with base in the Indian subcontinent, pushed northwest to make ingress into Central Asia. Conversely Czarist Russia saw an opportunity ripe for compensating her negative balance of sea power vis-à-vis Britain, by pushing southward through land offensive, securing River Oxus line by 1885. Afghanistan became the focal point of contest though Russia and Britain remained short of initiating war against each other. The game was triggered as both held each other in thick suspicions. Britain assumed that Russian grip over Central Asia would serve as their springboard for subsequent annexation of British territories in Asia and gain access to warm water ports. On the other hand Russia, having been severely mauled during Crimean War, thought it prudent to gain breathing space southward where weak 'khanates' were torn by mutual rivalries. At the same time Britain, gaining hold at the sub-continent when Robert Clive won the decisive Battle of Plessey in 1757, denied the French dreams about seizing of India's wealth. Lynn Montross comments, "The fantastic exploits of Robert Clive were made possible only by his country's sea power."[144]

By 1857, on suppression of 'sepoy rebellion' British hold over the subcontinent could not be challenged. By implication, she now threatened Russia from the south, also referred to as Russia's "soft underbelly". Thus, fertile ground existed to suspect each other and therefore play of the Great Game became conspicuous. To checkmate Russia's slow but steady expansion, British also intruded into Afghanistan. Conduct of First and Second Afghan War led them to little achievement except buying the hostility of Afghan people, which persists today. Finally, through lengthy spurt of diplomacy at St. Petersburg, a convention was signed on 31 August 1907 that marked an end of the Great Game, giving Afghanistan a buffer status particularly to separate the two powers. The urge to avoid war in a remote theater was also a marriage of convenience for both the contenders since balance of power had drastically tilted in favor of yet another European power, Germany. Compellingly both, Russia and Britain were drawn closer to deal with a threat that had built up at their doorstep.

According to Jennifer Siegel, international scenario for these powers forced certain compulsion and an element of relief also. For instance, Anglo-French 'Entente Cordiale' lessened Britain's Middle Eastern and African concerns. On the other hand, British reversals that she faced in Boer War and Japanese stunning victory over Russia after a surprise lynching of Russian fleet at Port Arthur on 8 February 1904 were some important strategic developments, which had sobering effect, both on Britain and Russia. Hence, the rapprochement through August 1907 Convention became possibility.[145] About the same time a British polymath, H J Mackinder would describe a region of the world in 1904 as the 'geographic pivot of the history'. His concept thus became the foundation of eminent geo-strategists approach to this region until today, which included our focus area i.e. Central Asia, Caspian and Caucasus. By 'pivot', he meant an area on the continent of Eurasia that is either land locked or whose rivers or littorals fed into inland seas or the ice locked Arctic Ocean. The Volga, Oxus, Jaxartes rivers drain into lakes and the Ob, Yensie and Lena rivers into the Arctic. Tarim and Helmand rivers fail to reach any ocean and peter out in the wilderness.

Most of the region Mackinder defined is Steppe land mottled with patches of deserts or mountain. Because of rapid mobility, Steppe land allows, as Mackinder pointed out to the historic tendency of the nomadic horseback or camel riding invaders coming from the east into the west. The pivot projection into the Central Asia is defined on one side by the Caspian Sea and Caucasus and on the other side by a mountain range from Pakistan northeast to Mongolia and Southern Russia.[146] The triangular projection 'south' into Central Asia was part of an area inaccessible to the sea powers like Britain, US, France and Japan. As such, land power could be generated into the rest of Eurasian land mass virtually unimpeded by the sea powers from strategically important area. This was the Mackinder's Theory on which some prominent geo-strategists built their respective concepts of geo-strategy as well as spatial strategy. Central Asia, incidentally, makes large chunk of this crucial space which, in, addition to geo-strategic factors, is now christened by hydrocarbon strategy as well. The region of strategic implications, however, had been successfully masked by the Soviets smoke screen until it petered out on dissolution of USSR when Russia withdrew to her core boundaries voluntarily. She soon realized that crucial vacuum thus created, when Mackinder's geographic pivot stayed denuded of military muscles, would be destined to see the rush forward from other power zones.

However, this time, the lead-power to fill the vacuum happened to be the USA and not Britain. Point finger to Russia or any other external power to contest influence or control over Central Eurasia, the mold of geo-strategy apply to the region anyway, "Power ingests weaker centers of power or stimulates rival centers to strengthen themselves."[147] It also marked end of Cold War era as the Capitalist's alliance established supremacy over the Communist ideology, which they labeled nothing more than utopian. Thus the Central Eurasian nations, at the dawn of new millennium, walked on a tightrope to maintain balance between getting out of their previous benefactor's (some may call occupier: Russia) hegemony and the need to prevent her wrath falling upon any of them because none alone or all combined could muster military muscles to face it. An observer opines, "This leaves Russia in a bind: on one hand it can not risk allowing Central Asia and Caucasus to fester, on the other it cannot afford to police the region. Fredrick Starr's suggestion that US can ensure stability by using surrogate such as Uzbekistan is a provocative proposition."[148] Napoleon was heard to have said that in order to understand geo-strategy of a power, know her foreign policy. It may be worth to see, what had been assessment of some prominent sages about US, Russia, and Central Eurasia on the close of 20th Century.

The Centurion Prognostics

Emergence of new world order at the collapse of Cold War left America as single super power in the global arena. The short span of Cold War era that lasted for only forty years also proves that historically the international systems are prone to severe shrinkage. For example, the one which grew out of Peace of Westphalia lasted for 150 years, followed by international system crystallizing through Congress of Vienna that had a life span of 100 years while Cold War had only forty years. In other words, the global turmoil and fast changing scenarios engineer the rapidity of collapse. By implication that would mean that unipolar world system will remain subjected to such stress of possible collapse while surviving for even shorter span of life in areas already identified by the prognostics. Central Eurasia is certainly to play a crucial role in the light of geo-strategic appreciations of H.J. Mackinder, Alfred T. Mahan, N.J. Spykman, G.F. Kennan, Henry Kissinger and Zbigniew Brzezinski. Some critics perceive that new world order orchestrated by USA created at the end of Cold War has led her to no better position to dictate world events unilaterally than during the conduct of Cold War. While USA has emerged more powerful, her larger potential of power application far and wide has rendered it diffused or overstretched. Some say that Wilsonian dreams of collective security happen to be the major casualty in the process of dilution of Cold War because there is dichotomy of threat perception as well as level of threat response among her allies which are also significant powers because Cold War threat lending cohesion to them has vanished altogether; at least for certain frame of time. On approach of 21st Century, when other global forces are at work, that would make US less exceptional. Despite having a robust economy, she is likely to face fierce competition that she never faced before. Henry Kissinger demarcates the parameters of the American global strategy for maintaining her superior foreign policy orientation. One could possibly mention and comment on those parameters[149] briefly because larger strands of his hypothesis are also applicable to Central Eurasian power game:

- Encroachment upon American exceptionalism and diffusion of power at universal level be not taken as a sign of decline. In addition, rise of other power centers in Western Europe, China and Japan should not alarm her because, traditionally development of other societies and economies have remained American objectives since the launch of the Marshal Plan. The proposition by Kissinger glorifies America's post WWII role but the clause would stand contradicted the soonest one would read succeeding segment of the concept when 'national interest' becomes predominant consideration.

- Though Richelieu's concept of 'raison d'etat' that interests of state justify the means, has always been repugnant to American but that does not mean that America has never practiced it. In fact, he opines that American leaders have to articulate a concept of national interest for the public and explain how the interest is served in Europe and Asia. The need to maintain the balance of power would require partners to preserve equilibrium in various region of the world. The contours of American intrusion in Central Eurasia starts taking shape here once one casts an analytical look at her massive military presence in this region 'proper' or on its periphery. In other words, the effort can be interpreted as devising a mean to articulate the concept of interests.

- The international system that survived the longest without war (Congress of Vienna) became possible only through shared values, legitimacy, equilibrium and balance of power, diplomacy. Henry Kissinger admits that Wilsonianism cannot be the sole basis for the post-Cold War era. It amounts to hint indirectly that perhaps America has to resort to discreet exceptionalism at places for enforcing the concept of national interest. The Iraq War is such an example while the aspects of the 'New Great Game' in Central Eurasia though potentially threatening, have so far remained within the ambit of or close to the criteria of Congress of Vienna.

- Growth of democracy will remain America's main aspiration but it is necessary to recognize the obstacles 'democracy' would face. Thus, he allows a margin for her to be flexible and tolerant of Central Eurasian Authoritarian Governments if that suits national interests. US stance in Central Eurasia and her history of being comfortable with dictators, monarchs and authoritarian rulers expose the weaker aspects of her foreign policy. Yet justifying 'means to achieve ends' remains a permissible clause of geo-strategic connotation for her.

- The fact has to be registered that America is an island offshore of the large land-mass (Eurasia) whose resources and population far exceed those of USA. Thus, the domination by single power of either of its two spheres, Europe or Asia would remain a strategic threat for America irrespective of the fact whether Cold War does not exist (as at the moment) or resuscitates itself on the world scene. Any move to offset such threat, when in theory Cold War does not exist, would mean some kind of interventionism. As remarked by John Pilger in a preface about Noam Chomsky, "It is characteristic of him that while many chose to celebrate the end of Cold War, he was cautious. He described it as an American nightmare - the domination of the Eurasian landmass by one unified power - Europe; and that what we are seeing today, is the gradual restoration of trade and colonial relationship of Western Europe with the East. He believes that big growing conflict is between Europe and United States. It's been true for years - they (the US establishment) really want to stick it to the Europeans."[150]

- As regards Russia, the American strategy of containment during Cold War may not hold ground for traditional foreign policy considerations. In fact, some fear that overestimating America's ability to shape Russia's internal evolution, America may involve itself to the limit that it generates a nationalist backlash at the cost of usual foreign policy. The symptoms are already on the surface that uneasiness of Russian leadership with USA on several scores suggests that if not the backlash; certainly harmonious views are non-existent between the two powers.

- The collapsing empires tend to generate two tension causes: attempt by the neighbors to take advantage of weakening imperial center or the effort by the declining power to restore its authority at the periphery. Rightly, too, perhaps the second cause of tension is significantly visible among Central Eurasian states, which splintered off the USSR. Oil and gas deposits discovered at massive scale through advance Western technology do allure Russia to perpetuate her influence and deny the same to others. It is an effort perhaps, which now triggers the geo-political maneuver of "New Great Game." The geo-strategic dimension are bound to get pro-active as the new concern about 'energy security' have arisen in the face of fast depleting oil and gas reserves 'panic'. Since the West, Russia, China, Japan, Turkey, Iran, Central Eurasian states, India and Pakistan would vie to benefit according to the mold of respective national interests, the facets of the 'New Great Game' will also multiply in discord and divisiveness among the competitors. Russia's attempt to monopolize 'peace-keeping' in her 'near-abroad' is indistinguishable from an attempt to re-establish their hold in post-Soviet space. It would thus remain a point of discord among the powers vying for corresponding influence in the region. Russia's security interests from the periphery are perhaps acknowledged by other powers as genuine but not the mode of realization of these interests. Instead of military option, it has to come through multilateral consensus and world body's role.

Eurasian Tangle

Quite relevant to US future role as the sole super-power versus others, the projected print also becomes vivid for the geo-strategists. With greater degree of alacrity, Zbigniew Brzezinski has made focus on Central Eurasia, but not without plausible criticism by others. He labeled Eurasia as the chief geo-political prize for America. Though he heavily draws from Mackinder, Mahan and Henry Kissinger, his assertions are direct and free of expediencies. In 'The Grand Chessboard' he sets the tone for his brand of 'strategy' by describing Russia and China as the two most important countries whose domination might threaten the US interests in Central Eurasia, also labeled by him as Eurasian Balkan. Of the two, he considers Russia a more serious threat. In the lesser context, he argues that Ukraine, Azerbaijan, Iran and Kazakhstan are essential nations that must be managed by US as buffers or counterweights to Russian and Chinese moves to control the oil, gas and the minerals of the Central Asian Republics. Picking up the relevant portions, he maintains, "In that context, how America 'manages' Eurasia is critical. Eurasia is the globe's largest continent and is geo-politically axial...75 % of the world population lives in Eurasia and most of world's physical wealth is there as well...Eurasia accounts for 60 % of the world GNP and about 3/4th of the World Energy resources."[151] His blunt mode is remarkable that he does not veil US ambitions for the riches of oil and gas, which is emerging as the most critical commodity for the World powers and more so for USA, to sustain her might. His detailed pinpointing of the level of relationship with Central Asia and Caucasus countries in particular is being meticulously followed by America through all kind of ethical slogans of human rights, democracy, morality and rule of law. Developments in Georgia, Ukraine, Azerbaijan, Afghanistan and expanding NATO from Baltic-Black Sea directions to offer PFP (partnership for peace) status to Central Eurasian states, expose the myths that 'New Great Game', which Brzezinski calls 'game' only, has deeper roots than envisaged by the scholars.

The intensifying effort to control oil and gas riches in the Middle East and Caspian Region is in fact the immediate prize for US and Europe without which their economies and hence the 'might' shall crumble. He makes the emergence of the 'New Great Game' irrefutable when he asserts, "The World energy consumption is bound to vastly increase over the next two or three decades. Estimates by US Department of Energy anticipate that world demand will rise by more than 50 % by 2015 with the most significant increase in consumption occurring in Far East. The momentum of Asia's economy is already generating massive pressure on the development and exploitation of new sources of energy and the Central Asian Region and the Caspian Sea basins are known to contain the reserves of natural gas and oil that dwarf those of Kuwait, the Gulf of Mexico or the North Sea."[152]

The assessment is valid but the point he circumvents here is that it would be the US which would face the worst crises after having reached her 'peak' production level in 1970. By mid of the current century, she is likely to become almost a net importer or at best left with only 10 % indigenous capability to meet her demand. Even today, America having only 5 % of the world population is consuming 25 % of the world's hydrocarbon energy. Thus, the 'starving scenario' becomes imminent reality that would decide how far she indulges on 'energy security' issues. Iraq is practical manifestation while 'Caspian' is the most sought for option. Therefore, onset of the 'New Great Game' for past about a decade with potential to multiply in intensity on each passing day is inevitable. "Now more than a hundred years later, great empires once again position themselves to control the heart of Eurasian land mass, left in post-Soviets power vacuum...The United States has taken over from the British. Along with ever-present Russian, new regional powers such as China, Iran, Turkey and Pakistan have entered the arena, and transnational corporations, whose budgets far exceed those of many Central Asian countries, are pursuing their own interest and strategies. The greatest difference in today's Great Game is the spoils."[153]

Design of the Game

The geo-strategy propounded by Brzezinski shapes itself as grand strategy once he writes, "to put it in a terminology that harkens back to the more brutal age of ancient empires, the three grand imperatives of imperial geo-strategy are: to prevent collusion and maintain security dependence among the vassals, to keep tributaries pliant and protected and to keep the barbarians from coming together."[154] It thus makes no exception if some state(s), which, hypothetically speaking, is/are democratic, having pleasant human rights record and follow rule of law and justice refuse to be pliant and collude against US instead. By design that would mean threat to the USA's interests meriting prompt dilution of such state(s). In other words, manifest pretenses in Central Eurasia are far more benign than the actual that could be ruthlessly diabolic. However, he is not shy to project military muscle as compared to Henry Kissinger, Spykman or Kennan once he asserts, "Hence forth, the Unites States may have to determine how to cope with regional coalition that seek to push America out of Eurasia, thereby threatening America's status as global power."[155] In fact, Kissinger presaging exercise and Brzezinski's assertion are hitting the accuracy 'bullseye'. Once it is known that human prognostic faculties are limited, one may see some kind of futuristic profiles of an event of limited scale but not the whole global blue print, which has to last for decades. Where could one place such geniuses? Michael C Rupert tells it all, "...major development of US and British forces had taken place before the attacks. Moreover, the US Army and CIA had been active in Uzbekistan for several years. There is now evidence that what the world is witnessing is a cold and calculated war plan – at least four years in the making and that, from reading Brzezinski's own words about Pearl Harbor, the World Trade Center attacks are just the trigger needed to set the final conquest in motion."[156] It is all about oil (energy). Such reactions, visible through Michael C. Rupert statement are not difficult to comprehend. Noam

Chomsky talks, "...of the process of reconstruction of imperial ideology that has been progressing step by step for the past years. It is hardly surprising that in Kuwait and other Middle Eastern states bitter resentment is expressed over the concept of legitimate American interests that may be protected by US armed forces...since it is assumed that the resources of the world are ours by right."[157]

For the purpose of Eurasian Chessboard hypothesis, Central Eurasia makes now a focal point under several claims by the West; not essentially pushed for the miseries of its people but obviously for lucrative myths of this region because in the opinion of Noam Chomsky, resources of the world are theirs, meaning America. Hydrocarbon riches make prominent projection on the imperial spectrum of their interests. In fact, political thinkers like Walter Laqueur suggested much earlier that 'Middle East Oil' be internationalized not for benefit of few oil companies but for the benefit of humankind. The statement sounds a pack of morals but who would define the 'benefit of mankind' and what shape it would appear when it shall go through magic wand-touch of interests of the powers that be. Certainly, it is a far-fetched conjecture. What Brzezinski called Eurasian Balkan and referred to the oil riches of Caspian Region; that meant, for the purpose of this 'book' as elaborated earlier; Central Eurasia.

Since this region remained 'blanket wrapped' by the Soviets for 70 years; for the better part of 20th Century, which saw industrial revolution reaching full swing, an argument may come up; why the 'New Great Game' is picking up acceleration in 21st Century. To give the subject a balanced treatment, the query has been raised because some 'oilists' shun the notion of any Great Game or Caspian riches. Some have even labeled the region's wealth as nothing more than 'Caspian Chimera'. Colin Campbell draws conclusion after a four pages commentary, "It is very evident that Caspian has proved a chimera, dashing hopes that it would lessen US dependence on the Middle East. This realization perhaps explains in part why it now turns its guns on Iraq. There is at the same time a serious lesson to be learnt: all that glitters is not gold."[158]

The comment is obviously rash because the scholar appears to have neglected the ground realities, a bunch of credible studies, confirmed oil and gas statistics, which have been examined so far. On one account he is on the dot to say, all that glitters is not gold, precisely because oil does not glitter and yet it is called 'black gold'. It may be apt to say that not only vacuum of power but also trails of vacuum of information persisted for quite long in Central Eurasia after the Soviets withdrawal, which the US Administration had crafted meticulously over several decades through Cold War strategy. Space thus became available, allowing others to fill the vacuum. The label of 'chimera' on the Caspian can also be perceived, say by Russia, as a part of the consolidation phase of the end of Cold War by the Western Camp.

One sees clearly that the combination of two potent incentives, which gave impetus to the New Great Game as the scholars mostly agree, are the theories of End of Oil and the Energy Security Crises even if some oil will be still trickling. It may be seen that the genie of 'end of oil' would keep gaining in its awesome apparitions and so would be the concern about the smooth flow of energy to the West from territories, generally held by friendly governments but hostile public. Thus, it makes the scenario 'nightmarish' for all the relevant powers to scramble against the odds, as seen through prism of realism or nearly a hallucination. Interestingly, a Pakistani author Ahmad Rashid coined the term 'New Great Game', when he wrote, "And so the much anticipated New Great Game between the major powers in Caucasus and Central Asia…became a reality."[159] To reinforce the logic it is imperative to:

- Dwell on end of oil, i.e. World Petroleum Cycle and World Oil Depletion Scenario.
- Elaborate the crisis of 'Energy Security', which looms large ominously at the international horizon and the leading powers are its compulsive viewers to much of their chagrin and disdain.

Those who follow the development in Central Eurasia that relate to 'making best out of the oil and gas' boom by the possible contenders, there appears no ambivalence among scholars about the kind of emerging scenario of the New Great Game. However the magnitude of clash of interest may generally follow the model what Eric Herring described once, "From the military balance perspective, the side which is militarily inferior will back down first... from the balance of interests perspective, the side with less at stake will back down first or concede most... The balance of interests is linked to the willingness of actors to suffer or risk suffering for what they value..."[160] The statistic and profiles of regional politics given earlier sufficiently provide the basis for deductions: whose balance of interest would hang perilously? Thus their role shall also become manifest to the corresponding intensity and detail. As regard 'backing out', perhaps this contingency would be seldom faced in case of energy squabbling, particularly once 'blinking' would mean death of their economies anyway. Staying in the arena firmly and also defiantly is likely to remain the most cherished option.

End of Oil Scenario

In global perspective, oil scenario is likely to grow grim because the scientific analyses hardly leave any margin of controversy to have any opinion otherwise. Those pointing out in mid 20th Century to an impending energy crisis by the turn of the century were branded as 'pessimists', 'doomsayers' or the scholars who could see only the 'negative'. They however demonstrated high degree of perseverance because their 'horrible' conclusions were based on arithmetical analyses. Only the world had no time to carefully listen to them. At the dawn of new millennium when energy crises are seen positively on the horizon, the doomsayer's camp has gained in size and credibility further. As the energy issue generates at the world level and its undercurrents persistently lash the Caspian Region, it would thus be relevant to have wider

134

evaluation to supplement our stance. For the sake of discussion, oil projections would be applied in the argument. However, why oil mainly? Reasons: one, that simultaneous discussion of full spectrum of hydrocarbon resources of energy shall render the focus on the issue as widely dispersed and hence gas, coal and non-hydrocarbon energy sources generated through lesser quantities of hydrocarbon fuel have been omitted. Where elements other than oil would enhance argument of sustainability of oil, these would be brought into discussion appropriately. Two: Oil pundits agree that oil is owner of 40 % of the world market. Since deposing King Coal in early 20th Century, it has wielded tremendous influence in shaping the world economies as well as politics. While coal's prospects stand dashed due to its ability of causing fatality to the world environments, gas is considered as a bridge-fuel, but not free from connected disabilities of several kinds. Thus oil being the leaders in the energy combination, it would be convenient to make it a tool of arguments, as its impact weight (40 %) versus coal (22-26 %) and gas (22-24 %) combined stands almost at parity on the lower side of estimates. Making use of crux of above statistics, because Central Eurasia shares every category by 4 to 5 %, reality emerges to comprehend the spin in the global politics and particularly in the oil regions. Paul Roberts appears on the dot once he writes, "Unstinting efforts by the United States, Europe, and other industrialized power to ensure access to Middle Eastern oil – by any means necessary and often with the help of Israel[161] – have helped foster a perpetual state of political instability, ethnic conflicts and virulent nationalism in that oil rich region."[162]

Fail not to perceive Middle East as part of Eurasia and Caspian Region, from the oil and gas point of view, the nucleus of Central Eurasia. The print and path of the oil geo-strategy in the backdrop of preceding chapters become clear. Though statistics have been quoted mainly from known authentic sources like World Oil, Oil and Gas Journal and BP previously, it may be apt to opt for BP statistics first. The world proven oil reserves are at 1,188

Gb with annual production at 80 Gb as of 2004. Obviously all the produced oil is consumed hence world oil consumption figures are almost the same as that of production. The world oil production as well as consumption increase was registered as 5.4 % in 2004 as compared to 2003. Assuming that by some designs the world increase in consumption shall stabilize, corresponding to the fresh exploration successes (though least likely) and proven oil reserves are drawn at current rate, in simple arithmetic, oil in hand (proven) at global level holds promise for about 14 years (2019). Yet another source of estimates (Table-21) places proved reserves at 1,265 Gb. That would give the consumption relief at current rate for 16 years (2020). The reserves growth of 730 Gb and the undiscovered, possible and prospective reserve of 939 Gb would mean with some fluctuations, having 1,669 Gb in hand. That leaves the total remaining oil beyond 2020, for another packet of about 21 years, allowing lease of oil life to the planet until 2040. The experts grant another 10 years for the possible margin achieved to sustain energy demand and the annual increases through other fossil fuels. Thus in this simple calculation, though proved also through mathematical determinants by the eminent energy scientists, the planet has to come to term with oil depletion shock anytime beyond 2050, intervention of miracles notwithstanding. The fact that geologists like M King Hubert made accurate 'peak' prediction about USA in 1956; the predictions made by the modern crop of geologists, equipped with the latest research tools are likely to be more accurate.

The crux of the conclusions of the studies by them establishes that: First; fossil fuel is not renewable; second, no other substitute can take up the role of oil or hydrocarbon fuels; third, world oil peak is placed at year 2005 or 2006 and fourth, ignoring oil depletion shock and not preparing for it would be a misleading fallacy. In fact famous geologists like Richard Duncan, Walter Youngquist, L.F. Ivanhoe, Jay Hanson, Graham Zabel and Albert A. Bartlett, a geo-physicist and score others have peripheral differences but converge on the major conclusions. Some even fondly quote Thomas Hardy who said, "Die off: if a path to the better there be begins with a full look at the worst,"[163] though Thomas Hardy had nothing to do with oil.[164]

Table-21: Estimated World Oil Resources, 1995-2025
Source: Energy Information Administration (EIA). www.eia.doe.gov/emeu/cabs/

Region and Country	Proved Reserves	Reserve Growth	Undiscovered	Total
Industrialized				
United States	22.7	76.0	83.0	181.7
Canada	178.9	12.5	32.6	224.0
Mexico	15.7	25.6	45.8	87.1
Japan	0.1	0.1	0.3	0.5
Australia/New Zealand	3.6	2.7	5.9	12.1
Western Europe	18.2	19.3	34.6	72.1
Eurasia				
Former Soviet Union	78.0	137.7	170.8	386.5
Eastern Europe	1.4	1.5	1.4	4.2
China	18.3	19.6	14.6	52.5
Developing Countries				
Central and South America	98.8	90.8	125.3	314.9
India	5.4	3.8	6.8	16.0
Other Developing Asia	11.0	14.6	23.9	49.5
Africa	87.0	73.5	124.7	285.2
Middle East	726.8	252.5	269.2	1,248.5
Total	1,265.8	730.1	938.9	2,934.8
OPEC	869.5	395.6	400.5	1,665.6
Non-OPEC	396.3	334.5	538.4	1,269.2

In case of Caspian Region when proven oil reserves are at 17 Gb on 'low' side and 44 Gb on 'high' side; the possible reserves in the region have been forecast at 167 Gb on low side and 194 Gb on high side (Table 3). As the economies boom, so would be the production, which so far at world level, is maintaining pace with demand. Because the world oil reserves are finite, the point or year has to be reached sooner when production peak shall commence downward journey on the graph. That year would be called world oil peak. Exxon Mobil identified this year as 2000 while Royal Dutch places the 'peak' year at 2005.[165] In fact, 'peak' phenomenon is so frightening that it is likely to force some of the leading powers to project an apparent unrealistic stance that they are not perturbed by the approach of oil crunch and at the same time would reinvent ethics to monopolize oil under several pretexts. The glimpses are already on the horizon; only intensity of such effort is awaited.

In the scenario of such a gloom or doom, Caspian Region presents a very lucrative option. As remarked by Duncan and Youngquist, "The world oil production peak, we assume, will be a turning point in human history. Our major goal is to forecast the all time world oil peak, not by one heroic effort, but rather by series of smaller efforts, much like an experienced team of mountaineers would climb the world's tallest peak."[166] Presently, the petroleum geology that holds energy promise of various magnitudes covers 182 nations; of which top 42 produce 98 % of world oil. The next 70 nations produce barely 2 % of oil while remaining 70 nations are devoid of any such luxury of oil and are hence net importers (Table-22). The table amply highlights the 'peak' reached by each of top 42 countries as well as that of the world.[167] The table serves as the bedrock of the argument that indicates that 33 out of the top 42 countries have already gone past the 'peak year' of their production. Only nine countries are yet to reach their peak. Vietnam and Venezuela are the latest victim to have dropped off, on having crossed their 'peak' by the end of 2005. Kuwait would stay on until 2018 that will be its 'peak' year.

Table-22: Top 42 Producers and Peak Years

Nation	Peak Year	Oil Prod Gb/yr Peak	1997	2040	Cumulative Gb 1997	2040	EUR	2040 vs Pk Yr	Remain Gb	RR,N/ RR,42N
1 Canada	2008	1.07	0.93	0.41	23.6	60.4	64.2	-62%	40.6	3.5%
2 Mexico	2001	1.32	1.24	0.11	26.4	56.1	56.6	-92%	30.2	2.6%
3 USA	1970	4.12	3.01	0.42	200.4	267.0	271.2	-90%	70.8	6.1%
4 Argentina	2001	0.33	0.31	0.05	7.0	14.6	14.8	-85%	7.8	0.7%
5 Brazil	2007	0.39	0.31	0.14	4.6	17.0	18.2	-64%	13.6	1.2%
6 Colombia	2009	0.29	0.24	0.11	4.4	14.6	15.5	-62%	11.1	1.0%
7 Ecuador	2002	0.15	0.14	0.05	2.5	6.7	6.9	-67%	4.4	0.4%
8 Peru	1982	0.07	0.04	0.02	2.1	3.4	3.5	-71%	1.4	0.1%
9 Trinidad	1977	0.08	0.05	0.02	3.0	4.5	4.5	-75%	1.5	0.1%
10 Venezuela*	2005	1.47	1.23	0.79	50.6	106.3	115.1	-46%	64.5	5.6%
11 Denmark	2002	0.10	0.08	0.02	0.7	3.1	3.2	-80%	2.5	0.2%
12 Italy	2003	0.05	0.04	0.01	0.7	1.9	2.0	-80%	1.3	0.1%
13 Norway	2000	1.27	1.23	0.18	10.4	41.2	42.4	-86%	32.0	2.8%
14 Romania	1976	0.11	0.05	0.01	5.1	6.3	6.3	-91%	1.2	0.1%
15 UK	1995	1.01	0.98	0.22	15.1	42.8	44.2	-77%	28.4	2.4%
16 FSU	1987	4.62	2.70	1.40	133.4	248.1	264.6	-70%	131.2	11.3%
17 Iran*	1974	2.21	1.36	0.85	47.8	116.9	129.6	-62%	81.8	7.1%
18 Iraq*	2010	1.95	0.44	1.08	23.9	95.5	109.0	-45%	85.1	7.3%
19 Kuwait*	2018	1.71	0.76	0.95	29.9	91.9	103.5	-44%	73.6	6.3%
20 Oman	2002	0.36	0.33	0.07	5.2	14.5	14.7	-81%	9.5	0.8%
21 Qatar*	2009	0.38	0.25	0.07	5.7	17.1	17.4	-82%	11.7	1.0%
22 Saudi Arabia*	2011	3.92	3.42	2.04	83.8	232.0	273.2	-48%	189.4	16.3%
23 Syria	1995	0.22	0.21	0.04	2.7	8.2	8.2	-82%	5.5	0.5%
24 UAE*	2017	1.77	0.99	0.62	18.8	82.2	85.4	-65%	66.6	5.7%
25 Yemen	2004	0.17	0.14	0.05	0.9	6.0	6.1	-71%	5.2	0.4%
26 Algeria*	2002	0.58	0.53	0.10	14.0	28.1	28.5	-83%	14.5	1.3%
27 Angola	2003	0.30	0.27	0.05	3.0	10.5	10.6	-83%	7.6	0.7%
28 Cameroon	1985	0.07	0.05	0.01	0.9	2.0	2.0	-86%	1.1	0.1%
29 Congo	2003	0.11	0.09	0.01	1.0	3.6	3.6	-91%	2.6	0.2%
30 Egypt	1993	0.35	0.32	0.06	7.5	15.4	15.5	-83%	8.0	0.7%
31 Gabon	2000	0.14	0.14	0.03	2.3	5.5	5.6	-79%	3.3	0.3%
32 Libya*	1970	1.21	0.54	0.27	20.3	46.6	48.2	-78%	27.9	2.4%
33 Nigeria*	2004	0.96	0.83	0.30	18.4	47.0	48.8	-69%	30.4	2.6%
34 Tunisia	2008	0.04	0.03	0.02	1.1	2.7	2.7	-50%	1.6	0.1%
35 Australia	2002	0.28	0.25	0.06	5.0	12.2	12.4	-79%	7.4	0.6%
36 Brunei	1979	0.09	0.06	0.02	3.0	4.6	4.6	-78%	1.6	0.1%
37 China	2002	1.23	1.17	0.46	22.5	62.5	66.1	-63%	43.6	3.8%
38 India	2003	0.31	0.29	0.08	4.9	13.3	13.6	-74%	8.0	0.8%
39 Indonesia*	1977	0.62	0.57	0.18	18.8	38.1	38.1	-71%	20.0	1.7%
40 Malaysia	2001	0.27	0.27	0.06	3.8	10.9	11.0	-78%	7.2	0.6%
41 P N Guinea	1993	0.05	0.03	0.01	0.2	1.0	1.0	-80%	0.8	0.1%
42 Vietnam	2005	0.09	0.07	0.02	0.3	2.7	2.7	-78%	2.4	0.2%
42 Nations	2006	31.00	26.00	11.50	836.0	1865.0	1996.0	-63%	1160.0	100.0%
WORLD	2006	31.60	26.50	11.70	853.0	1902.0	2036.0	-63%	1183.0	100.0%

There may be remote possibility for an odd country to renew their 'peaks' but majority would remain casualties of depletion. Surprisingly, the last to stay in the context for 'peak' reaching are all Middle Eastern players. e.g. Iraq 2010, Saudi Arabia 2011, UAE 2017 and Kuwait as already said would reach 'peak' in 2018. Column D of the table indicates the peak production rates. It appears that FSU, which also includes Caspian Region, will retain production record of 4.62 Gb/year. Saudi Arabia may soon exceed USA to get second place. There are other extremes as well. For example, Tunisia peaks at 0.04 Gb/year, which is barely 1% of the FSU 'peak' mark. Column E lists the production rate for each nation including Saudi Arabia, USA, FSU and Iran, which produced over 40% of the world oil alone in 1997 in contrast to the bottom four nations, Peru, Italy, Tunisia and Papua New Guinea that produced only 0.05 % of the world's oil. In column F, the tables are turned, when it shows production capacity in 2040. See that only FSU, Iraq and Saudi Arabia remain producers in whole numbers among the top 42, the other 39 countries, including USA, move to the decimal status. Next important column is J, which provides an insight to the future trends. It predicts the percent decline in production for each nation from its 'peak' to year 2040. Note that maximum decline is faced by Mexico (92%) and minimum is that of Kuwait (44%). However, by 2040, all the nations will be on steep decline. Column K forecasts percentage of RR for each nation (RR= EUR- Q1997). Saudi Arabia has the largest share of 189.4 Gb. Column L is also interesting. It gives the percentage share of each nation's remaining reserve to 42 nations remaining reserves from where one can see the future supply capability at a glance. Saudi Arabia, in this context with 16.3% share tops the list in this column. Table 23 indicates the 'peak' of the seven zones in which these 42 countries have been grouped. North America as a zone peaked in 1985, South and Central America peaked in 2005, Europe in 2000, FSU in 1987, Middle East is forecast to peak in 2011, Africa had gone past its peak in 2004 and Asia Pacific in 2002.

Here two important aspects need attention. One; Middle East, would remain vulnerable to energy security crises. Some observers have cogent reasons to suggest that

Iraq imbroglio, built up around Syria, Iran, Saudi Arabia, Caspian Region and lurking concepts of Greater Central Asia and Broader Middle East, NATO's PFP thrust forward are chain of the New Great Game. Keeping the theme restricted to Central Eurasia, while FSU has been indicated to have reached its 'peak' in 1987; it may not be confused with the Caspian Region status that is yet to grow with about 17-44 Gb of proved reserve and about 165-195 Gb of possible reserves. However, the time scale for reaching 'peak' tips faster if the oil is extracted faster. In other words enhanced production efforts in case of Caspian shall cause the 'peak' to materialize earlier though its time scale has yet not been calculated in isolation.

Table-23 also shows that by 2040, 60% of the world oil would be originating from Middle East. The second portion of Table 23 gives the statistics by geography and organization i.e. OPEC/non-OPEC that supplements the above argument. Since reaching of peak stage by any country or region forebodes end of oil, which is of course a finite commodity, questions have been raised, can 'peak' of a country, region, or world be delayed. At the global level, experts have worked out through combination of several mathematical hypotheses, curves and graphs, an approximate value of oil to be added to the available (EUR) reserves. As we know that world has peaked in 2005/2006. It can be extended but the required oil addition figures are extremely high, in reverse proportion to the oil discoveries, which are on decline.

Figure-2 indicates some results by two versions. The discoveries that picked up in 1910 with minor fluctuation in between peaked around 1965 and almost leveled out by 1995.

Table-23: Peaks by Regions, Geography and Organizations

Region	Peak Year	Oil Prod Gb/yr Peak	1997	2040	Cumulative Gb 1997	2040	EUR	2040 vs Pk Yr	Remain Gb	RR,g/ RR,42N
North America	1985	5.6	5.2	0.9	250.4	384	392	-84%	142	12%
So. & Cent. America	2005	2.7	2.3	1.2	74.2	167	178	-56%	104	9%
Europe	2000	2.4	2.4	0.4	32.7	95	98	-83%	65	6%
Former Soviet Union	1987	4.6	2.7	1.4	133.4	248	265	-70%	131	11%
Middle East	2011	12.1	7.9	5.8	218.7	664	747	-52%	528	46%
Africa	2004	3.3	2.8	0.9	68.4	161	165	-73%	97	8%
Asia Pacific	2002	2.9	2.7	0.9	58.4	145	150	-69%	92	8%
42 Nations	**2006**	**31.0**	**26.0**	**11.5**	**836.0**	**1865**	**1996**	**-63%**	**1160**	**100%**

The world's oil-producing nations can be categorized into: (1) geographic: Middle East and non-Middle East, and (2) organizational: OPEC and non-OPEC. (Source: Richard c. Duncan & Walter Young Quist, Petroleum Engineering Program,(University of South California, Los Angeles, October 1998.)

(Table-23 Continuing)

Region	Dominance	Peak Year	Oil Prod Gb/yr Peak	1997	2040	Cumulative Gb 1997	2040	EUR	2040 vs Pk Yr	Remain Gb	RR,C/ RR,42N
1a Mideast	> 2025	2011	12.1	7.9	5.8	219	664	747	-52%		46%
1b Non-MidEast	< 2025	2003	19.5	18.1	5.7	617	1201	1249	-71%	632	54%
2a OPEC	> 2007	2009	15.6	10.9	7.3	332	902	998	-53%	666	57%
2b Non-OPEC	< 2007	2003	15.9	15.1	4.2	504	963	998	-74%	494	43%
42 Nations		**2006**	**31.0**	**26.0**	**11.5**	**836**	**1865**	**1996**	**-63%**	**1160**	**100%**

Figure 2: The World's Conventional Oil Endowment/Discoveries

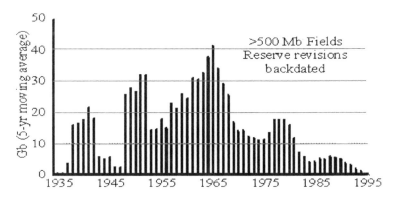

142

(Figure-2 Continuing)

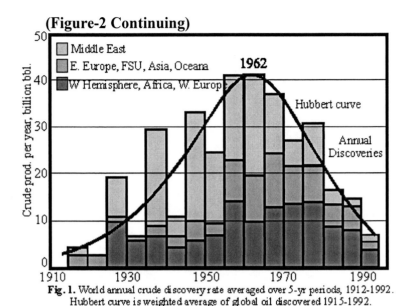

Fig. 1. World annual crude discovery rate averaged over 5-yr periods, 1912-1992. Hubbert curve is weighted average of global oil discovered 1915-1992.

[Ivanhoe, 1997]   (Disregard the words 'Fig.1' in above fig as these could not be deleted)

It however, does not mean that dwindling discoveries have dampened the oil companies' commitment to oil and gas exploratory efforts. In fact, as and when the oil is becoming more elusive, it is drawing added energies and resources of the countries in quest of oil and gas.

Table-24 indicates that, in fact, their exuberance is on increase in discovery ventures that is likely to face curtailment in certain regions for reason none other than that, there is no oil. The statistics of land rigs count with a time lag of a year in August 2005 and August 2006 proves that on the oil 'Regions' level, Canada score in land based operational rigs declined from 541 to 479.

Similarly, Europe has decreased from 25 to 21 rigs; Middle East surged from 173 to 225 rigs, Africa from 78 to 98 rigs, Latin America from 242 to 265 rigs, Far East remained constant around 134 rigs.

Table- 24: International Rotary Rig Count Monthly Average

Region	August 2006 Land	August 2006 Offshore	July 2006 Land	July 2006 Offshore	August 2005 Land	August 2005 Offshore
CANADA	479	3	550	3	541	5
EUROPE	21	56	18	49	25	46
Germany	4	1	3	1	3	0
Italy	4	3	3	2	4	1
Netherlands	1	5	1	5	2	1
Norway	0	20	0	15	0	18
Poland	1	0	1	0	2	1
United Kingdom	1	25	1	24	1	21
Others	10	2	9	2	13	4
MIDDLE EAST*	225	31	212	30	173	31
Abu Dhabi	9	4	9	5	9	4
Iran	45	8	46	8	36	13
Oman	41	0	40	0	34	0
Saudi Arabia	65	8	55	8	36	1
Syria	23	0	22	0	23	0
Turkey	4	0	4	0	4	1
Others	38	11	36	9	31	12
AFRICA	98	25	97	26	78	20
Algeria	27	0	27	0	24	0
Egypt	30	7	30	10	23	7
Libya	10	1	9	1	7	1
Nigeria	2	8	1	8	1	8
Sudan	23	0	24	0	19	0
Others	6	9	6	7	4	4
LATIN AMERICA	265	61	261	62	242	66
Argentina	82	0	84	0	79	1
Brazil	14	17	13	15	10	18
Colombia	24	0	21	0	16	0
Mexico	55	23	48	24	71	32
Venezuela	68	19	71	17	54	12
Others	22	2	24	6	12	3
FAR EAST	135	113	134	110	134	112
Australia	11	11	9	11	10	8
China, offshore	0	18	0	17	0	15
India	50	32	54	29	52	30
Indonesia	30	16	30	15	33	22
Malaysia	0	15	0	15	0	15
Myanmar	8	0	8	1	8	1
Pakistan	20	0	18	0	13	0
Thailand	2	8	1	8	1	8
Vietnam	0	9	0	10	0	9
Others	14	4	14	4	17	4
TOTAL	1,223	289	1,272	280	1,193	280

*No data available for Iraq.　　　　Sources: Baker Hughes Inc. & M-I SWACO

The rigs operational activity also confirms, on one hand, vanishing oil promise, say in Canada, Europe and Far East and on the other, that there are still vibrant regions like Middle East, Africa and Latin America.

Body search of the oil companies reveals that their virtues are no longer impressive. "Exxon-Mobil production had been flat since 1999."[168] BP and Shell are no better. In fact, BP has expressed serious doubts about further quest of oil, extending her acronym no longer for 'British Petroleum' but for 'Beyond Petroleum' as the world was running out of oil. To avoid facing censure, perhaps of the oil companies club, it later retracted her stance to state that BP was embarking on research fields beyond the oil vision, in the domain of other alternatives like hydrogen fuel cells etc. Shell as an oil company is also facing the crunch. An official of the Wealth Manager Magazine commented, "Shell has struggled with production...to replace a billion barrels every year is a real challenge."[169]

Unfortunately, the studies find that 1 Gb would delay world peak by just 2.5 days. Another test study allows 3.1 days per Gb and yet another permits 15.7 days per Gb. Professor Albert A. Bartlett, an eminent scholar and a geo-physicist, has made predictions based on empirical values. His exhaustive study deals with such issues as sustainability of oil, its relationship with population, growth and environments. His study deals with oil depletion scenario in a separate attempt that he essentially based on 'Hubert Curve', which empirically approximates the full cycle of growth peaking and subsequent decline to zero production.[170] His opinion is no different once he opines that to extend world oil 'peak' by one year; it would require added EUR of 66 Gb of oil. In other words, approximately 1 Gb for each 5.5 days will have to be produced. It would be in a setting when world EUR is 2.0 x 1012 (2.0 trillion bbl), a little less than half of this oil has already been produced through 1995 and then maximum of the world oil production (peak) is indicated to be in 2004.[171] Therefore, when such large discoveries are not ever in sight, the news is the 'oil shock'. As seen in Figure-2 oil discoveries, commencing with significant impact and volume in 1910 reached peak in mid 1960s and then gradually petered out by 1995. When the booming economies of the oil giants and the new entrants are faced with oil depletion shock, their struggle and stunt for oil would naturally pick up momentum that is already in the sight. As the reserves dwindle, productions drop and consumptions surge, the oil game can lead to unimaginable scenarios. Some say it would be end of the human civilization and some predict scenarios, triggering nuclear holocaust. Just seeing the oil dependency, one would allude to USA, Canada, China, Japan, India, Iran, Iraq, Saudi Arabia, UAE, Kuwait, Turkey, Caspian littorals, Europe and Australia that are either threatened by the 'oil shock' directly or would be caught in the crossfire of the dinosaurs' battle just because hydrocarbon strategic assets lie in their territories.

On the contrary, certain myths propounded by less informed scholars paint rosy picture that are based totally on assumptions. Some refer to sustainability of oil while scientists deny this. Hydrocarbon resources are finite, non-renewable and cannot be extended by any device. The logic of substitutes is so flawed that to mention it briefly, it does not stand the test of scientific merits or feasibility to replace illustrious oil. Detailed studies exist with reference to hydrogen, oceanic hydrates, nuclear, solar, and biomass options with gloomy conclusions that these do not afford a fraction of chance. Howard T Odum is rather frank to remark, "The fact, that our society cannot survive on alternative energy, should come as no surprise because only an idiot would believe that windmills and solar panels can run bulldozers, elevators, steel mills, glass factories, electric heaters, air conditioners, air crafts, auto mobiles and still have enough energy left over to support corrupt political system, armies etc."[172] Jay Hanson concludes about oil depletion scene, "Envision a world where freezing, starving people burn everything combustible---everything from forests (releasing CO2, destroying top-soiled species), to garbage dumps (releasing dioxins) to people (by waging nuclear war, biological, chemical, and conventional wars) and you have seen the future."[173] It therefore makes plausible deduction that panic seen but not admitted through world events including Central Eurasia affords yet another ground to believe that addressing energy depletion dilemma is beyond the leading powers capability. It also gives strong clue that depletion of oil phobia is a major stimulant of the New Great Game. At the same time, hydrocarbon man is being haunted by security of the energy resources as a consequence, which would be focused upon, but first an immediate proving symptom i.e. spiraling prices of the crude oil, which have baffled the oil pundits. However, those who conceive the petro-dynamics

146

are not taken by surprise anyway. For them inevitable demise of hydrocarbon society remains a clear writing on the wall.

Profligate Prices Syndrome

It has struck the oil world like a bolt unexpected. The weather wizards of ancient times could predict storms, earthquakes on seeing the restless animals, birds, omens and tidal pattern but it did not mean that they were never victim of these. The booming barrel is only an early symptom of the catastrophe, likely to afflict human civilization at a massive scale and magnitude anytime beyond mid century. If nature's revelation of gigantic oil fields in second half of 19th Century that continued soaring until mid 1960s were its gift to the humanity, depletion of hydrocarbon resources in 21st Century shrouded by severe contentious fall out would be the nature's horrific revenge though human follies can still be accounted for as its chief architects. Some specific aspects can be focused upon in this regard:

- **The Pattern.** Prices profligate view appears to have two patterns. One, by the 'economist' who sees it as routine event in the backdrop of massive economic growth, precisely according to economics laws, and the second view is taken by geological and petro-pundits who have reason to believe that world is becoming extra sensitive to supply disruption as one focused on the geo-strategic developments in the international arena. One could have perhaps right questions to raise that if economists could forecast growth of economies and the future price trends, why is it that they saw their barrel-related forecasts subsequently totally off the dot? Economists efforts to sweep everything under the carpet in the name of some regional 'typhoon' or hurricane, may justify prices profligate only partially. Probably sensitivity is triggered by other factors; one already covered, the fear of depletion of oil and second, emanating from the first that is the competition, who would bag how much of the oil, whatever is available? Consequently, the barrel booms in price, upping the stakes much higher for the actors to launch themselves in the oil regions. When 'national interests' of several powers of significance, let alone super power, converge over the same region(s) with question of survival or extinction, the clash of diplomacy to begin with would emerge as a necessary evil, leading possibly to unthinkable horrific scenarios. What all-maneuvering goes in-between is the New Great Game. Caspian Region is caught up in the full blizzard of the rivals' interests.

- **Dichotomy in the Interpretation of Facts.** The aspect enumerated above can be seen in better perspective through US State Department of Energy Annual Report 2005 wherein the Caspian Region emerges prominent. Quoting some relevant excerpts, how oil prices are viewed in wider context but in a rather simplistic manner as if all is perfect on the energy front. Only critical approach would reveal two dichotomies prone but veiled divergents. First, it circumvents the basic symptom-cause analysis to point out the balance of hydrocarbon sub-soil stocks which have or likely to commence downward slide on reaching the world oil 'peak' in 2005/2006. Conversely, the production and consumption surge would haunt the world's leading economies like a giant but the reserves would dwarf out each passing day. Second, the department driven by the commercial and national interests only, alludes nowhere emphatically as a plain truth to the mounting frenzy among the powers while addressing energy supply issues at the global level. The excerpts: 'IEO2005 projects that world crude oil prices in real 2003 dollars will decline from their current level by 2010, then rise gradually through 2025.....Much of the growth in oil consumption is projected for the emerging Asian nations, where strong economic growth results in a robust increase in oil demand. Emerging Asia, mainly China and India, accounts for 45 % of the total world increase in oil use over the forecast period in the *IEO2005* reference case... Producers in the Organization of Petroleum Exporting Countries (OPEC) are expected to be the major source of production increases. In addition, non-OPEC supply is expected to remain highly competitive, with major increments to supply coming from offshore resources, especially the Caspian Basin, ... Although OPEC production quotas (excluding Iraq) were raised from 23.5 million barrels per day in April 2004 to 28.0 million barrels per day in July 2005, world oil prices generally continued to rise [1]. In June 2005, crude oil future prices exceeded $60 per barrel, a record high price in nominal dollars [2]... Several factors have worked to keep world crude oil prices high in the near term. First, world petroleum demand grew at a robust 3.4 percent (2.7 million barrels per day) in 2004, reflecting dramatic increases in China's demand for oil-generated power and oil-based transportation fuels, as well as a rebound in U.S. oil demand. Second, oil prices typically are sensitive to any incremental tightening of supply during periods of high economic growth. On the supply side, there was very little spare upstream capacity, and the spare downstream capacity was not always properly configured to produce the required slate of products. World oil inventories, in terms of "days of supply," were unusually low. Next, geopolitical tensions in major oil-producing countries - including the continuing war in Iraq and uncertain prospects for a return to normalcy in Iraq's oil sector - and potential unrest in Nigeria and Venezuela contributed to the volatility in world oil markets.[174] One would not notice any statistical inaccuracy in the report that has been beautifully laid out but the plea and direction of the emphasis in the report may be a moot point. For instance, it admits the causes that push the prices to escalate thereby defeating the preamble of the report that prices would decline from their current level by 2010 then rise gradually through 2025. When there is no end in sight of the resolution of the causes, rather there are valid apprehensions that these would further deteriorate, how does the US DOE predict stabilization of prices by 2010 with corollary big 'ifs'.

- **The Shift of Onus.** The onus of the price spiral has been discreetly shifted to the emerging economies, particularly China and India that have shared the consumption increase by 45 %. Not even hinting about the US share of consumption of fossil fuel-based energy that alone is $1/4^{th}$ or 25 % of the world's total with her 4 % of world population, a fraction of China and India combined, proves that there is deliberate effort by the actors to manipulate figures and the facts. OPEC as a future worry clearly emerges in the text and that of geo-political turmoil, which is well poised to gain in intensity for obvious high stakes of the contenders. Occasional soothing statements, the 'oil men' know are always good for public consumption that help in lending an effective disguise to the game maneuvers. For instance a statement like, "Saudi Arabia produces about 3.7 million barrels per day while West Africa produces eight million barrels per day, primarily from Nigeria. West African production is expected to increase to 10 million barrels per day within five years, thus could soon be eclipsing Saudi Arabia's production,"[175] may boost public morale for a while but it cannot alter the course of nature. At first place, it may not fit well to pit almost a continent against a country. Secondly, only a few with focus on oil statistics would know that Africa as an oil continent is dying after having gone past its 'peak' production in 2004 while Saudi Arabia is still to stay young for six more years when it would touch its 'peak' production level in 2011(Table-22). Thirdly, it may be more prudent for Africa to stabilize the pace of dwindling resources rather than depleting them fast, merely to win merit over Saudi Arabia, which faces no dent on its oil order. Fourthly, the presaging exercise undertaken in 2002 by a responsible person of an oil organization went flung by the board when Saudi Arabia production mark crossed Van Dyke's production barrier of ten million barrels/day in 2004. Fast depleting resources of non-OPEC, and the OPEC capacity to survive longer with the fossil fuel makes the issue for the New Great Game meaningful when attention would naturally divert to the regions like Caspian as an alternative or a breather though the West prefers to refer to it usually as Former Soviet Union (FSU). Paul Roberts makes a pertinent comment, "Because price is so critical, players are for ever seeking to manipulate it. Big importers like US and Europe, whose economies are built on cheap oil do every thing they can to keep prices on the low side and will routinely bring pressure to bear on OPEC when prices get too high."[176] The report admits that while non-OPEC supply would remain highly competitive, a euphemism resorted to while describing the depleting oil resources of non-OPEC which have generally crossed their 'peaks', major increment to supply would come from offshore resources like the Caspian Basin. When Latin America's oil producing regions and those of Middle East are trapped in hot pursuit of oil by the world powers, by implication it proves that the Caspian Region is gradually but surely heading for the similar contest in a not too distant time scale as 'price' syndrome and geo-politics are now the two sides of the same coin. The report clearly acknowledges the OPEC capability to influence the 'price' pattern of crude oil with reference to the turbulent geo-political situation. In other words, Energy Security is emerging as major issue, which would certainly need 'appropriate' policies by the contestants to prevent, if not grab, the opportunities slipping by. The recent history of oil manipulation in post-Cold War era, some scholars opine, has earned the world a 'hot peace'. It would be pertinent thus to focus briefly on Energy Security concerns that have the potential not only to intensify the New Great Game but also to scuttle world peace. Through a generalized approach, since geo-politics of oil anywhere in the world swiftly trails the Caspian Region, the hypothesis would be kept adapt to Central Eurasia.

Energy Security and the Titans

The threat of disruption of oil supplies for the Titans is fraught with grave consequences that they would find it hard to swallow.[177] Therefore; the task to preempt such eventuality is placed at the highest priority, justified by ethics of their standards as well, in any foreseeable scenario. Thus, the struggle to obviate energy disruption, gaining control over energy flow in particular direction and denying the same to other rivals has crystallized as the New Great Game. Reminder: Caspian is the hub of proven and untapped hydrocarbon resources that sit underneath while Central Eurasia, since BC era, remained high on geo-strategic significance.

- **History of Energy Security Dilemma**. An event that struck the West on 20 October 1973 like a bolt continues to haunt the leading petroleum-dependent powers, which the West would not like to see recurring. Arab Oil Embargo, talked about by Arabs for two decades since early 50s was hardly heeded to and brushed aside by the West as an attempt to gain political mileage against Israel. Anwar Sadaat's resolve to use oil as a weapon just prior to 1973 Arabs-Israel War was also treated as nothing more than hostile posturing. The oil embargo was initially imposed on United States and Netherlands that was later extended to Portugal, South

Africa and Rhodesia. The use of such a queer kind of weapon by the Arab World generated immense shock. The prices of crude oil at $5 a barrel swelled to $17 a barrel within a month. The Arab Oil Embargo had two elements; first, Arab producers cut back production and second, they slapped 'zero supply' restriction on the above named countries. A brief mention about effects would be prudent option because fear of out break of hostilities through deliberate manipulation of geo-political pivots mentioned earlier and ultimate oil depletion in future scenario that presents much bigger and shattering challenge, would be placed in the right perceptive. In West Germany, the industry issued heap of desperate telexes that they could not bear 'oil-less' status even for a day. In Japan, the public confidence in strong economic growth evaporated with the blow. Some rowdy demonstrations rekindled Japanese specter of 'rice-riots' of late 19th Century, which spilled over to 20th Century. In United States, the public conviction of prodigality of US resources was the most fatal casualty as they did not know even that US was importing oil or at least, were ignorant of the magnitude of US dependence on imported oil. Gasoline prices jumped by 40% and long queues put them wise. In fact, some gasoline stations displayed 'no gas today' banners. Britain was not aimed at directly, but oil companies with multinational obligation were forced to evolve a system of proportionate distribution of available oil to mitigate the bite, embargo had exacted on their other client countries. Thus, Britain was caught up in the whirlwind of embargo. Mr. Edward Heath, Britain's Prime Minister was so desperate that he almost threatened the BP and Shell chief executives to keep Britain's 100% supplies restored. Internally, coal miners also chose to strike that accentuated Britain's energy crisis further. Mr. Heath had no option but to be patient with status quo. It is abundantly clear that these were merely the response symptoms of immense diplomacy that was launched to tackle the issue of geo-strategic significance. First time since World War II, two super powers, USA and USSR, went on nuclear alert. WMDs were sheathed only when cease-fire was brokered between Egypt, Israel, and mechanism agreed to pull back the forces. Suffice to say that Arabs secured their objectives through application of oil weapon, which could not be achieved by their armed forces. US had to review her policy orientation; making it amenable; not only predominantly for Israel but for Arabs also. In fact Richard Nixon, President of United States was overwhelmed by US vulnerability to an extent that to appease Arabs, he publicly demonstrated anti-Israel stance.[178] Such was the scale of turbidity on the global scene triggered by oil weapon against the target states that world started to recognize OPEC, through its effects as OPEC 'Imperium'. By now, once bitten by oil embargo, it is fair to assume the degree of intensity, with which the actors would launch themselves in the New Great Game, should they be threatened by any fabricated catastrophe.

- **The Approaching Challenge**. The one main and waiting in abyss (depletion) may be beyond human control to avert. Eminent scholars like A G Frank, Immanuel

Wallestein and other have anticipated realistic scenarios apparently in the backdrop of rivals' economic boom. Whole range of experts is fully aware that the entire economic edifice rests on a single slushy pillar, called oil. An eminent analyst puts it in rather straight language, "An even more intense battle is unfolding in the Caspian Region. Since the late 1990s, China, America, Russia and Iran have waged a diplomatic war to control the flow of oil out of Kazakhstan and Azerbaijan. Each country has not only proposed a different route for the Caspian pipeline but in many cases worked to undermine competing route proposals."[179] Some question whether Anglo-Saxon hegemony is vacating to accommodate ascending Asia; particularly China. Will 21st Century American supremacy be challenged by regional China that could grow to a global hegemon or China shall come across its pitfalls of demographic, resources and ethnic strains, that could generate upheavals for her in stark similarity to erstwhile USSR? Even if the stage setting of transition of hegemony from Anglo-Saxon-centric to Sino-centric world is accepted, remains a lot between the cup and the lips. Will the transition be peaceful or the two sides would end up locked in oil resources war as and when race for oil degenerates to oil stampede? Lastly the environmental worry: what shall be the fate of the planet, which is being pushed already to the precipice of catastrophe? In fact, these are perplexing issues to ponder over and perhaps beyond human genius to serve ready-made answers.

- **The Novelty of the Energy Security Issue**. The proponent of oil war and the New Great Game; in our case in Central Eurasia are struck by the novelty with which the New Great Game shall be executed. For instance, scholars are hoarse; not from Muslim countries soil but from Europe and US that war on terror is in fact a struggle to invest oil rich regions. They rightly point out that there is mystifying coincidence between the maps of war on terror and oil. Yet for the sake of staying directly tuned to the 'book' theme, one would grade such notions of 'coincidence' at this stage a far-fetched, though never irrelevant. For cogent reasons, comparison is being drawn between two Great Games, "Check out Rudyard Kipling or J.G. Farrell, the British were at least as sure of their manifest destiny, of their imperial, civilizing mission, and at least as arrogantly confident about an empire on which 'the sun would never set' and about the racial superiority of their kind as is the US today. Nevertheless, time was not long before the British abandoned imperial pretensions, packed their colonial kit and left.[180] One would earnestly hope that US think tanks draw useful lessons from history. In the course of coverage however, one finds inadvertent volley of arguments if not criticism directed towards USA as compared to others who have at least switched on, warming their energies to join muscle flexing in the arena. The answer is simple. Because being a single global hegemon on the globe, USA shoulders singular responsibility also to lead the world to catastrophe or an aura of peace and prosperity. Its might combines characteristics like unmatched military power, history of mature domestic governance mechanism, monopoly over modern technology, globally dominating economy, enviable savior role played during mega events of conflagration and exacting single handedly a diluting blow on USSR what Brzezinski called it 'phantasmagoria'[181], a term earlier used by Joachim C. Fest also in a different context. Though a secular state, it has never discarded Christian ethics as and when it felt necessary that these would augment her role-execution with pride and nobility. In other words, the state did not remain separate from the church. Therefore it justifies why US is commenced with in any discussion about flip-flop events going askew in the world. The New Great Game in Central Eurasia is one such event where major responsibility rests on US and then anyone else because majority of other compulsive actors like Russia, China, Iran, Turkey and Caspian littorals happens to share geography of Central Eurasia. Third layer of geographically remote actors only seek presence, lest they be left out of the game of energy that is fast sprouting from the nucleus of Central Eurasia called Caspian. After US, next player who dominates the scene or has the potential to pose threat is China. Mark Jones, an advisor to Lukoil, had warned shortly before his death in 2003, "The countdown to peak oil will cause, in the arena of great powers, rivalry. China and USA are sure and certain rivals. The final energy crisis will unquestionably reveal this fundamental rivalry, the need for conflict between these Titans dancing on the greasy slope of oil and gas."[182] One would wonder, whether Titans agree or not, surely both of them are destined to land up in the deep crevice if sanity does not prevail the soonest.

- **Caspian Littorals High on the Turmoil Index**. The critics are well stocked with security of energy arguments and their pessimism about inevitability of emerging conflict scenario; beside on-going struggle in Middle East; in Central Eurasia as well. Even if this region is assumed as an alternative, the security of oil situation is not rosy. Oil experts pinpoint other than Middle East, eight alternatives. "Five of the Alternative Eight - Angola, Azerbaijan, Columbia, Nigeria and Russia - have undergone civil wars or ethnic conflicts in recent years; the other three - Kazakhstan, Mexico and Venezuela have had riots, strikes or other form of political disorder."[183] Out of the eight alternatives cited here, reference has been made to three Caspian littorals, which constitute the arena of New Great Game. The list of possible threat is lengthy and daunting. The flash point pivots exist manifestly, which could plague the peace and tranquility of region that wears semblance of delicate peace now. The Caspian-Caucasus countries' territorial disputes, ethnic hostilities, clandestine threat of abetting hostilities by one power against another, horrific possibility and the accruing race to become a regional hegemon in Central Eurasia by the regional and external powers, economic deprivation and social discontent, fractured orientation of the Caspian littorals among themselves, radical Islam in the Western perspective, all combined in the backdrop of oil and gas depletion scenario have the monstrous connotations. "The governments of Central Asia and South

159

Caucasus face kaleidoscope of challenges... Most of these problems emanate from internal dynamics within each state that limit their ability to ensure stable and legitimate governments for the population. These are weak states characterized by personalistic rule.... Together the weakness of these states and absence of multilateral cooperation threatens Western strategic interests in maintaining regional stability, a favorable balance of power and access to energy supplies. These trends suggest that next 10-15 years could witness the large scale instability and conflict and the possibility of state collapse."[184]

- **War Plans Amidst Security Fears Exist Already**. The security concerns are best explained when US extended Carter Doctrine that also envisaged provision of security umbrella to over-seas flow of oil as a matter of national security. US Central Command (US CENTCOM) was thus created to enforce Carter's Doctrine of safe lanes in the Persian Gulf region. Later in 1999, it was given authority to expand over the Caspian littorals as well. In other words, US military muscles are in place in Caspian Region since long and securing toehold in Afghanistan, Uzbekistan and Kyrgyzstan in all probability is the manifestation of execution of Carter Doctrine in Central Eurasia as well. Here perhaps if evidence is brought to prove that since 2001, US installation of military camps and colonies in Central Eurasia including Afghanistan is an exercise to render security to oil and gas reserves including impending build up of favorable pipeline network, would not be out of place. Middle East and Central

Eurasia combined make the oil and gas inventory as over 55 % and 45 % respectively of the world total. Hence, it reinforces the antagonists' view that launching premeditated maneuvers based on the contrived pretexts of presence of WMDs and known 9/11 conspirators could not be ruled out. President Bill Clinton implemented Carter Doctrine vociferously, adding in its design the bid to secure US monopoly in the Caspian Basin over drilling rights and pipelines network. He was never shy to tell President Heyder Aliyev, "In the world of growing energy demand, our nation can not afford to rely on any single region for our energy supplies. We not only help Azerbaijan to prosper, we also help diversify our energy supply and strengthen our national security."[185] Expressing his resolve about 'not to rely on any single region', he obviously meant the adjoining Middle East. When stakes are so high that in the absence of energy security arrangements, fate of national security of a super power hangs in balance; it leads to logical deduction that other powers of any significance like Russia, China, Iran, Turkey, Japan, Germany, France, India, Britain, Australia, Israel, Pakistan and Canada by implication may stand mutually threatened proportionately in the later point of time to the scale of hegemony of any kind a single actor or a group attempts to achieve. These countries are aware of certain basic transitions brought about by historic events in the realm of energy economy. US enjoyed monopoly over energy distribution system in Cold War era until the blow of OPEC oil embargo of October 1973 to March 1974 struck it down. Thereafter sheer diplomacy and international relations exercise through out the world, largely divided in OPEC and non-OPEC spheres had been shaping the energy order. The delicate balance, hitherto fore, maintained in collective perspective is now turning out to be synonymous to walking on razor's edge when end of oil is in sight and oil stampede is likely as an inevitable specter. Otherwise too, in simple arithmetic, oil exploration of the possible reserves, other than proven reserves, extraction, transportation and refining would cost so much that even the most of sound companies financially may run out of breath, "Over the next three decades, according to International Energy Agency, the oil industry will need to invest $ 1.7 trillion simply to maintain its current oil production levels...on top of that, oil companies would need to spend an additional $600 billion to meet all the new demands, especially from Asia. Taken together, that means $2.2 trillions in oil investment- a pile of money, even for oil companies and petrostates- and it is not clear where it will come from."[186] The reference to Asia's Caspian Region is meaningful because this region is going to be strained to the limits. How would the strain affect this region? The experts opine that decline in non-OPEC oil would require the OPEC to increase their daily out put in a massive manner which would require financial potency. Nevertheless, this kind of commodity may be hard to find in OPEC including Venezuela and Nigeria whose economies are extensively mismanaged and are barely coping up with current levels. The focus, of necessity, has to shift to the untapped fields of Caspian littorals. The hopes and expectations rising now and finding expression through crystallizing of scenario of New Great Game; oil pundits opine that it might deteriorate to greasy, slushy game of conflicts which certainly sounds as an extremely tragic note for Central Eurasia as well as for the mankind.

- **Rival Scenarios and Urge to Develop Caspian-Caucasian Indigenous Security Capacity.** The rival scenarios to become the pivot of the clash in Central Eurasia are already on the horizon that leave no doubt about the "mischief" side of the ongoing geo-strategic dimension of the maneuvers and counter maneuvers. For the last couple of years NATO is being cited as an emerging tool of the western oil diplomacy that is already expanding south-eastward along Baltic-Black Sea-Caucasus and is also firmly planted in Afghanistan in the wake of "Operation Enduring Freedom." Paradoxically though, in Iraq and Afghanistan, nothing has 'endured' except destruction and devastation. To top it all, there is exclusive US military presence in Uzbekistan (wound up lately) and Kyrgyzstan. An abandoned base of Soviet era is being reconstructed in Atyrau, Western Kazakhstan, with US assistance. Similarly, Kazakhstan is also being given military capability by US to raise a rapid reaction brigade as a response to the impending terrorist threat to her installations, which are located in Caspian Region.[187] Seeing such development when Georgia also ranks high because of its being a conduit for the energy pipelines, hardly one would have any ambiguity about the direction "New Great

Game" is headed to. US Secretary Defense, Donald Rumsfeld when he asserted during his visit to Kazakhstan in February 2004 in response to a question about US interest, "It is Caspian security, the western portion of Kazakhstan which is important to this country,"[188] fixed official stamp on US posturing in Central Eurasia. The statement is no surprise because oil balance on discovery of Kashagan oil field of Kazakhstan has tilted in her favor if compared to Azerbaijan. As a response to this arrangement, China maintains a sizable force in her Central Asian province of Xingjian and also nuclear installation at Lop Nor. Russia having an advantage of contiguity or proximity to all the Central Eurasian states, maintains military presence in some form in Kyrgyzstan, Tajikistan, Armenia, Georgia, Turkmenistan and a lingering legacy of Soviet era naval fleet at Astrakhan on the lower reaches of Volga River on the Caspian periphery. In addition to above game players, Iran and Turkey have the means and flash points available to manipulate the situation. It would suffice to say that several fora tried by the Central Eurasian states in quest of a meaningful security mechanism, could not develop into any worthwhile military muscle but they do point to the level of deep suspicion, they harbor about each other. Russia, China and Iran hold expanding role of NATO, OSCE and US military presence in Central Eurasia with disdain. Likewise, some Central Eurasian states fear Russia, Iran, Turkey and China more than the influence of OSCE and NATO. In fact, almost all are inclined to lean for NATO's PFP status as of necessity. Rand Corporation study enumerates that the West has six strategic interests or objectives in the region.[189] Briefly these are, preventing establishing of a hegemony over the region, gaining and maintaining access to the Caspian energy resources, reduce likelihood of civil war, impede proliferation of WMDs, discourage spread of militant anti-Western Islamic movements and lastly prevent spilling over of the conflicts into area of concern, principally Turkey and the Persian Gulf. The situation becomes deplorably interesting when the aim to shoot other game players crisis-cross. On one hand, Russia needs moral support from China and Iran to outwit the West about their designs in Central Eurasia; on the other, she does not like even Iran and China fostering their influence in the region. "Externally, Russia has sought to demonstrate to the world that Central Asia has remained exclusively in the sphere of Russian interest, and that it will not allow any rival powers to emerge in the region."[190] The Caspian Region had been a geo-strategic 'hot-spot' through its history but now one thing is clear that because of its hydrocarbon reserves it has become 'spicy spot' as well for others to the relish of their national interests 'buds'. Shall NATO christen the New Great Game of oil in Central Eurasia as if it were their colony? The answer is NO. Of late, it has been observed that an instrument to rally around is already available which can be developed as a balancer, though to NATO by contrast, it is in embryonic form. It is even brief; three-letter organization called SCO (Shangai Cooperation Organization). Some have gone beyond to label it as NATO of the East. Others believe that with their six members; Russia, China, Kazakhstan, Uzbekistan,

Kyrgyzstan, Tajikistan, and India and Pakistan in observer status, in certain point of time; if the West pushes too far, SCO might develop into formidable military organization. Some may call it far-fetched but the geo-strategy can develop fast into alliance if there is mutual consensus and convergence of interests. SCO suits all as a tool of security for the weaker four and a platform for power projection for the stronger two. China for obvious reasons of her economic boom needs to project her influence and contain others. Russia, otherwise left out of consultation and commensurate universal role would obviously attempt short to medium scale alliances to fulfill her craving for 'imperial' status that lie beyond her capability at the moment. Thus, SCO has become a significant development in Eurasian geo-politics. In fact, optimist would hinge hope that it might transition into a formidable geo-political bi-polar block as against present unipolar world dominated by a sole super power. Yergeny Bendersky emphasizes however, "One of the key states (Russia) in SCO will be the deciding factor in judging the success of this bold geo-political venture."[191] Observers noticed that Russia and China delivered punch to Washington's ambitions in Central Asia on the eve of G-8 Summit once they put up perfect conceptual harmony on 'international order' followed by SCO meeting in July 2005. "While the combination was not enough, it was the most forceful challenge to US interests in Central Asia since invasion of Afghanistan in 2001."[192] As we see the history of US behavior, these developments, however, in the rubric of geo-politics are just rudimentary to force US to explore scenarios, which could avert New Great Game fraught with dangerous consequences. The last blow delivered by the Arab Oil Embargo in 1973 led US to adopt energy policy that was yet more fractured and focused on securing supply guarantees. Even post 9/11 opportunities have been lost. On the contrary, US Administration has rigidly stuck to her belief in the energy policy that security of energy supply was the bedrock of national security. Thus, the world has to put up with excessively myopic USA to the detriment of peace and stability in Eurasia once Middle East and Caspian Region are at the nucleus. She has ostensibly rejected the scenarios of peaceful diplomacy; energy conservation and alternative technology to explore viability of hydrogen fuel cell in favor of gaining monopoly over diversified resources of oil that are likely to become hard nut to crack. Thus goes the dilemma of energy security, which may gain monstrous magnitude and lethality at certain point of time in Central Eurasia, actors' identity not withstanding. Having discussed the ingredients of the New Great Game that add fuel to the fire, it would be pertinent to focus on main actors exclusively.

CHAPTER-FIVE

ACTORS' ROLE AND AMBITIONS

USA

Scholars see US and European geo-strategic and economic interests inseparable, often through some variants in the interpretation. Whatever the emphasis to prove whether economic (oil and gas) interests are contingent upon the geo-strategic constraints of 'Eurasian Balkan' a focal point has emerged for all the intellectuals from the east and the west, the south and the north; that is geo-economic rivalry in the region is helping geo-strategic competition to flourish. Nevertheless, there are lone exceptions like Stephen Sestanovich who testified otherwise, maintaining that US policy does not begin from an assessment of our economic interests, but rather from a geo-strategic standpoint.[193] Shall one assume that by asserting his country's geo-strategic stance; and being a USG functionary, he was by implication conducting a political counter maneuver 58 years later than Joseph Stalin and Adolph Hitler had conspired against USA to keep her out of Eurasia for geo-strategic considerations in November 1940? It is not only a new millennium but also a different kind of thrust and perceptions that exist abundantly among the comity of nations to pick up the covert as well as overt strands of geo-strategy in right perceptive. Mr. Sestanovich, in context to Central Eurasia certainly made a deliberate attempt to supplement his government posture. Yet the world knows US economic interests' priority is far higher than any other consideration because of the Caspian hydrocarbon riches. US involvement in and across Caucasus has picked up distinct momentum since the mid nineties.

For the Persian Gulf, an instrument of energy security in form of Carter Doctrine was already in place but debate heated up on the desirability of extending its umbrella to Caspian-Caucasus Region as well. That meant additional task for CENTCOM, which, in the event of simultaneous engagements could run out of breath. Therefore yet another alliance, NATO, was to roll over the region of interest with expanded scope and tasks. NATO's adjustments were not only executed but clearly defined also to become guarantor of the Western objectives. USG thus made her 'fractured energy policy' rather conspicuous. Some pertinent questions can be raised. Why did US resort to a sort of knee-jerk reaction in this regard when 'energy security' concerns could be addressed even through the instrument of 'diplomacy' in Eurasia? Did US conceive the trampling of Caspian-Caucasus sensitivities particularly when the region is skirted around by four regional powers, Turkey to the west, Russia to the north, Iran to the south and China to the east? A partial answer to these questions is available, "It is difficult to escape the conclusion that America's Caspian Policy has been predicated on the illusion of a unipolar moment: the notion that Washington can orchestrate and subsequently can maintain a convivial alignment of international forces. The implication is that it is possible to fashion relations in the region so as to constrain Russian decision making with little or no blowback from Moscow."[194] When such is the frank confession as well as approach, it is logical to perceive that Russia would not like to take it lying low.

- **US Struggle Goes Even Beyond**. In fact, the US struggle can be viewed even beyond the boundaries of 'New Great Game' when she is now seen floundering to construct an energy order in Middle East and Africa as well at an exorbitant cost.

Therefore, as a part of grand energy strategy, the US would perhaps never shy to foster 'the West' friendly integration of Mediterranean as well as the Caspian-Caucasus countries that would, of necessity, need force projection and hence at least in first stage the emerging proof is in sight: the expansion of NATO. Such expansion, the US claims, will have to be with consensus of these countries including Russia. Conversely, Russia does not appear inclined to support a mechanism of Cold War era. The act of switching the Russian dominated North-South pipeline direction to the West is a blow that must have been understood by Russian as well as Washington wizards, "The new approach, coordinated by the (US) National Security Council is designed to break Russia's grip on Central Asian oil export. The objective is to protect the survival of independent states in the region and to protect US corporate interests."[195] BTC, being celebrated by the Western camp as a unique marvel and a feat of engineering, has certainly the potential to divert oil flow from north or south to the west. In overall perception when policy appreciations of the Western think tanks clearly point to the need of engaging Russia to move on intimately, such perceived blows to fragile balance though credible for the West, introduce an element of dichotomy in their acts and facts about Russia. At least in this context: it amounts to blowing hot and cold in a single breath. Carter Page's admission sounds realistic, "Current USG policy towards Caspian Region could come under increased pressure in the years to come." He is of the view that, "the proximity to the conflict in Afghanistan and Iraq as well as the possibility of sustained high energy prices could potentially sharpen the US public's attention on this region at some stage."[196] The statement is meaningful. Either, Carter Page has omitted several indicators of US attention on the Caspian Region since mid nineties or indirectly censures fellow 'public' of their magnitude of oblivion to such crucial developments. Both the possibilities exist. At the international scene, the credibility of US administration is eclipsed by stigma of several kinds though American people have shown large heart to remain discreet in criticizing it.

- **A Unique Character.** In the long American history, it is the first US administration perhaps that has unique 'oil' character. Kaleem Omar comments, "So close are these links that there are times when it seems as if the interest of 'big oil' and those of the United States government are virtually synonymous in the eyes of Bush administration officials... Bush began his business career as an oil man... a buddy of US energy giant Enron's founder and CEO Kenneth Lay now facing criminal charges... Cheney was CEO... of energy services giant Halliburton for five years (1995-2000)... Condoleezza Rica is another. She once worked for US oil giant Chevron, which has even named one of its oil tankers after her..."[197] Articulating a coup against Venezuelan President, Hugo Chavez in April 2002 because he threatened US interests through his populist politics, was yet another pathetic jolt to US democratic ethics enough that William Blum could be thinking of churning out another volume of US rogue behaviors.[198] For the Caspian Oil, Turkey approves US moves in the region being a faithful ally who is also stocking her coffers with oil revenue dollars as a downstream country. As regards to Iran, US until recently has been caught up with ambivalence. ILSA in place since 1996 has emerged as haunting US tool for Iran. There had been tense diplomatic war moments when each contrived a crooked title for other; nevertheless, US fears about Iran abetting terrorism, push for WMDs and scuttling the Middle East process have stayed green though occasionally streaks of reconciliation were visible like a silver lining on the dark cloud. However, the mistrust has grown so much that it would take a Herculean effort for both the Governments to garnish public mood to any compromise. Therefore, in immediate scenario, Iran would woefully stay out of any substantial role for the regional peace and stability. Her discordant relations with Azerbaijan and of necessity, becoming chain link in Russia-Armenia-Iran nexus perhaps is sufficient to close this chapter of reconciliation with USG. While dealing individually with other Caspian littorals, US appear fully conscious of the minefield it is likely to come across that could put the whole energy security environments in jeopardy. Her readiness to act as an arbiter for inter-littoral disputes and having done it successfully in a few cases, there has been some dampening of the littorals worries except Russia and Iran. On the US part, increased commitment of forces in the region may be perceived as a 'stabilizer' but suspicions get even more intensified with these two countries and recently China joining their stance. Stephen Blank, quoting the Washington Post comments that, "the Pentagon also recently allocated areas of responsibility...US European Command (USEUCOM) got the Caucasus and the USCENTCOM received Central Asia. Although this is as much an administrative device to supervise the ongoing program of military cooperation...it also represents a major step for contingency planning, and Moscow knows it."[199] It is rather simple to include Iran and China in the 'know-list' as well.

- **US Bellicosity Not a New Phenomenon**. Since the Clinton era, the Caspian Region has been assumed as a back up source for oil and gas to the Middle

East. In fact, gradually the bellicosity is exaggerated, that shapes the aggressive mood of the US Administration and her European as well as Far Eastern allies. Some US analysts call on the United States not only to take the lead in pacifying the entire area now, arranging peace in Georgia, Nagorno-Karabakh, North Caucasus, Tajikistan, Afghanistan and perhaps Kurdish war with Turkey but also to overthrow the government of Iran or to orchestrate Brzezinski's grand coalition.[200] The list and the revealing events suggest that US has neither met any considerable success nor is likely to; courtesy, of the play of power politics of other players conceived with a stretch of imagination to any limit possible. Searching the soul of US role; two prominent thrust lines emerge; first, that US genuinely desires to bring in elements of peace, stability and popularism in Caspian-Caucasus Region at terms pliant to her interests. Secondly, any threat emerging to energy security scenario shall outweigh all the other considerations to stem out that threat. This recipe of specific orientation; call it grand strategy or Eurasian New Great Game, is bound to work with certain trepidation until such time a spoiler lands in the arena to challenge her with some novel contraption. In a desperate setting Russia, Iran and China have wherewithal to target her Eurasian interests because none other in the region is potent enough to even care about herself. In a lingering stalemate scenario, the present honeymoon between US and some Caspian-Caucasus states will be encroached upon by the time factor, rekindling the concept that a shrewd enemy nearby, is a precious boon than a remote friend. In that eventuality, Russia, Iran or China could emerge as acceptable hegemon. By dint of US presence, hopes are on the extreme. One; that the energy resources the region harbors, are ordained to raise the Caspian littoral societies to the Western level and second is like a metaphor of a pressure cooker, "What comes out of pressure cooker is always a matter of taste but on one point all cooks agree: the least desirable outcome, the one to be avoided at all cost, is an explosion."[201] Lutz Kleveman sees US role in the Caspian Region somewhat differently. He asserts that Mr. Bush's verdict, those who are not with us are against us, kicked discard as well as worry among USG and Moscow, Beijing, Tehran about the aggressive US foreign policy. Long before the Iraq war, the three governments had clearly suspected that the Bush administration was using the War Against Terror in Central Asia to seal the American Cold War victory against Russia, to contain Chinese influence and to tighten the noose around Iran.[202] As regards to Russia, she is aware of her potential strength in hydrocarbon reserves. Conversely, Russia also perceives clearly that despite rivalry over pipelines orientation, in the setting of New Great Game, Russia will remain indispensable to the US because of her immense oil and gas reserves. To compensate for her loss of ground partially so far in the Caspian-Caucasus region, her active cooperation with two of the links of 'axis of evil', Iran and North Korea, as US calls them, rescue Russia from a zero-sum game. Hence, it is becoming increasingly evident that the US may not find manipulation of Eurasian key geo-political pivots a hassle free enterprise on which would rest her longevity and global primacy. While Russia barricades herself against the Western venture into Caspian-Caucasus, US faces, yet another reverse that public mood in Central Eurasia is not predominantly favorable to her, a moment obviously warranting a realistic soul searching!

Russia

In the wake of Russian phantasmagoria, as fondly called by Brzezinski, a terrible power vacuum was created. The Caspian-Caucasus Region states were literally observed as rudderless; groping for political, economic and military evolution. While the former two essentials of a sovereign state were to be largely the initiatives of the native leadership, the third one, military orientation, could not be mustered overnight for absence of any worthwhile military muscles integral to the newly independent states. No sooner had the dust settled down in turbulent and reshaping Russian mainland and being hostage to the stupor of her imperial past; she quickly embarked on the exercise to shape 'instruments of stability' to claim her 'near abroad' in a manner that could afford her a pivot of influence over FSU space.

- **Tools Available to Russia**. CIS was first such attempt that remains splintered about perception of Russian role as guarantor of security. Pulling out of militaries by ambivalent Azerbaijan, Georgia and Uzbekistan and birth of GUUAM (Georgia, Ukrain, Uzbekistan, Azerbaijan and Moldova) alliance was such an association that symbolically ditched prospects of Russian security apparatus taking roots in Caspian-Caucasus Region. Though CSTO is the latest attempt of 2002 vintage by her, consequently Russia has not been able to consolidate her influence in the power vacuum game. On the contrary, Russia and other actors on the periphery like China and Iran are faced with a scenario when NATO appears set to eliminate the serious anomaly of persisting vacuum. US Command forces for Europe and Middle East; in the war contingency, shall be able to augment NATO forces, should the need arise. Since the mid nineties, Russia has appeared to have advanced three policy parameters: first; integration of CIS under Russian domination:

Secondly use of military, political and economic leverage to make CIS states pliant to Russian interests and thirdly, secure international recognition of Russia's exclusive peace-keeping role as a major bulwark of stability[203]. Russia may be having half a dozen of justifications to stay firmly planted in the near abroad but forgets basic advantage she has to accord to the emerging state with the label of sovereignty. That entitles all of them to choose the pattern of conduct of state affairs without any consideration of outside coercion or dictation. Russia did not stop here but shaped her military doctrine to gain her expansive objectives. Her role posturing this way in Central Eurasia is being termed as 'neo-imperialism'. It has also afforded moral high ground to the West that has effectively raised the Russian threat bogy to Caspian-Caucasus states through an orchestrated defamation campaign; allowing ethics space to the western military muscles to flex in the arena as an element of counter geo-strategy. As appropriately observed by Leppingwell that Russian military thinks of Central Asia (and hence Caspian Region) as a buffer zone along its southern border and had adopted a forward defense strategy predicated on belief that the defense of Russia's border starts at the CIS borders[204]. It is thus obvious that Russia has withdrawn from Central Eurasia physically, but her psychological fix remains focused on her imperial boundaries of 19th and 20th Centuries. She has, even in the new millennium, never relented in her pursuits of maintaining a vital position, preventing foreign influence, penetrating into energy consortia, securing complete monopoly over pipeline networks and to top it all, as the West perceives, resorting to coercion, subversion and blackmail. In such a comparative bullish environment, Russia's role is bound to be rebuked even by her old colonial subjects and allies. Perhaps for these reasons,

Russia's conceived role is shrinking in the face of Western influence.

- **Russias' 'Losing Ground' Largely Self-inflicted.** Completion of BTC, launching of KCP as agreed between Kazakhstan and China, SCP from Baku to Erzurum making Azerbaijan a gas exporter for the first time are nothing but firm proofs of her declining role. It may not be out of place to say that Russia afforded the West appealing grounds to pose her as future hegemon and thus slumped on popularity graph among CIS. Such symptoms have been correctly put in order by Oksana Antonenko, "However even today, Russia's regional policy is weakened by its inability to reconcile economic and security interests into a regional strategy which could guarantee stability and prosperity for both, Russia and its neighbors."[205] However, at coming of Vladimir Putin on the scene, the world noticed a touch of distinct pragmatism as it became manifest through a special meeting proceedings that was chaired by him on 21 April 2000 to reassess Caspian energy policy. A number of decisions were taken which aimed at the damage control by dropping confrontational stance. Yet these measures in the true sense become redundant in effect when world see nexus between Iran, Armenia and Russia. Iran already cornered by US sanctions and ILSA, Armenia sitting over a powder keg called Nagorno-Karabakh and Russia struggling to join main stream of oil game in the Caspian-Caucasus within full view of fleeting grip over the Caspian energy monopoly has rendered the three states (Russia included), powers of lesser significance.

- **Russia Weak but Vibrant.** Yet it does not mean that Russia's ability to muddy the calm water has been downgraded. Russia faces insurgency war in Chechnya and Dagestan but has influence over

Abkhazians and South Ossetians of Georgia; colludes with Iran and Armenia, outmatches in military strength any of the regional powers including China, if compared in nuclear capability perspective, and maintains potent naval presence over Caspian Sea from Astrakhan. Her strength is further reinforced once one has a look at her oil and gas inventory wherein she sits over 72 Gb of proven oil and about 48 tcm or 1700 tcf of gas proven reserves. When the belief is that Caspian Region is witnessing the 'New Great Game' at the strength of its energy resources, Russia has share directly and solid foundation away from Caspian in the context of oil and gas. Thus, she can neither be ignored nor treated roughshod by other actors of any significance. As the world sees Russia beaten in the pipeline politics; a lot perhaps is to be ascribed to the Russian own doing that proves that even her dynamics of conduct of internal affairs is also topsy-turvy. Jean Christopher Peuch observes that CPC project refurbished and made operational in collaboration with Western oil companies from Tengiz oil field in Kazakhstan to Russian Black Seaport of Novorossiysk is not threatened by lack of oil or technical deficiencies but endless ownership disputes among its members and hefty bribes that are to be doled out to greedy regions and autonomous republics as transit fees once it traverses through their territories. Should this project fail; through facing serious security situation, Russia would suffer a total loss of over $33 billion of her share of oil revenues[206]. If the investors and the upstream countries are to face such irritants in transportation of oil; it tantamounts conversely that Russia herself has thrown down the towel with sapped off competitive spirit; or else her confidence to meddle hinges on her imperial dreams revival. However, it does not require a genius to guess that Russian's pursuit of coherent foreign policy in the region is characterized by split and dysfunctional syndrome. When the 'traditionalists' prevail, it is made hostage to their historic imperial frame; considering coercion and domination as their granted privilege. Conversely, if the business as well as oil and gas companies lobby makes any headway; pragmatism returns to work in cooperation with universal energy ethics in the region. A RAND publication highlights, "Russia's ability to realize any 'neo-imperial' designs it may have on the region will be handicapped by these discordant voices and the fragmented nature of Russian foreign policy."[207]

- **Russian Perception about the Western Camp.** However, most Russian elites view Western influence backed by military capability as direct threat to Russian security. For this perception, they do not appear to be relenting ever or downgrading their resolve of maintaining grip over CIS borders that they assume, serve as an extended sphere of national security. The clash chemistry of percepts in the inner domain makes her stance on the region divisive and ambiguous, though the hardliner voices rattle through sharp and loud. The world understands the Russian sense of deprivation when her global posture melted down to regional level and accruing loss of her granaries of products and raw material. For example, Central Asia alone contributed 26% coal, 32% crude oil, 95% bismuth, 90% uranium, 95% phosphorus, 76% copper, 86% galena and tin for the Soviets economy; the loss of which has obviously dented the Russian economy. Yet as a responsible power, she ought to shape and execute her policies that strengthen her influence rather than eroding the level already existing. Mehdi Parvizi Amineh is of the opinion that Russia's current policy toward oil in the region is characterized by two competing political

179

strategies[208]. The first hinges on a traditional realist approach on need to maintain balance of power, the second on protecting Russian interests in the Caspian Sea. This camp views the Azeri-Western oil deal; not only as New Great Game, but a century long game. They assert that influence over the region meant control over oil resources in Caspian. Minus the oil, no influence can be maintained. 'Trans-nationalists' seeking active collaboration with the regional and extra regional actors to gain a foothold in the world market and the latest technology, propound the second policy strategy. What the Russian Government has failed however is to evolve an objective policy. Instead, it has remained torn between traditionalists or nationalists and transnationalists. If US energy policy has been labeled as 'fractured' in post-1973 scenario, Russian energy policy can be labeled as 'tethered to the lobbies' whims. With Mr. Putin's government's firm control, there should have been no impediment coming across. Question arises; what prevents Russia to evolve an amenable policy. Andrei Shoumikhin juxtaposes Russian imperial temptations and her 'pragmatic exigencies' to note that, "With diminished economic, political and military potential, Russia is still trying to play the role of hegemon in the Caspian-Caucasus Region… in the best tradition of Russian "Velikoderzhavie" (the big power omnipotence)."[209] He further dilates that 'traditionalists' who are ideologically and politically influential in the elite class have little doubt that most Russian problems still are being caused by the quintessential Western 'machinations' just like during Cold War. By implication, the reference to Cold War justifies to assume that larger number of Russians perceive that the New Great Game in Caspian Region has yet another face and that is an 'on-going Cold War'. The perception dichotomy of the West and Russia leaves little space for evolving an amenable energy order and thus the game is likely to go on. However, Russia can still be called as linchpin country among the actors that oppose Western military role in the guise of helping Caspian-Caucasus countries to recover and grow as vibrant democracies. Iran and Armenia gravitate in an orbit for the Caspian Region where Russia holds critical core position. The West appears to agree that while Russia may be too weak to re-impose its imperial domination but it is too powerful to be excluded.[210] Finding greater convergence of interests, not only China but also India and Pakistan are finding it expedient to enter the race for influence in the arena. Pakistan is crucial to Central Eurasia being geographically contiguous to it while India claims historic affiliation. In other words for all practical conduct of geo-strategic affairs in Caspian-Caucasus backdrop; the world stands demarcated as bipolar, the West versus others, while debris of unipolarity would smolder for years to come.

China

The observers appear inclined to perceive China's entry as a crucial element in the New Great Game that will lend to it the third dimension in geo-strategic connotations. The trio, US, Russia and China emerge as heavyweights, drawing more attention than others do, though not at the cost of ignoring them. China entered the arena convincingly in the late nineties and her intentions are driven by two main considerations. One is obvious that being low on indigenous oil and gas reserves her priorities would compel her to look towards Caspian Region. The second driver of the China's policy orientation is her security concerns that plague her in the context of Xingjian province, which is inhabited by Turkic race, Uighur Muslims predominantly. Beijing suspects that Uighur's radical Islamists have ties with those in Central Asia who encourage their separatist movement. According to some West's percepts, China has resorted to dilute low-level insurgency through obtaining favorable demographic balance by encouraging Han Chinese to migrate to this region from the east. In Uighur's interpretation, the move has added fuel to the fire. Conversely, China has right reason to offer even if it accepts Han work force transit to her western province that is seeing tremendous progress and Hans being equipped better with science and technological expertise than the Uighars. In the context of oil and gas politics China's dilemma is even serious because of her chronic dependence on imported energy; skirting long naval routes. China's oil proven reserves are barely 1.4% of the world total while her production is 4.5% of the world total oil. In other words, to meet her annual consumption requirement of 8.2% of the world total, she has to rely on imported oil that would be 3.7% of the world total annually. For the availability of natural gas, she holds 1.2% gas reserves of the world total but produces of necessity, 1.5% of the world total to meet ever-increasing demand for gas annually. Because of her economic boom, her oil consumption increase in 2004 over 2003 had been 15.8% and 19% in gas for the same year.[211]

- **China's perception about the West.** China perceives US meddling in the Caspian Region to monopolize the oil and gas resources to the detriment of the emerging economy of China. In Chinese view, the geo-strategic dimensions, work against her when she suspects America to be allowing improved military muscles to Taiwan. To off set such vulnerabilities, China has no option but to develop lasting relationship with Central Asia; and also with Caspian littorals for economic compulsions. On the Sino-US equation; China perhaps stays informed that her expanding influence in Central Eurasia shall not be contested by US as long as she does not assert herself as a rival military power to challenge US interests in the region.

China's massive forces system and fledging nuclear capability if seen juxtaposed to her economic boom does lead to the hypothesis that at certain point of time, China may undermine US role in conjunction with Russia and Iran. Already some experts are referring to SCO as NATO of the East. No matter how lustrous Chinese military might be, when compared to US, Russia and Iran; the myth of this eastern actor crumbles being somewhat analogous to Japan of World War II, which was military giant but could not sustain its military might because of oil factor. Not only in Central Eurasia but also in Middle East, China sees US preponderance of military infrastructure as a threat since bulk of Chinese oil supply emanates from Persian Gulf. As regards Gulf, had the production of Indonesia and other Southeast Asia not been declining, China would have preferred to be their client for the energy imports. Of necessity, she has to turn towards Persian Gulf where her dependence is accentuating. Assuming that supply lanes of Persian Gulf would stay reliable; even then, her 48% of (1997) dependence for oil shall rise to 81% in 2010. That indeed presents a bleak scenario.

- **Quest for Alternatives**. Entering into joint oil and gas venture with Kazakhstan are such moves that are likely to address her possible pitfalls. KCP is under construction with another similar gas pipeline planned to be extended to Xingjian initially and later to the Pacific Coast for the eastern market that is likely to grow ten times more in consumption than Europe. Oil and gas routes to the east are not palatable to the West; not perhaps even to Russia; on the ground of their cost-prohibitive factor and loss of oil revenues. However, China is not deterred by impediments as is evident from a Chinese official statement, "At the moment we are producing about four million tons of oil in

Kazakhstan but that is not nearly enough for us. In coming years we want to acquire many more fields in Central Asia."[212] Michael Klare is of the opinion, "Chinese know that the US forces are largely there to safeguard the outflow of oil (thus benefiting China, along with other nations), Beijing fears that the United States might someday cut off China's flow of oil (say in response to fresh crisis in Taiwan) and cripple its economy."[213] From the viewpoint of internal dynamics of Central Eurasian states, Iran, since isolated by measure firmly planted by USA, may welcome Chinese influence that can ill afford its loss of breathing space through traditional international relationing. Geographically, China is too far off and borders only three of Central Asian states. In Kazakhstan, Chinese and Russian interests clash with each other because of Russia's resolve to protect her ethnic Russian minorities, which make a very large chunk of Kazak population. Kyrgyzstan and Tajikistan are embroiled in domestic problems to an extent that China cannot rescue them by making such a large investment. Turkmenistan and Uzbekistan have generally shown tendency to muster independent stance and have soft corner for the West. According to RAND Corporation report, "It is hard to visualize an ascending China in Central Asia if these two countries prove resistant in Chinese political and economic penetration."[214] However, that does not mean that China would relent in her pursuits of the game of influence to a degree that it neither frightens the Central-Eurasian states nor tramples over Russian sensitivities that has much larger stakes than China in geo-strategic dimensions.

- **Prioritizing the Role**. Prioritizing China's role, her focus shall stay to her west. At least till next decades; China will conduct largely defensive political maneuver in Central Eurasia as future projection for sustaining economic growth. In her priority, shielding Xingjian from divisive influence would rate higher and simultaneously creating space in the energy game with certain constraints. True to their historic traditions of keeping 'time' on own side; Chinese envisage influence expansion sure footed like a glacier; slow and steady. For this measure, it has opted for enormous communication infra structure to connect Central Asia with about $1/5^{th}$ of her total world population. For Central Asian states that will be too alluring to refuse. Amineh views about China-Central Eurasia cooperation prospects are based on greater optimism. She takes into account certain basic pointers that indicate the magnitude of business with which China is in the New Great Game, "At the moment China is trying to develop so called Second Eurasian Bridge railway which connects the coast of Pacific Ocean to the coast of Atlantic Ocean."[215] Chinese have completed the development of this part (Urumchi-Altova) of railway, commencing in 1991, which is 446 km long. Thus, this 10,800 km transcontinental railway line is shared by China alone for 4,136 km. It would give advantage to the transportation effort over naval route from Chinese coast to Netherlands by over 11,000 km. That shows, other than being a model compatible to conservative societies of Central Eurasia, the Chinese level of seriousness to play her role on the Eurasian Chessboard. While Amineh also quotes certain other Chinese strengths to be in position to play a balancer role to the West, Turkish, Iranian or Russian hegemony, she perhaps ignores that addition of another actor in the arena shall strain fragile peace with corresponding intensity. The more the actors and stakes get higher; lesser chances to evolve harmonizing and stabilizing strategies for the region particularly when oil depletion specter has started haunting the globe and everything hinges on oil. Though China appears fully poised to play her role in a manner that it is in position to share Caspian riches because, "In the long run, energy resources of the region are bound to be of special interest to Beijing, and direct access to them, not subject to Moscow's control, has to be China's central goal."[216] What is evident from above school of thought is that China's role oscillates from being peripheral to central. The latter prognosis sounds reason if one looks at China as a booming economy, which has to project it for securing all possible energy resources for maintaining her economic, if not military ascendancy.

Iran

Prior to political change in Central Eurasia, Iran shared direct borders with Soviet Russia, both being the only Caspian littorals. The history of turbulent relations between the two spans over centuries as Iranian territories remained the direct victim of the Great Game of 19th and 20th Century. Until the late 20th Century, the historic Treaties of Gulistan (1813), Turkmanchai (1828), Treaty of 1921 and the Treaty of 1940 had governed their sweet and sour relations. Whereas in the first two treaties oblique references are available to the Caspian Sea; the Treaty of 1921 spells out clear provision, "Both committed parties agree equally to have the right of shipping under their flags in the Caspian Sea."[217] Treaty of 1940 was further improvement on the stance of both the countries when they declared shipping rights over the Caspian as an exclusive prerogative of the two littorals; Iran and Russia. Caviar trade booming at that time; the fishing rights were extended to both over the entire seabed except ten nautical miles exclusive coastal belt. The preamble reveals the chemistry of Russian and Iranian stance that recognize no other agreement valid except of 1921 and 1940 though there are three other littorals along the Caspian Coast, Azerbaijan,

Kazakhstan and Turkmenistan. The rigidity in the views about Caspian legal regime persists. While Russia negotiates with other littorals individually in an attempt to resolve off shore oil and gas exploration disputes, Iran does not enter into any meaningful bilateral negotiations. Russia soon joins the Iranian stance once the negotiated arrangements are labeled ad-hoc; until mutual consensus is evolved in the light of 1921 and 1940 Treaties. The Iranian role subsequently emerges from such psychological fix perspective of oil and gas politics. Observers note that Iran's initial stance towards other littorals was flexible that was rebuffed under US influence, "Yet US opposition to most of the projects Iran had promoted eventually led Tehran to side increasingly with Moscow and to adopt a policy which in particular could be described as: the Caspian for the Caspian."[218]

- **Iran's Role Significance**. In the setting of the New Great Game, Iran's role in Central Eurasia would remain pivotal. It not only possesses huge oil and gas resources, 133 Gb of proven oil and 91 tcf of proven gas; geo-strategically it has remained a bridge in the Eurasian corridor. To the Caspian Region; it offers most favorable exit routes for its oil and gas export to the international market though it has been successfully blocked by USA through such tools as sanctions and ILSA in the place since 1996. Iran has the capacity to play multi-directional role as it shares international borders with fifteen countries in the region. It makes Iran central on all the issues of Middle East, Caspian-Caucasus Region, and Central Asia including Afghanistan. US hostility has led Iran to lean towards Russia and China; the two potent actors of Central Eurasia that have the capability to challenge US interests. Iranian policy makers conduct usual business with other Caspian littorals and Central Asian states while pursuing some specific goals. Gaining political influence, profitable economic and commercial relations, the spread of religious ideology, acquisition of nuclear technology and Sino-Russian weapons system feature high on her agenda. While Azerbaijan-Iran relations are plagued by ethnic and political divide since Iran is a crucial link in Russian-Iran-Armenia nexus; she has not lost sight of attaining favorable edge in the New Great Game for oil and gas. Hence, her relations with Turkmenistan are cordial, that sends jitters to Uzbekistan and Kazakhstan who suspected her of supporting opposition during Tajikistan's internal crisis pioneered by Islamists. Iran and Turkmenistan have not only energy 'swap' arrangement through Iranian Caspian Seaport of Neka but also have alternative means in form of KKK gas pipeline and Meshhad-Sarakh-Tadzhen railway line which was made operational on 14 May 1997. It is 298 km long railway line, which stretches for 168 km in Iranian territory and 130 km in Turkmenistan territory. The plan is afoot to link Iran, through Central Asia railway, to China. Iran's position in the oil world and favorable geo-strategy has kept US administration under tremendous pressure to review ILSA like arrangement when US policy was jolted by French Oil Company "Total" that signed $2 billion oil and gas exploration deal in the Gulf on 29 January 1997, going way beyond ILSA restriction of up to $20 million dollars annually for foreign companies doing business with Iran. Thierry Dismarest, Total's Chairman remarked, "Nobody recognizes the extra-territorial character of the law, which goes against the principle of sovereignty in relation between nations... we reckon that we are free in our movements."[219]

- **Iran Manipulating Caspian Littoral Status**. Iran, when seen from the perspective of a regional power; forces a dilemma on her northern neighbors in Caspian-Caucasus Region. Iran has decidedly refused to be flexible on division of Caspian Sea resources. Iran eyes them with 'equal distribution' fix and considers Treaties of 1921 and 1940 as still applicable, though much has changed since. Being a potent regional power among the littoral states next to Russia; by implication Iran can lay claim of share technically even from the offshore oil field of Azerbaijan as well as Kazakhstan because 'Caspian legal regime' dispute is yet to be resolved. Iranian and Russian resonance in Caspian policy makes the nexus strong; considering Armenia; it further reinforces their role capacity. The new entrant, China, sympathetic to Iranian orientation and showing capability to coexist with Russia leads to a scenario that perhaps in the end may force the West to be dictated by her for vacating the arena. The West would obviously not bow down being led by the solitary global power, USA. The present mode of 'role play' through diplomacy if translated in military terms in a future scenario would mean ignition of Eurasian Balkan. It would not only be catastrophic scenario but deplorable as well. The emergence of such a military block is though a subject of numerous contradictions at the moment. However, until the mid nineties, Russia perceived Iran as a threat that focused on its obligation to Islam even within Russian boundaries, but now they reinforce each other's role despite contradictions; is a point to draw a lesson from. In a complex situation when Russian geopolitical thrusts point towards Azerbaijan and Kazakhstan, Turkey's thrust aims across Caspian at Kazakhstan, Iranian thrust is directed against Azerbaijan and Turkmenistan and now a far and wide thrust from China like a thunderbolt from the east across Central Eurasia; it becomes imperative to reckon, in Brzezinski's perception, that these would not only crisscross, they can collide also.

- **Pipeline Wrangling and Iran**. Completion of BTC and SCP pipelines would be an obvious blow to Iran if not China at the moment because the two pipelines will switch oil and gas flow from the erstwhile Russian dominated northern axis to the West's sponsored westward axis, terminating at Ceyhan and Erzurum respectively. This can take care of Azerbaijan's ability to export all of its oil and gas and yet stay short of designed 'through-put' capacity. TCOP from Kazakhstan and TCGP from Turkmenistan to connect these to Baku with BTC and SCP is a plan yet in the evolution phase when Russia and Iran are poised to resist fiercely as the two pipelines are to go through Caspian Sea, the status of which has not been negotiated. Should the West push her way through to accomplish these projects, it is likely that Caspian energy situation shall deteriorate. It thus becomes imperative that the West and the two Caspian littorals have to allay Russian and Iranian fears, an exercise likely to be riddled with big 'ifs'. US Administration scuttled the 'swap' arrangements between Kazakhstan and Iran, threatening Chevron and Mobil Corporations with legal sanctions since 'swap' oil originated from Tengiz oil field to Kazak Caspian Sea port of Aktau and delivered at Iran's Caspian Seaport of Neka for consumption of 80% of the 70 million Iranian population, which inhabit Northern Iran. The Kazak government succumbed to the pressure because the state shares were barely a quarter in the oil field. One would have the reason to believe that marked reduction by 75% in Turkmenistan-Iran 'swap' volumes were possibly engineered at the behest of US coaxing. In both cases, Iran's capability to handle high-sulfur contents were questioned technically that created prices adjustment puzzle. In other words, blame of 'swap' failure was made to rest with Iran. Under these circumstances, Iran's soft posturing towards US when bitten by such undercurrents of the New Great Game obviously stands precluded. Conversely, Iran is upbeat. In the words of an Iranian oil broker, Hamid Honarvar, "If we start doing serious business with the Kazaks, there is nothing the American can do about it."[220] He was of the opinion that for this reason, perhaps seeing oil and gas lying east of Caspian, slipping off America's domain, she created pretext of war in Afghanistan and subsequent military deployment, adding that it was US government herself behind terror attacks of 9/11 on WTC and Pentagon.

- **Iran-Azerbaijan Factor and other Irritants.** Iran admits that Azeri oil is firmly under US thumb, mainly for the reason that Azerbaijan, for several considerations, is more drawn towards Turkey and hence US. Now, massive Western investment and 'Turkey' factor has prevented Iran's forays into Central Eurasia to gain significant toehold, yet there are reasons to fear Iran other than its geo-strategic strengths and her collusion with Russia. Iran anti-imperialist stance and rhetoric raise her credibility among Muslims, even among Sunnis, once Iran directs calculated tirades against Israel to cash on popular sentiments. Iran foreign policy orientation towards Middle East affords her a leverage to counter US moves and compensate her loss she faces in Central Eurasia which certainly is not her primary concern but a stand-by playing field to share the 'New Great Game' and explore means to create bog for the rivals, mainly USA. Iran is also aware of political discord among her Azeri population in its province adjoining Azerbaijan. In fact, Iranian Azeris, ten million, outnumber the Azerbaijan Azeri majority that is barely eight million. To offset her vulnerability of weak flank, she has made shrewd move by wooing Armenia as counter weight to Azerbaijan in South Caucasus, which by design has led to Russia-Iran-Armenia nexus. Faced with Nagorno-Karabakh loss; Iran scores at Azerbaijan by convincing Iranian Azeris to desist from greater Azerbaijan dream, particularly when Azerbaijan cannot manage her present territory. Some observers see Iran as an effective actor while colluding with her regional allies but not as a major actor because of weak economic projections and inability to invest in cash-starved Central-Eurasian states. As intellectuals foresee space in US Administration diplomacy to soften stance on Iran and engage her influence in the Middle East and geo-strategic edge in Caspian-Caucasus region, they in the same breath urge Iran to rethink to break cordon around by reshaping her loquacious posturing on the international scene, particularly to the West. Iran's tit for tat foreign policy so far has cast her as a 'pariah' state. It may be pertinent to point out that any good will germinating among the Western people is thoroughly dashed by Iran through such proclamations that it was set to enrich Uranium and her leadership sloganeering to 'wipe out Israel from the world map'. While right to tap nuclear energy as a source and shrewd option to explore alternatives for her enormous but fast dwindling oil and gas reserves cannot be denied but it is also encumbered as a responsible member to allay international fears and move along the wind rather than flexing muscle in confrontational manner. Similarly Israel, whatever be the Iranian perception about her creation like some other Middle East countries; is very much an equal and sovereign state among the comity of nations. Hence, she is to be respected and differences resolved on the negotiation table or from the platform of existing mechanisms of conflicts resolution. As an analyst sums up, "For at least next decade, Iran strategy towards Central Asia will be defensive and cooperative rather than threatening and confrontational... Simply put, if Iran could not establish its hegemony over the Gulf Arab states where Tehran enjoyed many natural advantages, it seems hardly likely that the Caspian Zone will fall under Iran's domination."[221] One would partially agree with the comments because the Caspian chemistry and stage setting of the 'New Great Game' are much different than common to the Middle East. A point can however be made. Iran's capability to worsen the energy security situation cannot be underestimated as much as its ability to help restore stability in the region while working in concert with other actors. Discreet pragmatism would enable her to prove an assumption wrong, what Fred Halliday said about Iran, "Condemned to react, unable to influence."[222] Prudence demands that there is a need to muster a few Castlereaghs and Metterniches in the arena by all the actors combined to douse the dormant flames of the game otherwise it might engulf the myopic interests of all and sundry.

Turkey

The country that has contiguity to Caspian-Caucasus region wears two hats. One; it shoulders responsibility to take care of her national interests in individual nation-to-nations equation. Second; being a crucial NATO ally she has to represent and safeguard Western interests while nestling in well-defined and almost ideal geography. In the context of Caspian-Caucasus region; predominantly Turkic race of Muslim countries makes double plus for Turkey though Azeri population profess Shiite faith; yet on ethnic ground they own Turkey and not Iran. It makes Turkey a comfortable actor to wield and expand her influence that is backed by the Western camp also. The Soviet 'phantasmagoria' brought relief for Turkey on one hand that Russian borders shrunk away from Turkish borders after over 200 years; on the other hand, she was confronted with fellow kins high hopes and expectations. For instance; Turkey did utmost to extend credits to the emerging Caspian-Caucasian countries despite her weak economy initially but was likely to gasp herself for the breath since lacking potent economic stamina. Fortunately, the 'New Great Game' picking up intensity also brought Western investment that afforded a breather to Turkey. The second challenge, which it has to square off with, is the simmering turbulence in Caucasus and Central Asia, which had remained stifled through the Soviets 'cap on' strategy. Azerbaijan expects her active military support against Armenia over Nagorno-Karabakh issue. Very prudently, Turkey has done everything for Azerbaijan but has stayed short of military adventure against Armenia that could spill the conflict to other actors as well; like Russia in first instance. The separatist movements going on in Chechnya, Dagestan, South Ossetia, Azeri province of Iran, Abkhazia and turbulent but authoritarian Central Asia; Xingjian and Afghanistan included; bring tremendous strain on Turkish diplomacy to tread her path carefully; rushing somewhere and tip-toeing else where as an international actor in the arena. Turkey like all other actors is crowned with some strength and riddled with some weaknesses.

- **Strength.** In geo-strategic setting, it controls access routes of all Black Sea coastal states to the Mediterranean through Bosphorus and Dardanelles as well as air routes between Eastern Europe and Middle East. She is a crucial member in the Western alliance system including NATO and her economy may be weak by European standards but is strong and dynamic when pitted against Asian neighbors. With a large standing army, Turkey can deal with conventional threat though with limited war stamina. Against nuclear capability of nuclear or emerging nuclear states in Central Eurasian game setting, she stands perhaps compensated through NATO's security umbrella. These strengths make her standing significant in Eurasian Balkan; while Turkey itself is very much in it as a potential candidate along with Iran. Becoming the conduit to the Caspian oil, passing through Azerbaijan, Georgia (BTC pipeline), it has switched the balance of power in the Western favor which Brzezinski had commented very explicitly in 1997, "... pipeline issue so central to the future of Caspian Sea basin and Central Asia. If the main pipelines to the region continue to pass through Russian territory to the Russian outlet on the Black Sea at Novorossiysk, the political consequences of this condition will make themselves felt even without any overt Russian power plays... conversely if another pipeline cross the Caspian Sea to Azerbaijan to the Mediterranean through Turkey and if one goes to Arabian Sea through Afghanistan, no single power will have monopoly over access."[223]

- **Weaknesses.** Turkey's weaknesses that impede if not prevent her role as honest actor are also numerous. She is prone to severe internal ethnic conflict; Kurds versus others. A high rate of inflation makes serious dent on her economy. Her relations with five out of eight neighbors[224] remain traditionally strained; thus reducing her options for conducting exterior maneuvers successfully. Though certain apprehensions were expressed that the development in Middle East and her burden of responsibility towards Central-Eurasia might prompt her to drift away from the Western influence but it did not prove true. Instead Turkey now leans to the West to gain strength in the race of seeking influence in Central Eurasia versus Iran, Russia, and China; and also to lend credibility to her being European though on geographic basis, she is a little less than 1/8th 'European'. With NATO umbrella; her economic interests may partially converge on Russia with focus on her oil and gas reserves; her military interests do not. William Hale comments, "that is to say, that Russian power would be virtually ended. This expectation has clearly turned out to be wrong. Russia may be weak economically, but it is still the dominant power in a region in which the other ex-Soviet states are, if any thing, even weaker."[225] However, with dilution of USSR as a super power in bipolar world of Cold War era, Turkey's disillusionment with the West had to exacerbate. The dust had hardly settled down that Turkey found a new role in Central Eurasia in the face of growing fear that Russia may reclaim her lost territories or convincingly impose remnants of her might over Central Eurasia's newly independent states.

- **Turkey Indispensable for the West**. The West, by the mid nineties, redefined her economic and military objectives, particularly in Caspian-Caucasus Region that stood threatened by Russia, Iran and now China as well. In other words, Turkey's indispensability in the Eurasian Balkan has heightened in direct proportion to the simmering level of the 'New Great Game'. While Turkey, being a NATO member already could use its shield, threat of Eurasian Balkan hostilities have placed indirectly US CENTCOM and US EUCOM at her disposal; the former for the Central Asia and the latter for Caucasus region. That way, her imbalance in conventional and non-conventional military capability vis-à-vis Russia, Iran and China combined stands effectively addressed. It does not mean, however that Turkey would have free Bull Run in the arena. The dynamics of her pioneer and overbearing role in Central Eurasia may generate a blow back effect on her domestic politics, of which Turkey is aware, that would have a splintering effect on her survival. It is so because Turkey is bound to ride on two popular themes for elusive quest of extended role in Central Eurasia. One; it is the ethnic card and history of Turkic grandeur and second is the Islamic identity. Pan-Turkic and Pan-Islamic thrusts ought to go side by side. However while Turkey sees no harm to use Pan-Turkic side of the card but she would loath using Pan-Islamic side of the same card since that hits at the roots of her declared, 'secularist' status when Islamic surge could sweep Turkey's mainland also. Again a dilemma within; if she is found reluctant using Islamic card, there is another watchful actor, Iran, in the neighborhood that intends using it to the hilt and thus making Turkey's influence somewhat redundant. Such elements in her foreign policy force her to walk on the 'razor's edge' sort of situation. Turkey's developing tinge of arrogance and chauvinism has also offended the sensibilities of Turkish states of Caspian-Caucasus Region who assume that they themselves are more Turks than Turkey. As one expert in the region has noted, the people of the South Caucasus and Central Asia have a strong sense of national pride and having suffered under the yoke of Soviet colonialism were not about to become the "little brothers" of Turkey or any other outside power.[226] That does not mean, however, that Turkey would desist anyway from making incursion of influence into Caspian-Caucasus region; mainly to offset yet another emerging strategic disadvantage of energy dependence on imported oil which at the moment is 65% of her total needs. The limitation would accentuate when it soars to 75% in about two decades time. Lacking any worthwhile indigenous oil and gas reserve, her annual consumption share of energy is 0.8% of the world total, incidentally for both, oil and gas.

- **The Only Choice**. In order to sustain her economy in the future as well, she is left with no choice but to become an active actor of the Caspian-Caucasus 'New Great Game,' while it has already firm foot in the Middle Eastern arena. Commissioning of BTC pipeline has placed Turkey in the list of crucial conduit for Caspian oil, which is likely to be charged by December 2005 and start delivering one million barrel of crude oil daily at Turkish Mediterranean port of Ceyhan. Though inauguration of BTC project has brought jubilations to the West with Turkey on the front, it has shuddered the other two regional powers, Iran and Russia. The effects of BTC project stands further reinforced by SCP that would take care of Azerbaijan's gas export to Turkish gas installation at Horasan for onward transmission to international market. The West appears determined; not only to switch Russian dominated routes to the Western Turkey-destined corridor but also to perpetuate her monopoly. By implication if TCOP and TCGP dream comes true, as it did in case of BTC, from Kazakhstan and Turkmenistan respectively, little would be left to keep ASP wet from Kazakhstan to Russia or KKK gas pipeline blowing from Turkmenistan to Iran. Some question whether this scenario diversifies the routes at all! If the Russian monopoly was to be substituted with Western monopoly, though the latter may relatively be more compassionate, yet end result of the 'New Great Game' would hang in critical balance. Turkey on her part is well poised to make best use of oil thrust, shifting to her territories that would give her, in case of only BTC oil transit fees to the tune of $140 million initially, growing later to $292 million annually[227]. When such are the heavy stakes, it is logical that not only Turkey's role will gain the intensity in the 'New Great Game' but also other actors may resort to offset the Western sponsors monopolizing efforts dictated by considerations, similar and common among them in energy perspective. The region ridden by discord, social deprivation, ethnic divides in all probability may turn into a hostile arena, particularly when the global crunch of oil is encountered on its depletion. A stage may be set for the oil stampede in the Caspian-Caucasus Region as a consequence that would be the phase one of military hostilities. Certainly it would make a frightening drop scene of the New Great Game'.

India

Being an emerging economic giant when her economy grows at massive rate of about 8%, India has clearly seen the need to address her vulnerability i.e. lack of energy resources which slide inversely to the spiraling graph of her economy. India has proven oil reserves of 5.4 Gb and produces 0.8 million barrels a day while her daily consumption has gone past 2.2 million barrels a day, thus forcing her to import 1.4 million barrels a day. In the gas sector, India has about 30 tcf of gas reserves and produced 883 bcf annually. With her heavy dependence on coal as well, her gas imports remained zero. The reserves estimates in both categories are as of January 2004 while consumption and production statistics have been quoted as of year 2002-2003. In the energy ranking, despite not having a conspicuous position in oil and gas reserves, India is included in the top 25 countries, occupying 24th ladder just before UK, which is 25th. India and China have a lot of similarities in their domestic milieu: social, economic and military. Their responses in the energy domain have triggered off almost simultaneously. Erstwhile rivals, their militaries clashing in early sixties over territorial claim when Chinese forces humiliatingly vanquished the Indians, have landed in intense maneuvers in the energy arena. Jyoti Malhotra writes, "Clearly the Sino Indian scramble for the oil field of Central Asia is fast acquiring the proportion of New Great Game, in a region which has for centuries enjoyed being the strategic straddle between civilizations. But the truth is that as India grows at annual rate of 8% and demands commensurate source of energy to keep that growth rate going, it is coming face to face with China that is being driven by the same reason."[228] The Indian struggle to acquire maximum out of the global hydrocarbon scene is no longer a modest exercise when one finds India's ONGC officials hectically negotiating for oil field shares and pipeline blueprints across the globe, with particular focus in Caspian-Caucasus Region. Her latest bid to buy Kazak Company, PetroKazakhstan, for $3.9 billion was only scuttled at the last moment when China put in additional $0.28 billion (total $4.18 billion) and sealed the deal. Aware that her impending deal with Iran over gas pipeline through Pakistan would be ridden with US disapproval as well as geo-political threats, India seems poised to go ahead anyway[229]. If there is a delay of a sort, it is to make the energy environments more conducive and friction free for the future.

Now, hanging Iran-Pakistan-India pipeline in balance, India is comfortably gloating over the inventory of concessions that US would offer instead. A big concession she has already extracted conveniently by signing Indo-US nuclear energy deal in 2006 that by implication acknowledges her nuclear status in the club. Indian foreign policy pundits can rightly boast of it while not having given up the Iran project as yet that has potentials to defeat US designs, by nullifying her 'strangle' around Iran. The delay is bringing India two crucial dividends. One is aimed at USA to keep her on defensive posture with Indian potentials as a crucial actor to abet her efforts in suffocating Iran economically. The second is aimed at Iran to seek concessions to any degree possible, insinuating that how difficult it is for India to face the crunch of a super power bully. A corollary in between the two neutralizes Pakistani claim of India's dependence on her good will, as safe pipeline is either through Pakistan or nowhere else. Indian diplomacy has cleared successfully the litmus test when Iran discretely cut down trade volumes with countries that joined EU chorus of anti-Iran nuclear proliferation in October 2005. Though, India joined in opposing Iranian nuclear program, Iran denied any reaction towards India, being her 'strategic' partner. The Indian energy moves are infested with deceptions and perhaps India's 'wheeler dealer' Mani Shankar Aiyar acknowledges such a trait straightway through his name metaphor when 'Aiyar `in Urdu language has English equivalent as 'cunning'. India has ambitions to embark on expanded role in Central Eurasia once she would focus on its trade and energy dividends that can accrue from this region. Unfortunately, she is handicapped geographically as well as politically to gain any worthwhile toehold in the region for certain obvious reasons:

- Though some parts of the Western India are considered to be governed by the geo-strategic consideration of Eurasian strategy, her geographical insulation, when non-pliant if not hostile Pakistan lies in between, emerges as a geo-strategic reverse.

- Other regional powers like Russia, China, Turkey and Iran have much stronger claims and easy available wedges to make dent into the New Great Game than India from somewhat distant quarters.

- India lacks the ability to muster that level of economic or military muscle to invest in the region though her recent bid to buy 'PetroKazakhstan' Oil Company and securing a military base in Tajikistan, in all probability was driven by such considerations of teeming up her stakes for reaping more.

Some analysts contend that, "India views the evolving Caspian security environment through the prism of its rivalry with China and Pakistan. For instance India is deeply disturbed at greater Chinese inroads in Central Asia and could be tempted to play Chinese separatism card in Tibet or Xingjian - to keep China off balance. Tension between India and China is also likely to arise over Caspian energy development, since both countries are competing for access to oil and a share in the region's pipeline sweep stakes."[230] Perhaps one would grant Tibet card to India but it has been played so long that China may discard it summarily after having fastened her grip over Tibet through decades. India's Xingjian card is not potent enough; in any case, that would be desperate move to force China to commit 'mischief' covertly in Indian several unstable regions.

Even in the past when the 'New Great Game' had not simmered, both held each other in great suspicions on such accounts. On the energy front, other than China's win over India in 'PetroKazakhstan' case, India also lost to China (CNPC) in Angola in October 2004. In Iranian 'Yardavan' oil field, India (ONGC) with 20% share appears as pygmy against China who has 50% shares. In Greater Nile Petroleum Oil Company, CNPC out maneuvered ONGC by securing 40% shares as compared to India's, which could bag only 20%. India has not ventured to buy Russian company when China is set to stalk over $6 billion deal for their Rosneft. However, India perseveres in the energy game when it appears even stretched as far as Sakhalin Island resources to tap them. It thus proves that the Central-Eurasian theater of oil war is certainly on high priority with Indian design to play significant role in the 'New Great Game'. It is believed that until June 2002, India was a minor player in the game but a strong candidate. Its aggressive stance in the game became visible when Indian Prime Minster Vajpayee attended the summit meeting of the Kazakhstan sponsored Conference on Interaction and Confidence Building Measure in Asia (CICA: appears to have been abbreviated inadequately): he stressed the importance of the Caspian Basin energy supplies for India. He also concluded an agreement for the acquisition of stakes in a number of oil and gas fields, to be developed by Indian conglomerate ONGC Videsh.[231] Hereafter Indian role in the game becomes all too vivid.

Pakistan

Oil and gas stock inventory of Pakistan lacks luster to the extent that for Asia-Pacific Region, BP gives statistics of eight countries[232] only, and groups the rest of them under title 'the others'. Pakistan is one of 'the others'.

Her proven oil reserves as of January 2004 estimates are 288 million bbl, produces about 62,000 bbl/day and consumes 360,000 bbl/day, meeting her shortfall of 298,000 bbl/day through imports. In gas sector she holds proven reserves of over 28 tcf, produces 23 bcm and consumes 26 bcm with negligible imports so far. The statistics simply prove that her growing economy rate around 5% would necessitate her to tap energy sources from abroad. However, traditionally Pakistan has relied on Middle East oil. Prudence demands that she should look elsewhere to diversify her dependence and take advantage of her geo-political edge in the region. The options of letting energy exit through Iran or Russia have been foreclosed; the Caspian Caucasus energy exit has to be either through the Western corridor that is likely to congest with alternative option through Afghanistan, Pakistan, onward to India or Indian Ocean ports of Karachi and Gwadar. Observers point out that, "probably eventually we (Pakistan) will need two pipelines to support our economic growth. The pipeline from Turkmenistan across Afghanistan is the shortest."[233] In other words, urgency to import natural gas from Caspian Region stands highlighted. Conversely with simmering instability in Afghanistan, the prospects stand dashed, forcing Pakistan to look further south to Iran or Qatar. The size of Pakistan's economy and its potential growth do not equate her with other emerging giants like China or India but it is aware of its ability to act as Energy Bridge from the west to the east. Such a geo-strategic advantage puts her in the arena of 'New Great Game'. However seeing no end to Afghanistan imbroglio for years to come, her edge in being contiguous to Central Asian oil and gas regions has been neutralized. Her weak economic stamina too becomes a serious handicap to flex her muscle in the arena, except that geography has favored her to be an eastern conduit, somewhat similar but not to the same scale, as Turkey is for rapidly developing western energy corridor. The trio, China, India and Pakistan would consume much of the energies among themselves to outwit others in the Central Eurasian game. Sound economy muscles available to the former two are not available to Pakistan. China and Pakistan are at advantage to counter India while India has to exert against both China and Pakistan. Observers believe, however, "Pakistan's common ethnic and historical roots with Central Asian not withstanding, Pakistan has made only limited inroads in the region."[234] The foreign policy makers of Pakistan have designed a fine hinge, ECO that can render a very effective platform to play the game among others, the main being Pakistan, Iran and Turkey. It is also imperative that though Afghanistan cauldron is a major hurdle, but it is not so intense that it cannot be surpassed through negotiations with the warlords on grounds similar to those in some Caucasus's equally turbulent regions. Amineh's assessment also appears pertinent to conclude, "Pakistan must deal with the problems in their own country."[235] Thus, the job of Pakistan policy wizards appears no less easy.

European Union

Erstwhile impression of Europe being led by America was not totally out of place when USA opted to embrace 'responsibility' voluntarily under Truman Doctrine from across the Atlantic Ocean[236]. However when Europe recovered agility to pursue its agenda after sprouting from the debris of WW II, the constituent states rightly questioned each other ever since about the need to transcend historic hostilities for the sake of future generations of Europe. It therefore looked for certain platform, purely European to mold its own destiny. As a result, an institution developed on the principle of peaceful co-existence that is called EU. It now comprises Belgium, Czech Republic, Denmark, Germany, Estonia, the Hellenic Republic, Spain, France, Ireland, Italy, Republic of Cyprus, Lithuania, Luxembourg, Hungary, Austria, Poland, Portugal, Slovenia, Slovakia, Finland, Sweden and UK. What gives a clear edge to this organization over any other actor is its transparent chemistry claimed in preamble to its charter, "Believing that Europe, reunited after bitter experience, intends to continue along the path of civilization, progress and prosperity for the good of all its inhabitants including the weakest and the deprived; that it wishes to remain a continent open to culture, learning and social progress; and it wishes to deepen the democratic and transparent nature of its public life and to strive for peace, justice and solidarity through the world..."[237] True to its thrust on its transparency, EU has evolved its energy security parameters but recognizing at the same time, legitimate right of individual member states for ensuring security of energy supplies and deciding own energy mix. Similarly, those countries in the neighborhood as well as afar with which it has to deal in the energy spectrum, it makes unambiguous policy profiles to honor international laws with same kind of moral intent. EU dependence on others has been meticulously identified, according to 2004 statistics, Russia providing it 24% of gas and 27% of its total oil requirement. Norway comes next, supplying 13% of gas and 16% of oil that is trailed by Middle East providing 19% of oil only. Algeria meets its 10% of the requirement and North Africa, 12% of oil. Its indigenous production is 46% of gas and 21% of total oil requirement. Other regions supply 7% of gas and 5% of oil. The Caspian Region lies in the latter category that is likely to expand in scale and magnitude because it holds promise of further discoveries while world generally is prone to decline in production of oil in particular. It therefore becomes imperative that Russia as hydrocarbons power be not ignored in the interstate relation equation because of inevitable interdependence between Russia and EU. Similarly, the policy guidelines on bilateralism focus on the Caspian Region as well[238]. What clearly emerges from the possible role in the matters of energy in Central Eurasia is the fact that EU can pursue its charter with certain specifics comfortably:

- Russia receives a significant status because of her vast indigenous energy potentials, an aspect for which Russia is particularly starved now, when it faces a drought-like situation about its weight in the world affairs.

- Caspian-Caucasus Region is indicated to be integrated in the supply pattern but on equal state-like merit. Thus, here bilateralism and multilateralism is recognized and never any 'bully' behavior surfaces.

- EU as an actor in the arena would cast sobering effect on the hype in quest for energy, visible among other actors.

- By dint of its excellent smooth relationship with Russia and willingness to allow ample space to China and Japan, the EU earns an applause that would remain a scarce commodity for other actors.

- EU advocates tackling of approaching energy crunch through consultations with the members as well as neighbors.

- Pursuit of EU policies would remain a boon for Central Eurasia where it has come to be recognized an honest broker. Such an exercise of reposing confidence in EU by the regional actors has also rendered it an ability to venture into conflict resolution. Besides, her expanding influence is likely to serve as a beacon of inspiration for others.

Actors of New Dimensions

Because of the higher stakes directly in the Caspian Region, the actors that make the New Great Game rather conspicuous have found adequate exposure as regard their intent and extent of involvement. Some international and transnational actors also represented by their oil and gas companies create an added dimension to the New Great Game. In 1995, France launched a hectic diplomatic channel with Azerbaijan to seek increased shares in Azerbaijan consortium, which was dominated by US oil companies. Azerbaijan did not yield for obvious reasons. Behind the smoke screen of oil companies, US continue to force Iran's shift in the foreign policy that threatens US objectives in the Caspian Region, so far unsuccessfully. The influence of powerful Transnational Corporations (TNCs) and Transnational Oil Companies (TNOCs) with their multi billion dollar budgets and profits often becomes difficult to deter as and when they exert in the Caspian Region. To quote, in 1993 Exxon profit had been $5.8 billion when Uzbekistan GDP had been much less, $4.15 billion. Though the Caspian Region is generally dominated by the Western based companies, those located in Europe or Asia find restrictions on Iran rather a blessing. Precisely for this reason, 'Total' of France signed over $2 billion deal to enter into a venture in Iran, defying American ILSA of 1996[239]. The observers also read a trend initially that while US based companies led the FDI in Caspian-Caucasus Region from the front, the European companies were not enthusiastic because of the host countries' lack of economic viability. However, gradually the momentum has picked up. Not only European participation is becoming distinctly visible but Russian and Asian companies including those of China, India, Japan, Canada and Italy started showing interest positively. Yet US Companies dominated the scene, which, until the late nineties were committed to seventy-five ventures that make half of the total oil and gas activity in the region. Seeing the oil and gas companies' spurt of activities, transnational financial institutions like World Bank, IMF and EBRD have explored their role to help the regional countries develop their energy infrastructure. The composition of Azerbaijan offshore oil projects shareholders indicates that other than oil giants; there are actors like Norway, Japan and Saudi Arabia who have not missed the race either through representation by their oil companies. Similarly, 'Bridas' of Argentina is involved in developing Turkmenistan gas reserves along with Unocal. Besides, Ukrgaz, a Ukrainian gas company also operates on Turkmenistan-Uzbekistan border. With several dozens of billion dollars investment brought in by these organizations, it affords them maneuvering space for their native countries anyway in the New Great Game. As and when, out of the fragile cooperation, grouping and regrouping, the delicate balance of interest would shift to hostile posturing; the scenario would forebode an ominous situation. To execute the scenario or preempt its crystallization shall remain Herculean task for each actor. However what Jane Mayer says, is quite disappointing about a responsible superpower, USA. A top secret document of 3 February 2001, which he happened to see, suggests that US National Security Council directed its staff to cooperate in evolving military assessment of the administration's energy plan that would take care of two aspects of White House priorities: Stepped up pressure on rogue states and action regarding the capture of new and existing oil and gas fields[240] It is quite likely that similar top secret plans covering the security of energy contingencies may be buzzing around in the power corridors of all other actors, proportionate to their military might but possibly in much uglier tone.

CHAPTER-SIX

CONCLUSIONS

Strategic Significance and Historic Power Play Established

Central Eurasia, as described earlier, has unique peculiarities. To sum up all, in geopolitical and geo-strategic connotations, it meant a linchpin stretch of landmass to bolster or impede inter continental trade since BC era. Ethnic diversity has been its traditional strength as well as historic weakness. It was strength as long as each segment remained confined to its sphere of influence, thus ensuring mutual cohesion and ethnic homogeny. It helped each individual of the clan to stick to his exclusive brand of culture and traditions. The climatic conditions generally being harsh all over, while the chieftains enforced some sort of discipline code, it nevertheless had semblance of jungle life. The mighty and the fittest survived when the weaker lot perished. Same strength degenerated into weakness when the native clans were to face the onslaught of a formidable foe that incidentally emerged stronger through endeavor of his charismatic personality to achieve unity among two or more clans or within its large clan. The lesser cultural and ethnic units thus yielded to the might of the other(s) 'fittest'. The history of Central Eurasia is thus riddled by such vicissitudes that it was considered easy to conquer due to its ethnic diversity but difficult to rule, again because of ethnic diversity. Revolts and rebellions were the order of the day. A conqueror, subdued a city or a fort, planted allied governance mechanism, would hardly move one day 'march' distance that he would receive desperate call to fall back and deal with the rebellion. The interpretation of its significance may vary in different historic period but the character of Central Eurasia, a constant of all ages, sticks out at all times and that is its 'Centrality'. Alexander the Great, exacerbated by the obstinacy of Achaemenides who impeded east-west trade on Silk Road thought it expedient to punish the Persians in 329 BC, subduing and devising favorable mechanism for the West that stretched to the Indian subcontinent. The traditional east west bridge, called Central Eurasia, served pretty well. It flourished even more when Arabs appeared on the scene in mid 7th Century to make the prevailing governance system pliant to their economic interests as well as ideological pursuits.

At the beginning of the 13th Century, a blizzard originated from Karakoram Mountains of Southern Mongolia and swept the whole of Eurasia. Though for Changez Khan, expansion was itself a convincing reason but Khwarazmi king had afforded him immediate pretext that killed Changez Khan's emissaries and disrupted 'caravan' traffic heading to the East. During the next about 500 years, Central Eurasia saw emergence of local powers in its different parts, often one becoming more potent than the others to hold sway over larger chunk of territories for the time span that generally lasted for 100-200 years. Persians, Ottoman Turks, Imperial Russia remained the indigenous actors all along. Imperial Russia, in the time and territory factor dominated effectively once it consolidated her expansion up to Oxus River by 1885. With Bolsheviks emerging on the scene in early 20th Century, Central Eurasia remained in their firm grip. In latter quarter of the 20th Century, they opted to expand by capturing Afghanistan at the peak brewing of Cold War era since World War II. It turned to be the last nail driven in the coffin of Communist ideology at the hands of, what the West called, 'holy warriors'.

Central Eurasian Permanence

Central Eurasia has sung death songs of several occupants literally or proverbially but absorbing the alien culture, civilization and religious beliefs to the varying degrees at the same time, Islam being the most popular religion. In the recorded history, ingress made by Greeks, Arabs, Mongols, Ottoman Turks and Imperial Russia into Central Eurasia are the events that cannot escape the focus of the scholars. The latest being the defeat of communist's ideology, orchestrated by her potent adversary, USA, that forced the Soviet forces to pull out of Afghanistan, as it remained no more tenable militarily with huge economic drain on them. The turmoil in the Soviet orientation in the wake of Afghan imbroglio appeared as the final death sign of socialist ideology, which the West had been insisting long that it was nothing more than 'utopian'. USSR withdrew to her core boundaries, now called Russian Federation and allowed emergence of several independent states in the Central Eurasia. The number and rapidity with which these states emerged finds no parallel in history. To some this 'freedom' came as a shock and a challenge to stabilize. The lesson from the history to learn is that aliens come and go. If there is a character of permanence to anyone, it is the land and people of Central Eurasia.

Vacuum and the Non-Eurasian Power

When such a large power vacuum was created on withdrawal of the Soviets, it was logical to believe that proportionate power influence from adjoining power centers would flow into Central Eurasia consequently. However, the world saw, for the first time, that a non-Eurasian power opted to fill this vacuum as a right, perhaps through her belief that it staged managed the dissolution of USSR single handedly. No one could deny her role as the lone super power in post-Cold War era but certainly the free-license it contrived for it could be questioned on several moral grounds propounded in international laws that regulate the international relations among the world community. Similarly, other actors like Russia, Turkey, Iran, China and India have come to flexing their power muscles to the relevant degree for sharing the space of influence, bordering to neo-colonial pursuit if not venturing physical occupation or reoccupation. Among them Russia may be exception that sees Central Eurasia as her 'near abroad,' a 'soft underbelly' or a 'back yard,' slapping justifications to react to any move by others to any extent possible since Russia's security is at stake. In other words, a sure arena of the 'New Great Game' emerges as well attended if one goes by the prevailing geo-political environments in Central Eurasia or Caspian-Caucasus Region.

Potentials of Caspian Bonanza as Catalyst of Turmoil

Added to its historic geo-strategic significance since BC era, a definite overview is available by now that supplements Central Eurasian vulnerability for hot contest to the extent that some scholars have come to believe that World War III is already in the offing. That may be close to reality but an expression a little away from propriety at this juncture to spell ominous doom. The developments that lend weight to the arena of the 'New Great Game', it has been dealt with in details, are the burgeoning oil and gas riches of Caspian-Caucasus countries, emerging insecurity of supply lanes of oil and gas incidentally for the powers whose might hinges on the slushy pillars of hydrocarbon energy, the 'powers' hallucination based on their past experience of OPEC Oil Embargo of 1973, and end of oil scenario that make some predictions feasible not as a sage but by picking up certain definite pointers. One, the regions of oil and gas have become universally a major challenge to the leading 'powers' diplomacy. Two, when the interest would converge at a space, a country or a region beyond certain proportion, the diplomacy is likely to fall prey to 'frenzy' of events till such time there are hopes to stabilize the situation. Three, when the prevailing energy order cannot sustain too many actors, the energy security spectrum would degenerate in a manner that world may see visible military options being exercised by 'powers' to deny energy advantages to others that pose threat to their economic and hence 'national' interests. In fact, it may be an ugly scenario. Having seen the proven and possible hydrocarbon potentials of the Caspian, one stands wise to suggest that the region qualifies to be a perfect platform to see national and transnational struggles among the contenders, particularly when the aggravating shock of energy depletion is inevitable. The Caspian milieu already affords a maneuver space for non-native actors because of its immense geo-political fragmentation and hence an apparent urge to seek security by aligning to one power or another. When discord and disorientation plague the countries sitting over vast hydrocarbon resources, outside meddling, coercion and coaxing become a foregone conclusion. For such reasons precisely, the stage is already set and the 'New Great Game' brew is picking up to boil.

Inevitability of Oil 'Shock' and Hence of the Game

When the statistics of oil dependence of world leading economies prove that these 'powers,' hinged on oil and gas, would start gasping for breath any time around year 2020, correspondingly the game intensity will also pick up momentum. The actors have about three decades, until 2050, to adjust to energy challenges though at this moment no hope is in sight and geologists are already predicting end of the present facet of the human civilization. It is therefore logical to assume that even in Central Eurasia with host of actors surrounding the energy proverbial 'pie' that would shrink at certain point of time in magnitude, Central Eurasia may have a deep plunge into historic order and that is the 'disorder' or 'survival of the fittest'. It certainly paints horrific doom scenario.

Dangerous Portends and Symptoms

Pipeline politics is no longer a hidden component in the game. America and her allies have declared with a bang that they would not allow the oil and gas flow to the north to Russia or to the south to Iran, though these two routes, by geologists' perception, are touted as the most economical. Russia offers argument that it already possesses an infrastructure, albeit of an old vintage, to transport the oil and gas to the world market with minor refurbishing needed to upgrade its system. Iran, strangled by economic sanctions through ILSA like instruments has been ruthlessly cast away from any worthwhile role in the Caspian. Geologists agree that with Iranian oil and gas industry infrastructure in close proximity to the Caspian-Caucasus Region, it makes her most competitive conduit for the energy from the Caspian to the international market. Sheila Heslin rightly depicts this scenario "As a result, Caspian region vast energy reserves have made the region highly competitive commercial environment for the companies from the US, Europe, Russia, the Persian Gulf and Asia and have positioned it to become an important new player in the global energy market."[241] Despite being geological choice, what excludes Iran from the game is, first, that US-Iran traditional rivalry since the fall of 'Shah' seals Iranian option of energy exit. Second, that Iran in the international oil and gas market is also a competitor being a credible hydrocarbon giant. Third irritant perceived by the West is that Iran route by implication narrows down the scope of Caspian energy security because of destability continuing or resurfacing in the Gulf Region that would mean turning the Caspian source diversity practically redundant. In other words the pursued stance of interested 'power', to diversify not only the pipelines orientation as in case of Caspian Region but also to diversify sources of energy, will stand compromised. With such consideration in mind, even Caspian littorals would be hesitant to put all eggs in Iran's basket. The completion of BTC oil pipeline and SCP later for the gas has the potential to turn the oil

214

and gas flow virtually to the Western energy corridor. The matter would further aggravate if TCOP and TCGP dream comes true. It would mean perhaps, not much may be left for ASP, KCP and KKK Pipelines i.e. for the northern, southern and the eastern routes.

Widening Fault Lines and Energy Security Issues

The West now may have to modify stance and admit that such a design execution would amount to perpetuating her monopoly and thus be prepared to draw flak for substituting Russian monopoly over oil and gas pipelines. For these reasons, because Russia and Iran would bear the brunt directly, they are vocal players while China, though at relative geographical disadvantage, has also made dent into the region's share through KCP with plans for a similar gas pipeline as discussed earlier. As a euphemism, constraints have also been heaped on certain other factors to absolve some prominent players like USA, Russia and indirectly Iran. These constraints range from regional conflicts, disputed property rights, transport bottlenecks and sanctions, to the dimensions of multiparty negotiations. While most of the constraints would be forced by any pipeline project, traversing more than one country, the real one 'multi party negotiations' counts heavy among all others. It is so because it affords the actors a platform for the conduct of their game. Much touted 'security risk' for any major pipeline direction other than BTC, as Russian camp could plead, simply stands nullified because BTC direction is also riddled with similar if not even more serious security risk in war torn Georgia and its proximity to hostile Kurdish Region, assuming that Armenia may not 'shell' it unless there is a war between Azerbaijan and Armenia, a possibility high on the index. The pipeline politics, other actors see, has been pushed to the limit by America when it is harnessing its design of Caspian energy order with potent military capability by expanding NATO on the wheels of PFP clause, also additionally assigning Caucasus to her EUCOM and CENTCOM to Central Asia.

It leaves no doubt about the New Great Game. This way the security umbrella may become so over bearing for the other actors, particularly Russia, China, and Iran that it may draw their retaliation through 'devising a counterweight instrument of 'balance of power' in the region. SCO or 'NATO of the East' is one such platform, which if brought in to play its role, US unipolarity may fall in shreds, to face a hostile bipolarity, at least in Caspian-Caucasus Region. SCO has an inherent flaw that its efficacy for the years to come shall hinge on the Russian patronage and may become redundant, should Russia ever wish to ditch it while preventing the expansion of Chinese influence. Precisely for this reason, though least noticed by the world, Russia has loaded a double arrow in the bow by orchestrating in October 2002 yet another alliance called CSTO (Collective Security Treaty Organization). China is not a member. Its aim is to consolidate Russia's military control in the former Soviet space. The details so far emerging reveal, as observed by Kaczmarski that CSTO would practically take over the defense of its member states i.e. Armenia, Belarus, Kazakhstan, Kyrgyzstan, Russia and Tajikistan, which have remained the most faithful Russian allies. CSTO is made up of 20 command control units and 80 combat units including rocket regiments, air force punch and communication components to support the forces operations[242]. If SCO is being labeled as NATO of the East, CSTO has emerged undoubtedly a more formidable transparent alliance where Russia would perhaps have the liberty to unleash its punch in an obtaining situation. If SCO is the galloping battle-worthy horse perceived in certain point of time, CSTO is already fully harnessed. Russia has to jump the horse only for another saddle. These pointers lead to logical deduction that the New Great Game may accelerate from its covertly simmering phase to overtly hostile specter. There is no dearth of scholars who are already visualizing such a level of conflagration, becoming a reality.

Deceits in the Game

The unfortunate part would be that the actors, though inflicted with energy wounds, might not admit making the pipeline issues as pivot of political and diplomatic maneuver to retain high moral ground, posing that they shun the energy greed. Instead the region offers several pretexts to cash upon if the war phobia is to be built up which is an essential phase to ripen the nation's war psyche for the morale as well as moral ascendancy. Nagorno-Karabakh, Abkhazia, South Ossetia, Ingushetia, Chechnya, Caspian Legal Regime dispute, Ajaria, Dagestan, Farghana Valley's ethnic dichotomy, Azerbaijan-Iran stand off, Russo-Georgian tension, Russian military doctrine of seeking national security through CIS borders defense and host of others are the ready made recipes to ignite the Eurasian Balkan into a full fledged conflict which can spill over to Turkey, Iran, Ukraine, Russia and China. Such are the dangerous portends of the New Great Game that one would find hard to digest them. Expecting that conflict flash points, dormant so far, could be resolved through peaceful settlement of disputes, amounts to asking miracles to happen. In fact, the actors would prefer to remain equipped with 'powder keg' type capability through their influence on one or more alien territories so that they are not sidelined as and when it is time to show bargaining chips.

The Game-A Master Piece of Intricacies

The game is a masterpiece of intricacies and conflicting pursuits. When Russia and America are seen as opposing giants in isolation, Russia prefers to take Iran, Armenia and now Chinese interests along as a poly to counter the Western influence. At any stage however, if there is a threat of encroachment of interests, Russia despite being the leading actor tends to chart its individual course and hinders its own allies. Stephen Blank quotes Nurbulat Masanov, "When new transport routes, such as Trans-

Caucasus Corridor, become operational, Russia is expected to experience negative consequences... And with China, playing a larger role in Eastern part of Russia, the process is fraught with even greater unpleasantness."[243] The clash of interests proves that in ultimate analysis, none may be able to tolerate the other(s) when energy needs are translated to country-specific requirement. Russia is also blamed for engineering a coup in Turkmenistan in 2002 when prospects of its oil and gas transportation through Iran to Indian Ocean or through Afghanistan-Pakistan were becoming bright. In other words, seen in the perspective of hydrocarbon statistics and pipeline politics, the whole range of actors is assuming all their moves as 'fair' in oil and gas war. Thus emerges the haunting specter of the New Great Game that could ditch the global peace.

High Stakes of the Game and Survival Issues

Geo-strategic dimensions of the New Great Game, study of the pattern of responses by the game actors and gradation of their stakes can be arrived at with considerable accuracy. The West, personified mainly by the USA, is determined to achieve ascendancy over any other regional power, Russia, Iran and China, in the realm of transport corridor, orientation of pipelines and acquiring major shares in the hydrocarbon resources if not a sweeping monopoly. Completion of BTC pipeline, which was termed as a 'pipe dream', has vindicated its proponents, hence they are in position to dream of any other venture, and yet the public support would remain available to them being the unique achievers. The second dream venture, SCP to follow in quick succession to allow Azerbaijan export its gas from Baku to international market by connecting it to Turkish structure at Erzurum, like BTC, shall have strategic advantage for them, which if reversed, becomes a correspondingly strategic loss to Russia, Iran and China. Perhaps the West satiety for the strategic assets does not stop here. Third dream of funneling Trans-Caspian oil and gas from Kazakhstan (TCOP) and Turkmenistan (TCGP)

218

through TRACECA, that stands perfectly demarcated by BTC and SCP, would allow them consolidate their success chips. Such game maneuver has the potential to seal the fate of even other existing pipelines heading north, south or east, particularly when Caspian littorals would find free international market amenable to their bourses in stark contrast to Russia and Iranian irritants over prices issue The West is likely to remain a preferred customer on the merit of their strong currencies.

The enormity of the Western stakes, also observed by others with a grudge, becomes an open secret when 'energy security' is being given an unprecedented priority by taking elite forces like NATO, US CENTCOM and US EUCOM for executing contingencies if the energy environments are threatened by rival(s). The planning is meticulous to the levels that US has opted to afford the Caspian littorals favorable to the West, an indigenous capability through Rapid Reaction Forces, the size of which shall be commensurate to their visualized task. Raising and equipping such a brigade size rapid force of Kazakhstan Army should significantly help drawing conclusion about the extent to which US-designed security umbrella would function. It clearly acts as a pointer that the West is not only prepared to deal with rival militaries threats but also the disgruntled insurgent groups in certain territories through which the pipelines traverse. On the other end of polarity, Russia is a formidable nuclear power as well as conventional regional power. It has made clear in unambiguous terms that Russia's national security hinges on secure CIS borders. In other words, intrusion by any other forces apparatus in Central Eurasia has to be recognized by Russia, a direct threat to her national security. Russia is also well aware that loosing grip over strategic assets of oil and gas in Caspian-Caucasus region shall tantamount to be written off the influence it wields over the region. Similarly, China and Iran read Russian fate very closely to draw conclusions that their exclusion from the Caspian-Caucasus hydrocarbon riches would not only pose as an economic threat to them directly but their fate would also hinge on the 'Good Will' of the West which predominates Middle East oil sources and the sea lanes.

Overbearing Moves and Regional Powers

Overbearing maneuver by the West has come to be seen by Russia and possibly China, Iran and India as well, as an extension of the Cold War consolidation phase. Conversely the West, through an orchestrated media campaign is down playing her role in Central Eurasia, using such platforms as the necessity to help Caspian littorals benefit from their vast resources optimally, shield them from some regional hegemony, turn their sprouting democracies sustainable, establish rule of law, improve human rights record and check radical anti-West Islamic movements. In the sphere of diplomacy, one finds that some Caspian littorals are wary of Russian pressure. Such proclaimed motives put forth by the Western media have definite appeal. However, it does not meet the analysts' query whether the West could have gone that far to help Caspian-Caucasus Region in achieving their stated objectives if it was devoid of strategic energy assets. Conclusion certainly points to the 'negative' because some vast stretches of barren land and their starving people in Africa remain the lingering test of human compassion. The assessment of military situation suggests that Russia still has an edge over the West. Maintaining naval presence at Astrakhan, Caspian Sea for moving any force remains under its sway. Similar facility is also available to Iran from its Caspian Seaport of Neka. Russia either has contiguous borders or is in close proximity to all Central Eurasian countries. While breakaway movements plague her, she is capable to stoke insurgencies in several Central Eurasian regions that US, already overstretched in its military ventures, might find hard to contest and enforce even a semblance of peace. In the geographic advantage, Russia along with Iran is one of the five Caspian littorals and thus in comfortable position to play Caspian Legal Regime card at any forum. Last but not the least, Russia as well as Iran collaborate on all strategic issues against the West while both are major hydrocarbon-powers with capacity to out class the West. Russian proven oil reserves, 72 Gb, added to Iran's proven oil reserves, 132 Gb, if combined means both collectively possess over 17% of the world oil. Similarly, in gas inventory, Russian proven reserves of 1,694 tcf if combined with Iran's 971 tcf, place them in a very happy situation to own 42% of the world proven gas reserves. It therefore leads to a plausible conclusion that the New Great Game not only involves high stakes and intensity in the fold, but the survival of the current levels of power potentials as well.

Compounding the Game Arena

China and India are considered late but direct entrants in game arena. Indian efforts to seek share in the oil and gas fields and buy oil companies generally in competition with China come as no surprise to the world because it has to maintain its $560 billion economy as per year 2003 estimates and its growth rate, 6.4% as of 2004. India, other than launching itself in the New Great Game has shown the diplomacy flair for making best out of the situation prevailing on the Central Eurasian periphery. Her possible oil and gas pipelines options already talked about render her maneuver space that it would consume to the hilt to extract concessions from USA, Iran, Russia and Pakistan. As long as she milks the situation, her ambivalence, 'on' today and 'off' tomorrow with the project prospects, would continue to reap enormous dividends in the economic and foreign policy spheres. Similarly, China sees intrusions in Caspian-Caucasus region by the West as unwarranted in the present volume and intensity that is in fact likely to grow. By coincidence in the overall energy perception at the New Great Game level, China finds Iran, Russia and to an extent Pakistan as natural allies but in minor details it may be scared of the notions what Russia and Iran perceive about its influence. Therefore her game maneuver has to be very calculated

221

against the West as well as Russia, Iran and Caspian-Caucasus countries, knowing at the same time its vulnerabilities that could become exploitation pivots against China. Her share seeking of energy fields in Africa, Middle East and Central Eurasia is clearly understood as the compulsory option since she has to ensure growth of $1.41 trillion size economy, which for 2004 was recorded to grow at the rate of 8.1%. In fact, China by virtue of its size of economy, military and geo-strategic potentials, is considered, as a potent threat to the West globally though the West pursued demonstrated stance would remain 'keep China engaged'. Alive to her strategic fuel assets vulnerability, China's purchase of Kazakh's oil company, stalking for Russia's Rosneft Company and US Unocal are strong indicators to conclude that China would not only endeavor to secure favorable pipeline infrastructure but shall pile up heavy stakes at oil and gas fields as well as technology.

Seeing the overbearing West in the Caspian-Caucasus Region, China and Russia, the two powerful members of SCO will be drifting nearer, allaying other members fear as well as rendering them hope that the mechanism can become guaranteed shield against threat what CARs (less Turkmenistan not being SCO member) face internally and externally. Given the optimum military capability, SCO is likely to become an effective counterweight to the Western military capability allocated to Central Eurasia. Though Chinese border disputes with Russia are losing gravity, it nevertheless maintains a formidable force in her Western Xingjian province including the nuclear capability. Russia and China being a part of Central Eurasia would stand at advantage in point of time if ever assembly of forces were to be executed vis-à-vis the Western forces system that will have to secure base(s) of operations in territories, not always pliant to them except a narrow segment of the authoritarian rulers. With such a colossal degree of machinations, some already enacted and some clearly looming large on the horizon, the complexity of the New Great Game will multiply with least hope from any actor to retract her stance. While conflict options predominantly show up consequently, denial scenario of energy share to a particular actor or a group would also sound death knell for them. As the events and the shades are unfolding; the actors are likely to be drawn to 'conflict' scenario willingly rather than deliberately drifting away from conflict, an option that has least luster or incentive for them. The limitation ridden scenario of the New Great Game in such a backdrop enables to draw a logical conclusion that none among the 'Titans' in the arena may emerge as 'Titus'[244].

Caspian-Caucasian Rulers are the Party by Default

Hypothesizing that some extraordinary favorable development forces a sort of a glimmer of hope, contrary to the growing crunch of the New Great Game, it may be apt to dilate on frequently but briefly aforementioned Caspian littorals discord, orientation dichotomy, fractured mutual relations and fear of state collapse, described already in 'regional perception inequities'. The reviews so far have led to conclusions that portray very dangerous portends for which 'destability' would be a prerequisite. A query may be pertinently raised to determine, what Caspian-Caucasus countries can contribute to achieving stability because the 'destability' conditions and their ongoing groping for viable orientation are right now under analysts observation and hence need to be meditated upon. "Initially, at home as well as abroad, there had been general assumption that the newly independent Caspian states had already reached such a high level of socio-economic development that they would have little difficulty in making the transitions from the Soviet system to Western political and economic model. During the 1990's it became increasingly clear that it was not happening."[245] The causes, which deny the Caspian-Caucasus transition, not to afford them the excuse of conflict flash points, are in all probability their own doing, self-generated and rulers have no inclination to relent on them. If dissolution of the Soviet Union left them in vacuum and also exposed to such severe challenges that they failed to chart out a viable course but the rulers, generally the extension of communist legacy, considered it a boon as well. The state concerns were sidelined in favor of individual concerns whether these were of political, financial or social implications. Under these circumstances when their economies soared under the petrodollar push, particularly from the mid nineties onward, the resource rich states were victim to the traditional malady that has the history of gripping such countries. It is nicknamed as Dutch Disease, Paradox of Plenty, Economic Indigestion or 'Devil's Excrement'. When the oil revenue made easy gains, all the states ignored development of other crucial sectors. As a result, oil monoculture developed that could not mitigate such phantom issues like diverse education needs and massive unemployment because entire state activity gravitated on energy sector.

Beside the lingering leadership legacy of communist era, an evil called 'blat'[246] also passed on to the governing mechanism, which took monstrous shape of seething 'corruption'. It is clear to visualize the fall out effects emanating out of corruption. State mechanism of governance became crippled. Emergence of elite class and mafias introduced elements of social injustice and deprivation. Rich got richer and poor went down the poverty drain. It led to burgeoning of illegal economy. Alec Rasizade's commentary fits well to portray the prevailing situation once he asserted that such is the native mentality characterized by pervasive corruption and of course personal profiteering by those with political powers who have the tendency to view national wealth as a pool from which to draw individual fortunes[247]. When such social syndrome gain criticality, it thus becomes convenient to conclude that Caspian-Caucasus societies stand extremely fragmented with tendency to build on smaller ethnic divisions for seeking social security which ordinarily should have been the state obligation. The rulers in all states, because of corrupt and 'above the law' status turned unpopular with passing of each day. Repression works for a while but there are true voices that find way upward which are certainly ear grating for them. Under several pretexts, they resorted to repression tactics, putting even the Bolsheviks history of tyranny to shame. It is the characteristic of dictators that instead of listening to reason, they are inflated by their cronies in misplaced ego and expanding 'hubris'. As an exercise of survival, being weak internally and lacking popular support, in the frame of the New Great Game all of them had no choice but to be pliant to any actor approaching them and assuring them personal security, lease of governance and stocking their coffers with dollars, generally in the Swiss banks. In other words, their role in crystallizing the New Great Game stands collectively to the same volume and intensity as any other actor performing 'game' maneuver, focused on respective interests. Divided thus, they remain as pawns on the Central Eurasian chessboard. With such a collective plight, the New Great Game arena will stay very conducive to the regional and extra regional actors. A mere wish by Central Eurasian states that they prefer multi-lateralism and are averse to see the clash of 'Titans' in their court yards shall not have even an iota of deterrence unless their leadership comes up to match these facts with honest acts, always keeping people cause before 'self'. At the earliest they learn, how to resist the glitters of wealth and squandering of their strategic assets, the better it would be for their masses ultimately.

The New Great Game is in Full Swing

When short-listing the actors of the New Great Game who have stamina to survive longer in the arena with the requisite perseverance, a trio emerges on the scene i.e. USA, Russia and China. There is an exclusive brand of scholars which is projecting optimism that the trio in strategic dimensions have the commonalities to the extent that an agreed consensus and cooperation will prevail and the simmering tension would fade away. However, the scenarios discussed so far point to the probabilities on the contrary. Scholars, with their benign and humanitarian approaches are compelled to see some stark threats as less daunting. Thus, they wrap the threats with flexible logic to dab their intensity. A perfect humane tendency but when the 'threats' achieve undue magnitude and become all too evident, not sounding warning about them may be placed as scholarly negligence. It is the negligence part, which may encourage the actors to expand on their mutual obstinacy. Three fundamental omissions lead us to conclude that the New Great Game shall exacerbate and not abate in near future[248]:

- US legitimacy in the Caspian-Caucasus Region has emerged as an extremely controversial issue. Having punished the 'Taliban' and won an easy war in Afghanistan, Russia and China see little justification for the lingering US military presence in the Central Asia. Though for the public consumption, US has made clear that her military advantage thus achieved is not to be directed against any regional power, Russia and China with long history of mutual suspicions stay wary of American perpetuating military presence, whatever is the pretext.

- There exists no viable mechanism that could afford them a platform of dialogue to engage each other. Even in this context, America has, for its public consumption, underlined the need to take Russia and China along but her deeds have shocked Russia as well as China. Once they see America planning to squeeze every drop or bubble of oil and gas away from the Caspian-Caucasus Region, it needs no prophet to prophecy her ultimate designs. To top it all, elaborate secret plans are being churned out to allocate military effort as a contingency to 'diversify' oil and gas transport routes as well as the sources. Russia and China are likely to come to the brink soon to believe that in US lexicon 'monopoly' has been substituted with 'diversity'.

- The analysts see deplorably that no road map yet exists to put the New Great Game genie back to the bottle. In fact, the Western camp has not even admitted that their struggle in the Caspian sphere of hydrocarbons, presents even more devastating and complicated analogy than the Great Game of the 19th Century. Zhao Huasheng observes, "Russia, China and the US stand like a triad in Central Asia but with no path for them to get together."[249] Russia and China are modest to spell the doom because, should they speak out loudly, even their native intellectuals would put them on the dock for accelerating the game, as do the Western writers toward USA. The New Great Game, intensely supported by grave but practical maneuvers shall not fade away by ignoring any reference to it. In fact it might surface as a bombshell. While the drop scene of the New Great Game is not difficult to perceive, logic variants will remain about the point of time only.

With these kinds of drawbacks, the triad suffers; little doubt is left about the hollowness of the perceived approach of those who ephemerally sound optimistic. Their conclusions draw largely from the ability of these powers to cooperate during the events of mega crisis. In case of Russo-US relationship, at the occurrence of 9/11 holocaust, President Vladimir Putin was among the first foreign leaders to pledge her country's support to George W Bush in the war against terrorism. Russia also confirmed its prompt approval to concede to the US plan of using former Soviet bases in Central Asia as forward locations during US led war in Afghanistan. Both the powers extended every possible military and logistical support to Northern Alliance, an anti-Taliban native outfit, who acted as the coalition forces' scout for the land as well as air operations. It was a unique opportunity that Russia harvested. One, by active cooperation, it enabled Russia to gain remarkable stature as a responsible power at international fora. Two, letting US slip in the quicksand desert called Afghanistan, where Russia had received a bleeding nose only over a decade ago, Russia straightened her score over US supporting the erstwhile 'holy warriors'. Three, US made Russia see Taliban bashing by US forces in such a short span of reversed history, which could otherwise remain her fond dream for centuries. Four, accusations being heaped on Russia to be ruthlessly suppressing Chechens freedom movement by launching incessant military operations were totally wiped off for the time being. However, the US President, who had entered office, "to proceed with foreign policy and military initiatives that were known to displease Moscow, including the eastward expansion of NATO, the abrogation of Anti-Ballistic Missiles Treaty and the establishment of National Missile Defense System,"[250] found it tempting to oscillate rather to a positive stance towards Russia and move hand-in-glove after 9/11. The spirit of cooperation, as Russia perceived, was bound to collapse on conspicuous expansion of American military presence in the Caspian-Caucasus Region. It did not confine itself to demurring only but moved practically by locating potent air force contingent at its base, near US air base at Manas, Kyrgystan. Russia beefed up security forces presence in Tajikistan and her naval fleet for Caspian Sea. To counter her loss of ground in Georgia after ouster of Eduard Shiverdnadze, Russia appeared inclined to renege on its promise to vacate a Georgian air base. Obviously, it afforded her the capability to register her role effectively in Southern Caucasus. With such dangerous military moves, for which Russia cannot be exonerated of its responsibility of hammering the fragile fiber of balance of power in Central Eurasia either, though compelled to react, it is not hard to conclude that Caspian-Caucasus Region is another potentially threatening arena that would haunt the world peace through its manifestation as the, New Great Game.

Some hinge hope on EU that may emerge as an honest broker in the whole issue but the Union is also a 'dependent' force on the good will of Caspian-Caucasus region players, Iran and Russia included. Her capacity to evolve any mechanism, whatever the noble intentions it maintains, shall rest on the degree of cooperation the regional powers extend to it and the scale of flexibility US would demonstrate. At the moment, no such symptoms are visible. Thus, the observers find it logical to see striking similarity between the Gulf and Caspian Regions and that is their conflict potentials among the actors, which would be triggered by the relentless pursuit of achieving a sort of near monopoly over the strategic assets by the great powers. The unfortunate part is that soon a stage would arrive when, as one sees enormous stakes of these great powers piled up in Central Eurasia, more they would struggle to manage the conflict risk, more they are likely to drift towards it. Latest events in Georgia and Ukraine are only the advance indicators. In other words, with some variation in the magnitude of involvement of all actors, big or small, they may be igniting the cauldron, probably unwittingly. While Russia and China's involvement out of the triad is stupendous, US military expenditure, likely to cross \$150 billion a year for the Gulf, Caspian and Colombia, affords an empirical proof that 1/3 of her total defense budget is consumed in these ventures. Such a quantified involvement in the Greater Gulf or the Broader Middle East, of which Caspian Region is being considered as its integral part, leaves little doubt that grand designs are subjective tools of promoting grand supremacy that has come largely to hinge on Caspian strategic assets as well. The scenario further becomes haunting, as US energy import bill would be touching \$3.5 trillion mark from 2001-2025.[251] Based on these indicators, the intensity of actors' maneuvers has to yield further in rabidity on the onset of and during permanent foreseen energy crisis. It may be pertinent to quote Michael Klare, "Several new developments account for this new and dangerous reality. The first is the risk of chronic petroleum shortage. The second is the surging demand for oil and gas from the newly industrialized countries, especially China and India. The third is recurring turmoil in the major oil-producing regions, leading to shortfalls in output and deliveries. And the fourth is the noticeable lack of progress in limiting energy use and in developing alternatives to the existing oil intensive energy system. These factors were certainly present when I wrote, Blood and Oil' but in the year they have become far more pronounced."[252] Put all these ingredients in a grind and the monstrous scenario, in the light of preceding arguments, emerges undisputedly as the 'New Great Game'. A point to note is that of late where reference to oil is made in Central Eurasia; a concomitant allusion to 'blood' also follows... a 'finding' though unfortunate but christened by reality[253].

CHAPTER-SEVEN

RECOMMENDING A SYNOPSIZED WAY-OUT STRATEGY

Cool Down the Cauldron

The magnitudes of powers' worry about fast depletion of oil and inevitable oil shock around mid 21st Century, no sane person on God's earth would disagree about the need to cool the cauldron down. The Caspian-Caucasus Region in particular, in the context of the 'New Great Game' and Eurasia in general have emerged prominent that are picking up heat much faster than perhaps the global warming ghost, which haunts us with no less intensity. While both the menaces are potent enough to sound death knell to the humankind as a deplorable consequential tragedy, fingers unfortunately, point to powers, euphemistically speaking, that are not mustering desired level of responsibility they owe to the planet.

Analytical study of geo-strategic dimensions of the 'New Great Game', actors' role and ambitions and accruing conclusions augment our belief that the region is simmering with latent heat of hostile posturing. The internal and external dynamics of dormant as well as manifest conflict flash points are not only the direct threats to 'peace' but also remain the stumbling block whenever any effort, albeit rudimentary in scale and sincerity, is launched to address any issue in isolation. In Caspian-Caucasus Region as long as Caspian Sea Legal Regime and other issues like Nagorno-Karabakh, Abkhazia, South Ossetia, Dagestan,

Chechnya, shifting pipelines' orientation to the West, intra border demarcation disputes, tremendous deficit of good governance and abuse of human rights shall prevail, ominous discord, with potential to lead to the complicated chemistry of conflicts shall loom large on the Region's horizon. The external dynamics of the game are no less complex. Unfortunately, when the specter of end of fossil fuel or the ability of hostile masses to disrupt energy supplies stalk the might of some powers; the divisive scenario in Central Eurasia readily affords them a perfect wedge to clobber the obtaining situation to cut out respective power games no matter how myopic they are.

Application and extension of the Carter Doctrine, NATO, OSCE, SCO, CSTO, GUUAM, US CENCOM, US EUCOM and the emergence of particular axis-based diplomacy has rendered the breathing space for 'peace' extremely narrow. Interestingly all the discordant voices sound values irrespective of the perception-orientation they maintain towards each other. Conversely, the new generation of concepts in International Relations has emerged with highly controversial tag called, 'globalization'. Anthony Mcgrew defines it as "a historical process which involves the widening, deepening, speeding up and growing impact of worldwide interconnectedness."[254] Four theories supporting this phenomenon are proven with fine logic. Nevertheless, it does not escape the careful scrutiny to raise plethora of queries, some skeptic enough to explore answers to, is globalization a positive or negative development. Is it the latest stage of capitalist development? Does it make the state obsolete? Is globalization merely western imperialism in a new guise?[255] The irony of fate is that while the candid side of globalization is not even understood by the masses in Central Eurasia; its negative impact has already struck them with varying degree of intensity through globalization license, the actors waive to them. This makes the scenario rather horrendous when the New Great Game is likely to thrust forward by the contenders under the label of several ethics, coined exclusively to muffle the negative side that points to possible conflagration. Thus, recommendation in reverse is apt to suggest that evolve a strategy to cool down the simmering cauldron, tackling the catalysts of turmoil one by one judiciously but in a sure-footed manner.

Mushrooming of several security apparatuses in the region, discussed earlier, point emphatically that no common platform is available to address the energy issue effectively. In fact, willful, blatant neglect by the actors, not even admitting that energy-triggered threat of conflicts exists, points to the need that world intellectuals must take a dispassionate stock of the emerging situation. Think-tanks' efforts sponsored by institutes of particular leaning that are busy round the clock to sweep every grain of 'cordite' under the rug is certainly not a viable option. They are the architects of horrible powder keg sort of device themselves. Need of the hour is that the scholars, who have reputation to pursue conscientious approaches; no matter how hard they hit influential countries or organizations, must teem up their energies to cool the cauldron down. A realistic diagnosis would tantamount to first success in remedying the dysfunctional system.

Evolve a Viable Energy Regulation Platform

The prognostic pursuits, as relevant to this region where the 'New Great Game' is being played, would certainly claim success even if the 'will' to tackle scores of rampant issues is pooled in by the influential actors and international organizations simultaneously; admitting in the first instance, the urgency with which they need to commence their effort. By implication thus, stepping stone stage would be reached to take on the resolution strategies. It amounts to asking for moon if one recommends that through a magic wand touch; resolve the region's thorny issues at once. It would certainly be a wish, perhaps next to impossible. What is needed to shape the crisis management strategy pillars; that would logically lead us to certain plausible approaches?

- Devise a common platform; say Platform Alpha or P-A, integrating all actors of the New Great Game under the auspices of UN charter that will predominantly employ 'diplomacy' as a mean to promote understanding of the issues which plague Central Eurasia in the realm of energy security. Other regional or non-regional organizations casting ominous shadows of the New Great Game should vanish altogether or become corollary to UN, P-A's mechanism.
- The above would be feasible only if the existing security instruments, operating in the region or on its periphery are relegated in substance and purpose. It will enable suspecting actors on all sides to concentrate on their role within the frame of new platform, P-A, without any intimidation or hassle.
- The target states that sit on vast energy resources must be treated on merit and no alien power be allowed to abet the authoritarian regimes' efforts of survival that are wreaking havoc on their own masses in return for allowing the aliens a monopoly over their resources.
- If the oil and gas export diverse orientation can become a soothing phenomenon, it must be attempted in letter and spirit by accounting for each drop or bubble of oil and gas going the diverse ways. No single power should be allowed to hijack earlier 'monopoly' by the Soviets under the pretext of diversifying the energy exit routes.
- Energy must be delinked from the list of tools employed for arm twisting of rival states. Like an 'ambulance' bearing 'Crescent' or 'Red Cross' mark, it must go through barriers without having to stop for the approving nod of any country that intends implementing an imperial strategy or grand energy policy of its own brand.
- The world community must be educated to conserve energy and the large consumers encumbered with responsibility to develop alternate energy resources. UN, P-A should even consider commencing global rationing system for collective supplies and gradually

cut down the oil and gas-guzzler countries' quota to force them implementing passive as well as active measures. They would thus learn to live within the rationalized energy parameters.

- Alien forces must pack off from the region, no matter how convincing their pretexts are to stay. Such a move by P-A shall obviate the actors' ambitions to militarize Central Eurasia, the retaliatory moves largely taken as counter to other power(s).

- P-A must take up the lingering territorial or ethnic disputes; one by one; thus augmenting peace in Central Eurasia. P-A has to devise a mechanism in its charter that 'axis' syndrome of powerful countries does not impede its efforts and thus render it ineffective, no matter which hemisphere it belongs to or how influential that country may be.

- The representation mode of the actors and consumer nations can be worked out by categorizing all countries into A, B and C levels. For instance, 'A' category countries are those, 42 in number that sit over 98% of total world oil and gas. Grant category 'B' to next 70 countries possessing the remaining 2% of total oil and gas. Category 'C' will comprise the other countries on the UN inventory in the capacity of consumers only. Hallmark of the total exercise has to hinge on transparency and justice to ensure that energy resources acquisition as well as distribution contributes to regional as well as global 'peace' and 'stability' through reconciliatory approaches and not brandishing of arms.

Rethink and Re-align Energy Policies

Suggesting some workable mechanism to ensure energy security in Caspian-Caucasus Region or in Middle East, even in embryonic form as above, is certainly not a new phenomenon. Experts in this field have been attempting certain recipes once driven by the conflict symptoms of varied intensity. Robert M. Cutler did so in 1999; recommending evolution of Eurasian Oil and Gas Association (EAOGA), largely based on the possible lessons from the imminent conflicts. He wrote that EAOGA..., a dedicated association of governmental, non-governmental and intergovernmental organizations that would rally all levels of world society responds to Western interests in the newly independent states. It is possible with or without Russia.[256] No matter how sagely these prescriptions are worded, the shortfall in a sample proposition as that of Robert M. Cutler above hinges on defective chassis. See that his entire perception envisions response to 'the Western' interests only 'with or without' Russia. It is a fact that the West has developed economies and America had been oil and gas giant whose oil production went past the 'peak' in 1970 but the statement by Robert M. Cutler is rather simplistic. He accords no recognition to ground realities that raise the dilemma of energy security and accompanied grievance of exploitation and blackmail of the oil rich region like Caspian and its neighbors, which are buying the West's' expanding level of animosity. Only from this brief logic, one assumes that such a vision would lack any luster. The second segment of the statement 'with or without Russia' smacks of arrogance of the kind with which America is pursuing its energy strategy. World knows that Russia, a Eurasian power and direct actor in the New Great Game holds formidable position when it owns 6.1% of the proven oil reserves of the world total away from Caspian-Caucasus Region and 26.7% of gas proven reserves of the world total. Iran already excluded under the US influence through several kind of machinations, holds 11.1% of proven oil reserves and 15.7% of proven gas reserves of the world total. If the option to clobber a mechanism 'without' these countries is exercised, that would mean the world has missed 17.2% of proven oil reserves and 42.4% of proven gas reserves of the world total. Any mechanism, no matter how elaborately cut out, is bound to crash like a bumblebee without the two crucial regional powers like Russia and Iran. 'With or

236

without' and 'going alone' syndrome has pushed such powers like USA into the precipitated conflicts several thousands of kilometers away from their mainland. Its endeavor to be present and strong everywhere has inevitably led it to strategic overstretch and thus weakened everywhere. American soldiers are shedding blood on the black tar swamps in the regions, particularly in the Persian Gulf where oil conflict is picking up intensity than abating by any degree. As already said, America stands out as lone super power and anything going askew anywhere on the globe draws her opposition for its ability or disability to control the smoldering arena. For the Caspian Region, US is caught in the cross criticism for the same reasons otherwise other actors' ambitions discussed earlier, are not less malignant.

The experts of the caliber like that of Michael T. Klare's opinion about US options in the region sounds reason, "Politically and morally the price will be just as steep to retain our access to oil and secure permission to deploy our troops where we deem them necessary, in oil rich states as…Azerbaijan, Kazakhstan and Uzbekistan. We will have to crawl into bed with some of the worlds most corrupt and despotic leaders … And the numerous victims of those regimes will come to view America not as standard-bearer of democracy but as a greedy prop of dictatorship."[257] Though one would agree with his list of the countries partially that forced me to omit some in the quote by hopping over, he nevertheless, gave considerable concession to other a few that deserve to be called 'despotic' through and through. In fact by the time he wrote thus, America already stood soaked in such stigma. In the preceding chapters, US energy policy has been amply discussed as fractured one. It is therefore imperative for her and for other actors to probe pitfalls in respective energy policies. As for America, scholars are increasingly and impatiently suggesting her to delink energy pursuits and commitment to foreign governments, a venture worth billion of dollars and thousands of Americans corpses falling on the most hostile territories. The world would heave a sigh of relief if America picked up an added sense of responsibility, above its myopic gains. By implication, other lesser but lethal actors shall become focus of global scrutiny, leaving them no choice but to emulate USA in evolving peaceful energy strategies. Prevalence of diplomacy imperatives as opposed to intrusion strategies will then emerge as a logical phenomenon. Earlier these anomalies are eliminated, better for the world peace through obtaining stability in Central Eurasia.

Inward Containment Measures

It is not only the inevitability of death of 'King Oil" and "Queen Gas" by mid 21st Century that haunts the planet but also the issue sparks awesome streaks of pain and despair in another field of concern, that is universal environmental degradation. Reference to preceding tables proves that world total oil consumption increase over 2003 was registered as 3.4% in 2004. Similarly, in the sphere of gas the increase for the same duration has been 3.3%. The pace of consumption increase universally, if seen exclusively through prism of environments presents unsustainable risk at the hand of ever growing levels of carbon emissions that directly threaten the mother earth. Scientists see added frequency and intensity of earthquakes, floods, cyclones, drought, desertification, glaciers melting at abnormal rapid rate and incessant rains in certain parts of the world as unexplained phenomenon that leads to single culprit i.e. earth warming due to expanding scales of energy consumption. As if it was not enough, when some countries are facing energy crunch after sky rocketing prices, they are naturally inclined to dig deeper and wider to bring back 'King Coal' that was dethroned in the beginning of 20th Century. It is irony that coal, which remains a formidable pollutant in the face of limited technologies available to most countries to render it clean, has become the choice source despite its potential to damage the environments critically. As a result, its increased consumption in 2004 over 2003 was registered as almost twice the scale of oil or

238

gas i.e. 6.7% for that year. Here again some of the leading actors of the New Great Game incidentally are the leading coal consumers. USA consumes 20.3% and China alone consumes 34.4% of the world total. For the same reason, EU, Canada, Japan and a few others only, though ratified by about 180 countries to protect the world degradation of environments, embraced the Kyoto Treaty, wholeheartedly. Conversely some scholar opine that the leading champ had the continuing honor to stall this treaty to protect US citizens' indulgence for the energy in exchange for its formidable role in killing the planet. It seems certain that no one could nudge America to compliance or cooperation in such treaties because their 'big business' and 'military' do not approve of it. "Estimates by various US think-tanks and Republican-oriented consulting groups have heaped on the bad news, arriving at figures of 3,300 billion dollars of lost national output through to 2020; if the US were to ratify and apply the treaty from 2010. Perhaps worst of all, some shocked defenders of US integrity and world role (that is, its war capacity) discovered mainly by imagination that ratifying this Treaty would severely hamper national security..."[258] There is no doubt that price to pay for conserving the energy to cut down dependence on imports, cutting carbon emission level and discovery of the efficient and clean fuels, will be extremely exorbitant. Yet, earlier the world, particularly the leading actors took the inevitable bitter pill, that much larger and swifter relief to the planet will accrue. Reduced dependence on imported oil and gas shall also cause them an element of sobriety and enable them to cast away hallucinations that are now main drivers of their fractured energy policies, sought and implemented through, in exchange of very precious 'blood'.

BIBLIOGRAPHY

Abrams, M.A and Narimanov, A.A; "Geo-chemical Evaluation of Hydrocarbons and Their Potential Sources in the Western, South Caspian Depression, Republic of Azerbaijan," Maritime and Petroleum Geology: 14(4), 1997.

Ajam, Mohammad, "Names of the Caspian", Payam-e-Darya No.131, October 2004 (CNetiranArticlesCultureIranologyNames of the Caspian Sea.htm)

Akiner, Shirin, (Ed): The Caspian: Politics, Energy and Security, Routledge Curzon, Taylor & Francis Group, Oxford shire-London, 2004.

Akiner, Shirin: Islamic People of Soviet Union; 2nd, London: Keg and Paul International, 1986.

Amineh, Mehdi Parvizi: Towards the Control of Oil Resources in the Caspian Region; St. Martin's Press, New York-1999.

Asaf, K M and Barakat, Abdul: Central Asia: Internal and External Dynamics, Pan Graphics (pvt) ltd Islamabad -1997

Atabaki, Touraj; Kane, John O: Post-Soviet Central Asia; Taurus Academic Studies, London, New York, 1998.

Azmat, Hayat Khan, Dr, "Central Asia-A Geo-Strategic Analysis, "Central Asia Journal No.46; Area Study Center University of Peshawar; Pakistan, 1999.

Azmat Hayat Khan, Dr, "Russia and Central Asian Republics," Central Asia Journal No.43, Area Study Center, University of Peshawar, 1997.

Azmat, Hayat Khan, Dr, "The Game of Oil and Security in Central Eurasia", Central Asia. No. 52, Summer, Area Study Center, University of Peshawar, 2003.

Azmat, Hayat Khan, Dr,"Oil and Security in Central Asia and the Caspian Region," "Central Asia Journal No.50." Summer, Area study Center, University of Peshawar, 2002.

Azmat Hayat Khan, Dr, "Ethnic Factor in Central Asian Republics", Central Asia Journal No.47 (Area Study Center, University of Peshawar 2000.

Baev, Pavel; "Russian's Happiness in Multiple Pipeline"; Analyst; Central Asia Caucasus Institute, June 2004.

Banerjee, Neela, "For Exxon Mobil Size is a Strength and a Weakness", New York Times, March 4, 2003.

Banuazizi, A and Wiener M (Eds): The New Geo Politics of Central Asia and the Borderlands; IB Taurus London, New York. 1999.

Bartlett, Albert A, "An Analysis of US and World Oil Production in Patterns Using Hubbert Style Curves," Mathematical Geology, Vol.32. No.1, 2000, Department of Physics, University of Colorado, Boulder, Colorado, USA.

Beckwith, Christopher I: The Tibetan Empire in Central Asia: A History of the   Struggle for the Great Power among Tibetan, Turks, Arabs and Chinese During Early Middle Ages; Princeton University Press, 1987

Baylis, John & Smith, Steve (Eds): Globalization of World Politics; 3rd, Oxford University Press Inc New York, 2006

Bendersky, Yergeny, "Russia in SCO", Power and Interest News Report; PINR,"(www.pinr.com), 3 November 2005

Betta, Chiara "Xingjian or Eastern Turkistan: The Conundrum of Chinese Central Asia" Central Asia Journal No.50, Area Study Center, University of Peshawar, 2002.

Blum, Douglas "The Sustainable Development and the

New Oil Boom: Comparative and Competitive Outcome in the Caspian Sea," Working Paper Series No. 4, Harvard University, 1997.

Brawer, Moshe: Atlas of Russia and Independent Republics; Simon and Schuster, New York, 1994.

Brownback, Sam (Senator), "US Economic and Strategic Interests in the Caspian Sea Region," Caspian Crossroads (US)" Vol. 3, Issue No. 2, Fall 1997, accessed www.ourworld.compuserve.com.homepage, 14 January 2004.

Brzezinski, Zbigniew: The Grand Chessboard: American Primacy and its Geo-Strategic Imperatives, New York Basic Books: 1997.

Bur Leigh, Nina, "Missing the Oil Story," The Washington Post, 12 October 2001.

Capisani, Giampaolo R: The Handbook of Central Asia; IB Taurus Publishers, London, New York 2000.

Caspian Oil: not the Great Game Revisited, Strategic Survey 1997/98, International Institute for Strategic Studies; London 1998.

Ceragioli, Paola and Martellini, Maurizio, "The Geopolitics of Pipelines," Asian Times: 29 May 2003 (www.atimes.com)

Cheney, Dick, "Defending Liberty in Global Economy," (Speech) Cato Institute, 23 June 1998

Chomsky, Noam, "Towards A New Cold War', the New Press, New York, 2003.

Christian, David: A History of Russia, Central Asia and Mongolia; Vow-I, Blackwell Publishers 1998.

Coe, Charles, "Sea's Legal Status Remains beyond Grasp of Caspian Leaders," News and Trends Central Asia; Vol. 7. No: 10, 16 May 2002.

Cohen, Marjorie, "Cheney's Black Gold: Oil Interest May Drive US Policy," The Chicago Tribune, 10 August 2000.

Cordesman, Anthony H: The Lessons of Afghanistan: War Fighting, Intelligence and Force Transformation; Vanguard Books (Pvt) Ltd, Lahore Pakistan-2003

Cornell, Svante, "The Caucasian Conundrum and the Geopolitics of Conflict," <u>Marco Polo Magazine</u> No. 4. May 2000.

Country Analysis Brief, "The Caspian Sea Region", EIA, US Department of Energy, December 2004 (eia.doe.gov)

Croissant, Michael P; Aras, Bulent (Eds), "<u>Oil and Geopolitics in Caspian Sea Region;</u> Praeger, Westport, Connecticut, London-1999.

Dorian, James P, "<u>Minerals, Energy and Economics Development in China,</u>" Oxford University Press, Oxford, 1994

Dorian, James P., "China and Central Asia's Volatile Mix: Energy, Trade and Ethnic Relations," <u>East-West Center</u> No. 31 May 1997.

Duncan, Richard C; Youngquist, Walter "OPEC Oil Pricing and Independent Oil Producers," Presentation at PTTC Workshop, Petroleum Technology Transfer Council, Petroleum Engineering Programme, University of South California, Los Angeles, California-1998

Dyke, Van "Oil Production: West Africa May Overtake Saudi Arabia", <u>Vanguard</u> (Newspaper), Lagos, 23 November 2002.

Ebel, Robert; Menon, Rajan (Eds): <u>Energy and Conflicts in Central Asia and Caucasus:</u> Rowman & Littlefield Publishers Inc, 2000.

Energy Information Administration, US Department of Energy (<u>www.eia.doe.gov</u>) 10 Dec 2003

Endghal, William, "Central Asia, Washington and Beijing Energy Goe-Politics," <u>Open Caucasus Forum,</u> (<u>www.globalresearch.ca/index),</u> December19 2005.

Escobar, Pepe; "Pipelinistan, Part 1: The Rule of the Game," <u>Asia Times,</u> (atimes.com) 24 August 2004.

Farwick, Dieter "Globalized Geopolitics in 21st Century" <u>WSN News Letter,</u> World Security Network Foundation, New York, www.worldsecuritynetwork.com, 24 August 2005.

Fest, Joachim C: Hitler, (Trans), Richard and Clara Winston, Penguine Books, 1973

Forbes, R J: Studies in Early Petroleum History; Lei den, E J Brills, 1958.

Forsythe, Rosemarie, "The Politics of Oil in the Caucasus and Central Asia," Oxford University Press Inc New York, 1996.

Gibbs, H. A. R: The Arabs Conquest in Central Asia, AMS Press, London, 1970

Gleason, Gregory "Upstream Downstream: The Difficulties of Central Asian Water and Energy Swaps," Eurasianet.org February 6, 2001

Gokay, Bulent (Ed): The Politics of Caspian Oil: Palgrave Publishers Ltd.2001.

Hanson, Jay, "The End of Fossil Fuels," (Die off. Org) 8 March 2003

Henry, J.D: Baku: An Eventful History; Archibald Constable & CO, London, 1986

Herring, Eric: Danger and Opportunity: Explaining International Crisis Outcomes, Manchester University Press, Manchester and New York, 1995.

Heslin, Sheila N, "Key Constraints to Caspian Pipeline Development: Status, Significance and Outlook," James A Baker Public Policy Paper: Caspian Sea Library (www.eia.doe.gov) 8 February 2004

Holms, Olive, "Thesis to book: What to do with what is left", in Harman, Eleanor and Montagnes, Ian (Eds): The Thesis and the Book; Vistaar Publications, New Delhi, 1987.

Huasheng, Zhao "China, Russia and the United States: Prospects for Cooperation in Central Asia," CEF (Quarterly), the Journal of the China-Eurasia Forum, February 2003.

Huntington, Samuel P: The Clash of Civilizations and The Remaking of World Order; Penguin Books, 1997.

Battuta, Ibn: Travels in Asia and Africa, trans/published, Routledge & Kegan Paul, London, 1929

Jaffe, Amy Myers and Manning, Robert A, "The Myth of Caspian Great Game: The Real Geopolitics of Energy," Survival, Winter 1998-1999(Council of Foreign Relations (US) www.treemedia.com/cfrlibrary/library

Jagchid, S and Hayer, P: Mongolia's Culture and Society; Boulder, West View Press, 1979

Jonas, Theodore "Caspian Sea Legal Status", Azerbaijan Oil and Gas; 2001, United States-Azerbaijan Chamber of Commerce Paper (http://users.javanet.com)

Kaczmarski, Marcin "Russia Creates a New Security System to Replace CIS," PINR: Power and Interest News Report; www.pinr.com, 21 December 2005

Khawari, Farid A: Oil and Islam; Roundtable Publishing Inc, Malibu, CA. 1990.

Khodakov, A "Legal Framework for Cooperation in the Caspian Sea," CACR Vol. 4 No.10, Summer 1995.

Kissinger, Henry, "Does America Need a Foreign Policy: Towards the Diplomacy for the 21st Century", Simon and Schuster Ltd, New York, London, Toronto, Sydney, Singapore, 2001.

Kissinger, Henry: Diplomacy; Simon and Schuster Ltd. London, Sydney, New York, Tokyo, Singapore, Toronto, 1994.

Klare, Michael T: Blood and Oil: The Dangers and Consequences of America's Growing Dependency on Imported Petroleum, Henry Holt and Company New York-2004.

Kleveman, Lutz: The New Great Game: Blood and Oil in Central Asia" Grove Press, New York, 2003.

Leppingwell, John W R "The Russian Military and Security Policy in the Near Abroad," Survival. Vol.36 No.3 Autumn 1994.

Levine, Steve "High Stakes," Newsweek, 17 April 1995.

Ludendroff, Erich: The Nation at War; trans, A.S Rappoprt, London: Hutchinson, 1936

MacDonald, Scott B, "Central Asia Back on the Frontline, "KWR International Advisor No.12; December 2000, P.5 (KWR. advisor@kwrintl.com)

Mackinder, H.J, "The Geographical Pivots of History" Geographical Journal Vol. 23 No. 4, 1904.

Malhotra, Jyoti, "From Border Conflict to Oil Rivalry", The News, 10 September 2005

Masud, Khawaja, "The Promethean Savant", The News, (Pakistan) 8 August 2005.

Mayer, Jane "Contract Sports," New Yorker, 16 and 23 February 2004.

Mckillop, Andrew and Newman, Sheila: The Final Energy Crisis; UCL Press Ltd London, 2005.

Monbiot, George, "A Prowestern Regime in Kabul Should Give the US an Afghan Route for Caspian Oil", the Guardian, 23 October 2001.

Montross, Lynn, "War Through the Ages," Happer & Row: New York, Evanston, and London, 1986.

Muhammad Anwar Khan, Dr: England, Russia and Central Asia: (A Study in Diplomacy), 1857-1878, University Book Agency, Peshawar, Pakistan, 1962.

Muhammad Anwar Khan, Dr: Central Asia; An Introductory Reference Booklet; Area Study Center, University of Peshawar (n.d.) Pakistan.

Muhammad, Anwar Khan, Dr, "Age of Imperialism", Central Asia. No.52, Summer, Journal of Area Study Center, University of Peshawar, 2003.

Muhammad Aslam Khan, Dr/Brig(R), "NATO's Expansion: Prospects and Pitfalls" Central Asia, No. 55, Winter, Area Study Center, University of Peshawar, Pakistan, 2004.

Odom, Howard T, "Energy and Environmental Decision Making," Wiley; 1996

Olcott, Martha Brill, Central Asia's Second Chance, Carnegie Endowment for International Peace, 2005.

Olcott, Martha Brill: Central Asia's New States; Independence, Foreign Policy and Regional Security: US Institute of Peace, Washington DC 1997.

Omar, Kaleem "Concerning America's Deadly Role as Global Oil Police", The News (Pakistan), 4 September 2005

Paula, Christopher "Russian Caspian View Violates Law in Eyes of Kazakhstan's Minister", Platt's Oil gram News, 22 November 1994.

Peterson, Erik; Gaita, Anthony "Danger in Caucasus: Pipeline Politics are Leading Yeltsin into a Potential Quagmire in Chechnya" CSIC Watch, January 1995.

Picerno, James "If We Really Have the Oil", Wealth Manager Magazine,(www.wealth.bloomburg.com) 6 September 2002.

Pipeline Poker, The Economist, 7 February 1998

Pope, Hugh, "US Plays High Stakes War Game in Kazakhstan", The Wall Street Journal, 16 September 1997.

Rashid, Ahmad: Jihad: Rise of Militant Islam in Central Asia," Vanguard Books Pvt Ltd Pakistan and Yale University Press USA-2002.

Rasizade, Alec, "Azerbaijan and the Oil Trade: Prospects and Pitfalls," Brown Review of World Affairs, Vol, IV, No.2, Fall 1997.

Riasanovsky, Nicholas V: A History of Russia: Oxford Press; 3rd, 1976

Roberts, Paul: The End of Oil: The Decline of Petroleum Economy and the Rise of New Energy Order, Bloomsbury London-2004.

Roy, Arundhati "Most Cowardly War in History," The Nation, 9 July 2005.

Rubin, Barnet R: The Search for Peace in Afghanistan; Oxford University Press, Pakistan 2003.

Ruppert, Michael C: A War in the Planning for Four Years: How Stupid They Think We Are" Wilderness Publications, 22 June 2002(www.fromthewilderness.com)

Saivetz, Carol R., "Caspian Geopolitics: The View from Moscow": The Brown Journal of World Affairs; Summer/Fall 2000-Vol. VII, Issue 2.

Scraton, Phil(Ed): Beyond September 11- An Anthology of Dissent, Pluto Press; London, Sterling, Virginia 2002.

Siegel, Dr Jennifer: End Game: Britain, Russia and the Final Struggle for Central   Asia; IB Taurus Publishers, London, New York, 2002.

Skolosky, Richard; Paley, Tanya: NATO and Caspian Security: A Mission too Far, The Rand Corporation, Santa Monica California-USA, 1999.

Skrine, F H and Ross, E D: The History of Asia; Oxford Press London 1999

Spectrum of Strategy, Handbook of 1992 Armed Forces War Course; National Defense College, Rawalpindi.

Starr, S. Frederick and Cornell, Svante (Eds): Baku-Tbillisi-Ceyhan Pipeline; Oil Window to the West, Upsala University Press, Sweden-2005

Statistical Review of World Energy 2005; Annual Report; British Petroleum Company, Pauffley Ltd London.(www.bp.com/statisticalreview), June 2005.

Sullivan, Patrick O' and Miller, Jesse W: "The Geography of Warfare," Croom Helm Ltd London, Canberra, 1983.

Talwani, Manik; Belopolsky, Andrei and Berry, Dianne L, "Geology and Petroleum Potential of Central Asia," (Presentation); Baker Institute, Rice University, 23 June 2003.

Thomas, Timothy L. "Russian National Interest and the Caspian Sea," Perceptions; December 1999-February 2000, Vol. IV, No. 4, 1999.

Times Atlas 2005 (www.infoplease.com/ipa)

Turabian, Kate L: A Manual for Writers of Term Papers, Theses and Dissertations. 4th, University of Chicago Press, Chicago and London, 1973.

US Department of State, "Congressional Budget Justification; Foreign Operations", Fiscal Year-2005 (report).

Vivian, Frank, "Perilous Lifelines to West: Conflict-Ridden Caspian Basin is the World's Next Persian Gulf," <u>San Francisco Chronicle</u>, August 10, 1998.

Wikipedia: <u>The Free Encyclopedia</u> (www.answer.wikipedia /library), 24 September 2004

Wolfe, Adam "The Great Game Heats up in Central Asia, "<u>Power and Interest News Report: PINR;</u> (<u>www.pinr.com</u>) 3 August 2005.

Wright, John F. R; Goldenberg, Suzanne & Schofield, Richard (Eds); <u>Transcaucasian Boundaries</u>, UCL Press-1996.

Ziegler, W.H, "Reflection on Political Implication of Oil Depletion," <u>News Letter,</u> No 13, January 2002, ASP-OADC London, UK.

Appendix-1
Tables 4,5,6,7

Table-4	Oil statistics (high case) (Mt)					
Kazakhstan	**1990**	**1995**	**2000**	**2005**	**2010**	**2020**
Production	25.2	20.5	45	70	100	160
Consumption	27.2	10.4	20	33.7	45.5	84.2
Net exports	-2	10.1	25	36.3	54.5	75.8
Azerbaijan						
Production	12.3	9.2	14	30	70	120
Consumption	8.6	7	10.2	13	15	25.9
Net exports	3.7	2.2	3.8	17	55	94.1
Turkmenistan						
Production	3.4	3.5	10	11	12	14
Consumption	4.8	5.7	7	7	7	8
Net exports	-1.4	-2.2	3	4	5	6
Uzbekistan						
Production	2.8	7.6	10	11	12	14
Consumption	10.2	8.6	8.7	9	10	12
Net exports	-7.4	-1	1.3	2	2	2
Total						
Production	43.7	40.8	79	122	194	308
Consumption	50.9	31.7	45.9	65.6	77.5	130.1
Net exports	-7.1	9.1	33.1	56.4	116.5	177.9

Table-5	Oil production, domestic consumption and net exports (low case) (Mt)					
Kazakhstan	**1990**	**1995**	**2000**	**2005**	**2010**	**2020**
Production	25.2	20.5	40	55	75	130
Consumption	27.2	10.4	15.6	24.4	31.6	51.9
Net exports	-2	10.1	24.4	30.6	43.4	78.1
Azerbaijan						
Production	12.3	9.2	14	25	45	90
Consumption	8.6	7	10.2	12.9	14.8	21.9
Net exports	3.7	2.2	3.8	12.1	30.2	68.1
Turkmenistan						
Production	3.4	3.5	6	6.5	7	8
Consumption	4.8	5.7	6	6.5	7	8
Net exports	-1.4	-2.2	0	0	0	0
Uzbekistan						
Production	2.8	7.6	9	10	11	13
Consumption	10.2	8.6	8.7	9	9.5	11
Net exports	-7.4	-1	0.3	1	1.5	2
Total						
Production	43.7	40.8	69	96.5	138	241

Consumption	50.9	31.7	40.4	52.8	62.9	92.8
Net exports	-7.1	9.1	28.6	43.7	75.1	148.2

TABLE -6	Gas production, domestic consumption and net exports (high case) (Bcm)					
	1990	1995	2000	2005	2010	2020
Kazakhstan						
Production	7	5.9	9.8	14.7	29.4	34.3
Consumption	14.7	12.5	14.7	18.4	29.4	34.3
Net exports	-7.7	-6.6	-4.9	-3.7	0	0
Azerbaijan						
Production	9.9	6.7	7.4	17.3	23.5	29.6
Consumption	13.6	7.3	7.4	9.7	12.1	19.8
Net exports	-3.7	-0.6	0	7.6	11.4	9.9
Turkmenistan						
Production	84.3	35.6	42.9	61.2	85.7	129.8

				11.3		
Consumption	14.5	9.8	9.4			
Net exports	69.7	25.8	33.5	50	71.9	111.1
Uzbekistan						
Production	40.4	48.6	51.4	56.3	62.5	73.5
Consumption	37.6	44.2	49.4	55.9	61.6	74.4
Net exports	2.8	4.4	2	0.4	0.8	-0.9
Total						
Production	141.6	96.8	111.5	149.5	201	267.2
Consumption	80.5	73.8	80.9	95.2	117.1	147.2
Net exports	61.1	23	30.6	54.3	84	120

TABLE-7	Gas production, domestic consumption and net ex			
	1990	**1995**	**2000**	**2005**
Kazakhstan				
Production	7	5.9	8	12.2
Consumption	14.7	12.5	12.9	15.9
Net exports	-7.7	-6.6	-4.9	-3.7
Azerbaijan				
Production	9.9	6.7	7.4	11.1
Consumption	13.6	7.3	7.4	8.6
Net exports	-3.7	-0.6	0	2.5
Turkmenistan				
Production	84.3	35.6	36.7	49
Consumption	14.5	9.8	9.6	10.2
Net exports	69.7	25.8	27.2	38.8
Uzbekistan				
Production	40.4	48.6	50.2	53.9
Consumption	37.6	44.2	46.8	50.9
Net exports	2.8	4.4	3.5	3
Total				
Production	141.6	96.8	102.3	126.2
Consumption	80.5	73.8	76.6	85.7
Net exports	61.1	23	25.7	40.6

Appendix-2
(Tables 9-20)

Table-9: World Oil Proved Reseves-2004

Proved reserves	At end 1984 Thousand million barrels	At end 1994 Thousand million barrels	At end 2003 Thousand million barrels	At end 2004 Thousand million tonnes	At end 2004 Thousand million barrels	Share of total	R/P ratio
USA	36.1	29.6	29.4	3.6	29.4	2.5%	11.1
Canada	9.4	10.4	16.8	2.4	16.8	1.4%	14.9
Mexico	56.4	49.8	16.0	2.0	14.8	1.2%	10.0
Total North America	**101.9**	**89.8**	**62.2**	**8.0**	**61.0**	**5.1%**	**11.8**
Argentina	2.3	2.3	2.7	0.4	2.7	0.2%	9.7
Brazil	2.0	5.4	10.6	1.5	11.2	0.9%	13.9
Colombia	1.1	3.1	1.5	0.2	1.5	0.1%	7.0
Ecuador	1.1	3.5	5.1	0.7	5.1	0.4%	25.8
Peru	0.7	0.8	0.9	0.1	0.9	0.1%	27.3
Trinidad & Tobago	0.6	0.6	0.8	0.1	1.0	0.1%	17.5
Venezuela	28.0	64.9	77.2	11.1	77.2	6.5%	70.8
Other S. & Cent. America	0.5	1.0	1.5	0.2	1.5	0.1%	26.9
Total S. & Cent. America	**36.3**	**81.5**	**100.3**	**14.4**	**101.2**	**8.5%**	**40.9**
Azerbaijan	n/a	n/a	7.0	1.0	7.0	0.6%	60.2
Denmark	0.5	0.8	1.3	0.2	1.3	0.1%	9.2
Italy	0.6	0.7	0.8	0.1	0.7	0.1%	19.3
Kazakhstan	n/a	n/a	39.6	5.4	39.6	3.3%	83.6
Norway	4.9	9.6	10.1	1.3	9.7	0.8%	8.3
Romania	1.2	1.0	0.5	0.1	0.5	*	10.8
Russian Federation	n/a	n/a	71.2	9.9	72.3	6.1%	21.3
Turkmenistan	n/a	n/a	0.5	0.1	0.5	*	7.4
United Kingdom	6.0	4.3	4.5	0.6	4.5	0.4%	6.0
Uzbekistan	n/a	n/a	0.6	0.1	0.6	*	10.6
Other Europe & Eurasia	33.2	63.9	2.5	0.3	2.5	0.2%	13.8
Total Europe & Eurasia	**96.7**	**80.3**	**138.6**	**19.0**	**139.2**	**11.7%**	**21.6**
Iran	58.9	94.2	132.3	18.2	132.5	11.1%	88.7
Iraq	65.0	100.0	115.0	15.5	115.0	9.7%	*
Kuwait	92.7	96.5	99.0	13.6	99.0	8.3%	*
Oman	3.9	5.1	5.8	0.8	5.6	0.5%	19.4
Qatar	4.5	3.5	15.2	2.0	15.2	1.3%	42.0
Saudi Arabia	171.7	261.4	262.7	36.1	262.7	22.1%	67.8
Syria	1.4	2.7	2.4	0.4	3.2	0.3%	16.1
United Arab Emirates	32.5	98.1	97.8	13.0	97.8	8.2%	*
Yemen	0.1	0.1	2.9	0.4	2.9	0.2%	18.2
Other Middle East	0.2	0.1	0.1	†	0.1	*	4.6
Total Middle East	**430.8**	**661.7**	**733.9**	**100.0**	**733.9**	**61.7%**	**81.6**
Algeria	9.0	10.0	11.8	1.5	11.8	1.0%	16.7
Angola	2.1	3.0	8.8	1.2	8.8	0.7%	24.0
Chad	–	–	0.9	0.1	0.9	0.1%	14.6
Rep. of Congo (Brazzaville)	0.8	1.4	1.4	0.3	1.8	0.2%	20.3
Egypt	4.0	3.9	3.5	0.5	3.6	0.3%	13.8
Equatorial Guinea	–	0.2	1.3	0.2	1.3	0.1%	10.0
Gabon	0.6	1.4	2.3	0.3	2.3	0.2%	26.6
Libya	21.4	22.8	39.1	5.1	39.1	3.3%	66.5
Nigeria	16.7	21.0	35.3	4.8	35.3	3.0%	38.4
Sudan	0.3	0.3	6.3	0.9	6.3	0.5%	57.3
Tunisia	1.9	0.3	0.5	0.1	0.6	0.1%	25.2
Other Africa	1.0	0.6	0.6	0.1	0.5	*	8.6
Total Africa	**57.8**	**65.0**	**111.8**	**14.9**	**112.2**	**9.4%**	**33.1**
Australia	2.9	3.9	4.0	0.5	4.0	0.3%	20.4
Brunei	1.5	1.2	1.1	0.1	1.1	0.1%	13.6
China	16.3	16.2	17.1	2.3	17.1	1.4%	13.4
India	3.8	5.8	5.7	0.7	5.6	0.5%	19.6
Indonesia	9.0	5.0	4.7	0.7	4.7	0.4%	11.5
Malaysia	2.9	5.2	4.3	0.6	4.3	0.4%	12.9
Thailand	0.1	0.2	0.5	0.1	0.5	*	6.3
Vietnam	–	0.6	2.0	0.4	3.0	0.2%	19.0
Other Asia Pacific	1.1	1.0	0.9	0.1	0.9	0.1%	13.2
Total Asia Pacific	**38.1**	**39.2**	**41.6**	**5.5**	**41.1**	**3.5%**	**14.2**
TOTAL WORLD	**761.6**	**1017.3**	**1188.3**	**161.8**	**1188.6**	**100.0%**	**40.5**
of which: OECD	118.7	110.6	84.0	10.9	82.9	7.0%	10.9
OPEC	510.8	777.4	891.1	121.5	890.3	74.9%	73.9
Non-OPEC	170.8	177.7	177.5	23.8	177.4	14.9%	13.5
Former Soviet Union	91.0	62.4	119.7	16.5	120.8	10.2%	28.9

255

Table-10 : World Oil Production Statistics-2004

Production* Thousand barrels daily	1994	1995	1996	1997	1998	1999	2000	2001	2002	2003	2004	Change 2004 over 2003	2004 share of total
USA	8389	9322	8295	8269	8011	7731	7733	7669	7626	7400	7241	-2.5%	8.5%
Canada	2276	2492	2480	2588	2672	2604	2721	2677	2659	3004	3085	3.5%	3.8%
Mexico	3142	3065	3277	3410	3499	3343	3450	3560	3585	3789	3824	1.0%	4.9%
Total North America	13807	13789	14052	14267	14182	13670	13904	13996	14869	14193	14150	-0.3%	17.3%
Argentina	645	759	823	877	890	847	919	830	818	806	766	-5.9%	1.0%
Brazil	633	718	807	868	1003	1133	1268	1337	1499	1595	1542	-0.7%	2.0%
Colombia	460	591	635	667	775	838	711	627	601	564	551	-2.1%	0.7%
Ecuador	389	395	393	397	386	383	409	416	401	427	535	25.8%	0.7%
Peru	129	123	121	120	116	107	100	98	98	92	93	-1.3%	0.1%
Trinidad & Tobago	141	142	141	135	134	141	138	135	155	164	155	-6.1%	0.2%
Venezuela	2752	2959	3137	3321	3510	3248	3321	3233	3219	2622	2980	13.8%	4.0%
Other S. & Cent. America	90	96	102	108	125	122	129	138	155	155	152	-2.8%	0.2%
Total S. & Cent. America	5347	5782	6159	6499	6928	6828	6895	6814	6944	6385	6764	6.2%	8.8%
Azerbaijan	193	185	183	186	230	279	281	300	311	313	318	1.3%	0.4%
Denmark	187	188	207	233	226	301	364	347	372	371	394	6.6%	0.5%
Italy	94	101	104	114	108	98	88	79	106	107	104	-2.2%	0.1%
Kazakhstan	430	434	474	536	527	631	744	836	1018	1111	1295	15.5%	1.6%
Norway	2033	2903	3232	3280	3139	3129	3346	3418	3333	3264	3188	-2.1%	3.9%
Romania	145	145	142	141	137	133	131	130	127	123	119	-3.1%	0.1%
Russian Federation	6419	6288	6114	6227	6169	6178	6536	7056	7698	8544	9285	8.9%	11.9%
Turkmenistan	87	84	90	108	129	143	144	162	182	202	202	0.5%	0.3%
United Kingdom	2675	2749	2735	2702	2807	2909	2667	2476	2463	2257	2029	-10.0%	2.5%
Uzbekistan	124	172	174	182	191	191	177	171	171	166	152	-7.8%	0.2%
Other Europe & Eurasia	609	576	548	528	507	475	467	487	503	510	496	-2.7%	0.6%
Total Europe & Eurasia	13657	13825	14003	14233	14188	14475	15449	15443	16244	16968	17583	3.9%	22.0%
Iran	3730	3744	3759	3776	3855	3600	3819	3730	3414	3903	4081	2.3%	5.2%
Iraq	505	530	580	1166	2126	2641	2583	2376	2036	1350	2027	50.8%	2.6%
Kuwait	2395	2130	2129	2137	2176	2000	2104	2092	1661	2238	2424	8.7%	3.1%
Oman	819	868	897	909	905	911	959	961	900	823	785	-4.4%	1.0%
Qatar	461	461	568	719	747	737	855	854	783	917	990	9.0%	1.2%
Saudi Arabia	9084	9127	9265	9481	9544	8911	9511	9203	8979	10222	10584	3.7%	13.1%
Syria	583	596	586	577	576	579	552	585	547	564	536	-4.7%	0.7%
United Arab Emirates	2482	2410	2479	2492	2668	2302	2539	2430	2126	2547	2667	5.2%	3.3%
Yemen	346	351	357	375	380	405	450	471	461	454	429	-5.4%	0.5%
Other Middle East	52	52	50	50	43	48	47	48	48	48	48	0.2%	0.1%
Total Middle East	20118	20270	20669	21684	22916	22097	22376	22809	21145	23163	24571	6.4%	30.7%
Algeria	1324	1327	1396	1421	1481	1515	1579	1562	1681	1857	1933	5.0%	2.1%
Angola	557	633	716	741	731	745	746	742	905	885	991	12.3%	1.3%
Cameroon	115	105	110	124	106	95	88	81	75	68	62	-8.7%	0.1%
Chad	-	-	-	-	-	-	-	-	-	24	168	▲	0.2%
Rep. of Congo (Brazzaville)	185	180	200	225	264	293	275	271	258	243	240	-1.0%	0.3%
Egypt	921	924	894	873	857	827	781	758	751	749	708	-4.9%	0.9%
Equatorial Guinea	5	7	17	60	83	100	119	191	257	249	350	41.0%	0.4%
Gabon	337	356	366	364	337	340	327	301	295	240	235	-2.1%	0.3%
Libya	1431	1439	1452	1489	1480	1425	1475	1425	1376	1488	1607	8.4%	2.0%
Nigeria	1991	1998	2145	2316	2167	2066	2155	2274	2103	2263	2508	10.8%	3.2%
Sudan	2	2	5	9	12	63	174	211	232	252	301	18.4%	0.4%
Tunisia	90	90	89	81	83	84	78	71	75	68	69	2.6%	0.1%
Other Africa	42	51	62	84	63	56	61	64	70	75	92	22.4%	0.1%
Total Africa	7004	7112	7411	7767	7642	7609	7857	7942	8059	8464	9264	10.1%	11.4%
Australia	614	583	619	669	644	625	803	733	731	624	541	-13.9%	0.6%
Brunei	179	175	185	162	157	182	193	203	210	214	211	-1.5%	0.3%
China	2930	2989	3170	3211	3212	3213	3252	3306	3346	3401	3490	2.9%	4.5%
India	708	804	776	800	787	788	780	795	801	800	819	2.9%	1.0%
Indonesia	1589	1578	1580	1557	1520	1408	1456	1389	1288	1183	1126	-4.5%	1.4%
Malaysia	674	724	726	764	815	731	791	736	828	876	912	3.6%	1.0%
Thailand	87	97	97	116	121	132	164	174	191	223	218	-2.2%	0.2%
Vietnam	144	155	179	205	246	296	328	350	354	364	427	17.8%	0.5%
Other Asia Pacific	259	231	240	229	219	219	193	194	192	196	184	-5.1%	0.2%
Total Asia Pacific	7184	7325	7571	7715	7720	7454	7972	7914	7942	7881	7926	0.9%	9.8%
TOTAL WORLD	**67116**	**68189**	**69096**	**72160**	**73686**	**72229**	**74860**	**74029**	**74468**	**77664**	**80269**	**4.5%**	**100.0%**
of which: OECD	20528	20737	21255	21686	21490	21099	21517	21297	21426	21161	20732	-1.9%	25.2%
OPEC	27424	27792	28479	29976	31143	29816	31554	30628	28955	30686	32927	7.7%	41.1%
Non-OPEC‡	32300	33164	34244	34906	35052	34965	36960	36541	38056	35878	35916	0.4%	44.5%
Former Soviet Union	7391	7297	7171	7277	7391	7551	8010	8619	9532	10499	11417	8.8%	14.4%

*Includes crude oil, shale oil, oil sands and NGLs (natural gas liquids – the liquid content of natural gas where this is recovered separately).
Excludes liquid fuels from other sources such as coal derivatives.
‡Excludes Former Soviet Union.
▲More than 100%.
Notes: Annual changes and shares of total are calculated using million tonnes per annum figures rather than thousand barrels daily.
Because of rounding, some totals may not agree exactly with the sum of their component parts.

Table-11: World Oil Consumption-2004

Consumption* Thousand barrels daily	1994	1995	1996	1997	1998	1999	2000	2001	2002	2003	2004	Change 2004 over 2003	2004 share of total
USA	17719	17725	18309	18321	18917	19519	19701	19449	19761	20033	20517	2.8%	24.9%
Canada	1742	1776	1819	1886	1913	1926	1937	2122	2047	2137	2286	2.9%	2.6%
Mexico	1772	1650	1660	1787	1844	1842	1984	1909	1867	1895	1896	1.3%	2.3%
Total North America	**21232**	**21150**	**21793**	**22275**	**22674**	**23286**	**23622**	**23571**	**23695**	**24049**	**24619**	**2.1%**	**29.8%**
Argentina	418	415	432	461	467	445	431	405	364	371	393	6.6%	0.5%
Brazil	1418	1496	1601	1729	1900	1879	1855	1806	1853	1795	1839	2.7%	2.2%
Chile	190	209	223	242	247	248	236	230	225	223	232	1.5%	0.3%
Colombia	246	260	263	272	280	238	232	245	222	222	223	1.2%	0.3%
Ecuador	115	112	125	142	145	131	129	132	137	134	140	4.1%	0.2%
Peru	134	135	155	154	153	159	158	148	147	141	153	9.5%	0.2%
Venezuela	436	446	426	452	475	474	486	545	594	526	577	10.0%	0.7%
Other S. & Cent. America	1022	1044	1065	1098	1128	1129	1125	1138	1148	1172	1192	1.9%	1.5%
Total S. & Cent. America	**3976**	**4136**	**4390**	**4519**	**4583**	**4704**	**4659**	**4739**	**4684**	**4560**	**4739**	**3.7%**	**5.9%**
Austria	216	234	242	246	255	250	244	265	271	260	284	-3.0%	0.4%
Azerbaijan	161	171	140	120	151	149	124	74	73	84	91	7.3%	0.1%
Belarus	257	247	166	193	167	147	122	118	164	123	150	22.8%	0.2%
Belgium & Luxembourg	556	540	606	603	656	670	702	683	681	749	779	4.5%	1.0%
Bulgaria	118	115	116	92	100	90	84	87	90	90	98	5.2%	0.1%
Czech Republic	149	158	177	170	174	154	169	178	174	165	202	8.6%	0.3%
Denmark	209	217	235	229	223	222	215	205	200	190	189	-1.8%	0.2%
Finland	216	208	216	213	227	224	221	222	226	229	224	-7.0%	0.3%
France	1978	1892	1930	1943	2015	2044	2002	2023	1967	1965	1975	0.9%	2.5%
Germany	2880	2882	2921	2913	2915	2824	2760	2804	2714	2664	2626	-1.2%	3.3%
Greece	346	361	372	279	374	380	406	411	414	434	411	2.0%	0.5%
Hungary	169	158	148	150	157	151	149	142	148	122	136	2.2%	0.2%
Iceland	15	16	18	19	18	18	19	18	19	18	19	4.3%	♦
Republic of Ireland	116	118	124	130	152	172	176	186	195	194	187	2.1%	0.2%
Italy	1920	1987	1968	1969	1974	1960	1956	1945	1943	1927	1871	-2.8%	2.4%
Kazakhstan	247	242	204	207	171	141	146	113	133	177	192	8.1%	0.2%
Lithuania	72	64	66	60	78	60	49	66	53	61	62	2.9%	0.1%
Netherlands	792	828	810	850	854	880	891	642	902	962	1003	4.8%	1.2%
Norway	212	212	218	223	215	216	201	213	206	219	209	-3.5%	0.3%
Poland	314	321	368	391	424	431	427	415	420	425	462	7.1%	0.6%
Portugal	253	272	359	290	322	330	324	327	308	317	325	3.3%	0.4%
Romania	226	274	300	276	242	195	202	217	226	199	212	7.0%	0.3%
Russian Federation	3267	2904	2606	2595	2484	2534	2474	2456	2480	2503	2574	3.1%	3.4%
Slovakia	70	68	71	72	90	73	72	68	76	71	74	5.1%	0.1%
Spain	1120	1177	1221	1290	1391	1423	1452	1509	1526	1559	1593	2.8%	2.1%
Sweden	354	338	362	336	308	307	318	318	317	322	319	-0.9%	0.4%
Switzerland	272	282	278	278	279	271	268	267	259	264	258	-5.4%	0.3%
Turkey	553	610	605	642	649	638	677	685	656	668	648	-2.4%	0.8%
Turkmenistan	60	54	69	60	68	72	70	74	80	90	98	8.9%	0.1%
Ukraine	398	380	284	277	287	255	240	255	249	309	344	13.0%	0.5%
United Kingdom	1777	1757	1798	1752	1741	1729	1704	1764	1664	1712	1756	2.3%	2.1%
Uzbekistan	145	134	148	135	141	145	136	141	137	121	129	-0.9%	0.2%
Other Europe & Eurasia	392	395	414	437	451	443	437	456	470	495	500	1.4%	0.6%
Total Europe & Eurasia	**19752**	**19625**	**19430**	**19610**	**19743**	**19671**	**19452**	**19692**	**19513**	**19726**	**20017**	**1.8%**	**25.4%**
Iran	1098	1264	1249	1221	1180	1142	1271	1272	1395	1472	1551	6.1%	1.9%
Kuwait	134	130	126	139	180	202	202	206	222	208	260	12.9%	0.4%
Qatar	30	34	38	41	43	42	44	54	79	77	84	9.1%	0.1%
Saudi Arabia	1287	1321	1286	1342	1440	1455	1466	1500	1522	1629	1729	6.6%	2.1%
United Arab Emirates	353	349	346	345	292	256	243	272	284	296	306	4.0%	0.4%
Other Middle East	1147	1214	1219	1278	1308	1331	1356	1364	1425	1322	1354	2.5%	1.7%
Total Middle East	**4044**	**4160**	**4263**	**4364**	**4417**	**4488**	**4591**	**4794**	**4919**	**5034**	**5288**	**5.2%**	**6.7%**
Algeria	209	198	187	187	194	187	192	200	222	231	242	4.3%	0.3%
Egypt	427	474	501	531	559	570	564	548	554	550	566	2.9%	0.7%
South Africa	407	427	437	445	451	402	475	488	501	513	525	2.9%	0.7%
Other Africa	1099	1099	1117	1150	1190	1229	1231	1241	1249	1272	1314	2.5%	1.6%
Total Africa	**2130**	**2199**	**2241**	**2313**	**2394**	**2482**	**2462**	**2476**	**2506**	**2567**	**2647**	**3.4%**	**3.3%**
Australia	753	781	794	805	828	840	837	845	840	851	864	1.3%	1.0%
Bangladesh	45	58	63	69	75	68	64	80	80	93	95	2.3%	0.1%
China	3145	3390	3672	3995	4047	4416	4866	5030	5379	5791	6684	15.8%	8.2%
China Hong Kong SAR	165	186	184	192	194	190	201	243	208	289	314	17.9%	0.4%
India	1413	1580	1700	1829	1983	2134	2254	2264	2374	2450	2555	5.5%	3.2%
Indonesia	734	820	868	963	914	980	1049	1088	1115	1102	1150	1.4%	1.5%
Japan	5746	5794	5813	5782	5825	5618	5577	5435	5309	5463	5288	-3.0%	6.4%
Malaysia	372	381	406	421	407	439	441	448	484	480	504	5.2%	0.6%
New Zealand	121	125	127	131	131	134	134	136	142	147	151	2.2%	0.2%
Pakistan	291	315	329	369	373	383	372	366	357	320	296	-8.1%	0.4%
Philippines	306	344	360	389	382	375	348	347	332	330	336	2.2%	0.4%
Singapore	590	617	566	690	651	618	654	736	609	668	748	12.4%	0.9%
South Korea	1940	2009	2144	2373	2030	2178	2229	2235	2282	2300	2240	-0.6%	2.9%
Taiwan	645	719	717	741	768	820	874	919	844	868	877	0.9%	1.1%
Thailand	617	717	778	745	738	734	726	761	768	848	909	5.2%	1.2%
Other Asia Pacific	222	245	261	299	324	337	366	386	408	398	411	6.6%	0.5%
Total Asia Pacific	**17083**	**18077**	**18842**	**19686**	**19321**	**20246**	**21054**	**21159**	**21739**	**22337**	**23446**	**5.7%**	**28.9%**
of which: European Union 25	13596	13765	14049	14199	14501	14528	14402	14562	14456	14509	14637	0.9%	18.4%
OECD	44099	44475	45616	46498	46902	47800	47962	47711	47679	48282	48777	1.3%	59.8%
Former Soviet Union	4720	4333	3779	3751	3650	3597	3468	3440	3482	3657	3729	5.2%	4.9%
Other EMEs	19090	20538	21474	22622	22900	23751	24836	25101	25914	26453	26251	7.0%	39.3%

*Inland demand plus international aviation and marine bunkers and refinery fuel and loss.
♦ Less than 0.05%.
Notes: Annual changes and shares of total are calculated using million tonnes per annum figures rather than thousand barrels daily.
Differences between these world consumption figures and world production statistics on page 6 are accounted for by stock changes, consumption of non-petroleum additives and substitute fuels, and unavoidable disparities in the definition, measurement or conversion of oil supply and demand data.

Table 12 : World Oil Consumption by Product-2004

Regional consumption by product group — Thousand barrels daily	1994	1995	1996	1997	1998	1999	2000	2001	2002	2003	2004	Change 2004 over 2003	2004 share of total
North America													
Gasolines	9100	9235	9389	9560	9649	9999	10106	10211	10523	10675	10897	2.1%	44.3%
Middle distillates	5895	5934	6192	6396	6450	6629	6911	6812	6955	6861	7105	3.6%	28.9%
Fuel oil	1671	1338	1349	1351	1506	1415	1518	1411	1208	1271	1274	0.2%	5.2%
Others	4965	4645	4863	4967	4969	5245	5086	5137	5278	5242	5343	1.9%	21.0%
Total North America	**21232**	**21150**	**21793**	**22275**	**22574**	**23286**	**23622**	**23571**	**23965**	**24049**	**24619**	**2.4%**	**100.0%**
of which: USA													
Gasolines	7893	8026	8167	8324	8679	8716	8913	8890	9167	9275	9436	1.7%	46.0%
Middle distillates	5084	5132	5342	5502	5546	5700	5952	5884	5735	5886	6087	3.4%	29.7%
Fuel oil	1003	805	831	777	969	814	880	734	886	762	795	4.2%	3.9%
Others	3751	3732	3969	4017	3924	4290	4143	4082	4172	4109	4199	2.2%	20.4%
Total USA	**17719**	**17725**	**18309**	**18621**	**18917**	**19519**	**19701**	**19649**	**19761**	**20033**	**20417**	**2.4%**	**100.0%**
S. & Cent. America													
Gasolines	1105	1149	1167	1257	1274	1287	1274	1258	1233	1216	1246	2.5%	26.3%
Middle distillates	1398	1476	1538	1625	1700	1684	1680	1720	1718	1714	1815	5.9%	38.3%
Fuel oil	721	734	789	821	860	740	788	715	731	698	687	-0.1%	14.7%
Others	752	777	807	836	869	893	917	1039	1031	953	980	2.8%	20.7%
Total S. & Cent. America	**3976**	**4136**	**4300**	**4539**	**4683**	**4704**	**4659**	**4729**	**4644**	**4580**	**4739**	**3.5%**	**100.0%**
Europe													
Gasolines	4115	4196	4209	4256	4297	4311	4194	4088	4024	2920	3651	-1.8%	22.6%
Middle distillates	5890	6050	6271	6431	6630	6700	6748	6994	6892	7129	7297	2.3%	44.8%
Fuel oil	2280	2263	2260	2206	2195	2093	1971	1969	1886	1958	1900	-3.0%	11.7%
Others	2737	2773	2812	2967	2971	2970	3077	3092	3129	3162	3240	2.5%	19.9%
Total Europe	**15023**	**15292**	**15652**	**15860**	**16093**	**16074**	**15989**	**16162**	**16061**	**16169**	**16288**	**0.7%**	**100.0%**
Middle East													
Gasolines	708	762	773	812	828	842	890	920	996	1021	1120	9.7%	21.2%
Middle distillates	1336	1435	1466	1483	1458	1435	1541	1591	1640	1668	1768	5.9%	32.3%
Fuel oil	1183	1199	1221	1248	1236	1281	1266	1284	1301	1276	1354	6.2%	25.6%
Others	818	764	803	841	895	880	903	909	981	1060	1106	4.4%	20.9%
Total Middle East	**4044**	**4160**	**4263**	**4364**	**4417**	**4488**	**4601**	**4704**	**4919**	**5034**	**5289**	**5.1%**	**100.0%**
Africa													
Gasolines	539	554	552	559	568	574	577	587	591	603	619	2.7%	23.4%
Middle distillates	840	809	894	921	951	999	1012	1026	1049	1077	1119	3.9%	42.3%
Fuel oil	416	439	447	471	500	504	481	460	445	451	461	2.1%	17.4%
Others	335	342	343	362	374	385	392	403	423	436	448	2.7%	16.9%
Total Africa	**2130**	**2199**	**2241**	**2313**	**2394**	**2462**	**2462**	**2476**	**2506**	**2567**	**2647**	**3.1%**	**100.0%**
Asia Pacific incl. China and Japan													
Gasolines	3977	4234	4531	4991	5057	5331	5597	5648	5958	6100	6597	8.7%	27.9%
Middle distillates	6237	6714	7167	7437	7225	7821	7810	7907	9870	8146	8697	6.8%	37.1%
Fuel oil	3860	3856	3800	3832	3576	3651	3517	3359	3241	3369	3397	0.8%	14.5%
Others	2990	3212	3344	3425	3463	3483	4127	4192	4264	4722	4846	2.6%	20.6%
Total Asia Pacific	**17063**	**18017**	**18842**	**19685**	**19321**	**20248**	**21054**	**21109**	**21739**	**22237**	**23446**	**5.0%**	**100.0%**
China													
Gasolines	849	904	966	1111	1098	1184	1313	1282	1387	1440	1686	17.1%	25.2%
Middle distillates	979	937	1080	1282	1277	1465	1632	1709	1766	1905	2352	23.4%	35.2%
Fuel oil	662	669	719	750	726	684	725	728	706	791	907	14.7%	13.6%
Others	755	919	886	871	846	1083	1314	1342	1520	1654	1739	5.1%	26.0%
Total China	**3145**	**3390**	**3672**	**3995**	**4947**	**4416**	**4965**	**5030**	**5379**	**5791**	**6684**	**15.4%**	**100.0%**
Japan													
Gasolines	1442	1548	1576	1646	1611	1702	1738	1720	1759	1798	1796	0.4%	34.0%
Middle distillates	1905	1971	2027	1991	1949	1979	1968	1957	1990	1904	1861	-2.2%	35.2%
Fuel oil	1300	1135	1067	977	879	867	804	860	649	770	672	-12.7%	12.7%
Others	1100	1130	1142	1148	1086	1079	1079	1067	1021	980	960	-2.2%	18.1%
Total Japan	**5746**	**5784**	**5813**	**5762**	**5525**	**5618**	**5577**	**5436**	**5369**	**5455**	**5288**	**-3.1%**	**100.0%**
World excl. Former Soviet Union													
Gasolines	19545	20191	20841	21436	21843	22443	22629	22710	23326	23544	24241	3.0%	21.5%
Middle distillates	21595	22475	23929	24275	24415	25108	25665	26109	26096	26694	27741	4.2%	26.0%
Fuel oil	10007	9945	9642	9934	9662	9683	9542	9251	9821	9024	9063	0.7%	11.9%
Others	12298	12513	12977	13391	13421	14116	14613	14742	15293	15576	15964	2.5%	20.7%
Total World excl. Former Soviet Union	**57849**	**65912**	**67999**	**69035**	**68840**	**71357**	**72449**	**72812**	**73568**	**74277**	**76006**	**3.1%**	**100.0%**
European Union 25													
Gasolines	3773	3818	3808	3892	3914	3844	3844	3741	3670	3583	3514	-1.9%	24.1%
Middle distillates	5219	5459	5717	5822	5991	6080	6129	6351	6287	6466	6607	2.2%	45.2%
Fuel oil	1953	1931	1897	1874	1948	1838	1713	1712	1732	1684	1652	-2.5%	11.3%
Others	2409	2433	2455	2580	2583	2615	2870	2899	2717	2748	2810	2.2%	19.3%
Total European Union 25	**13402**	**13641**	**13902**	**14169**	**14446**	**14417**	**14561**	**14703**	**14406**	**14481**	**14590**	**0.7%**	**100.0%**
OECD													
Gasolines	15273	15721	15969	16415	16728	17028	17089	17064	17390	17499	17685	1.1%	26.2%
Middle distillates	14414	14777	15466	15799	15781	16119	16279	16530	16394	16686	17021	2.1%	54.0%
Fuel oil	5605	5115	5036	4904	4821	4671	4842	4416	4174	4318	4140	-3.9%	8.5%
Others	8892	8862	9145	9442	9283	9691	9682	9701	9821	9790	9928	1.4%	20.3%
Total OECD	**44959**	**44475**	**45616**	**46560**	**46613**	**47509**	**47892**	**47711**	**47779**	**48293**	**48774**	**1.0%**	**100.0%**
Other EMEs													
Gasolines	4186	4459	4672	5020	5146	5415	5559	5646	5935	6045	6556	8.5%	23.2%
Middle distillates	7382	7698	8161	8527	8644	8990	9326	9579	9703	9813	10717	9.1%	37.9%
Fuel oil	4646	4729	4807	5091	5082	4912	4900	4835	4747	4715	4943	4.8%	17.5%
Others	3406	3651	3802	3849	4148	4427	4850	5041	5469	5782	6036	4.4%	21.4%
Total Other EMEs	**19620**	**20537**	**21442**	**22487**	**23020**	**23744**	**24635**	**25101**	**25854**	**26355**	**28252**	**7.2%**	**100.0%**

* European Union 25 excludes Estonia and Latvia prior to 2004 and Lithuania prior to 1997
† Excludes Former Soviet Union
Notes: For the purposes of this table, annual changes and shares of total are calculated using thousand barrels daily figures.
Gasolines consists of aviation and motor gasolines and light distillate feedstock (LDF). Middle distillates consists of jet and heating kerosenes, and gas and diesel oils (including
marine bunkers). Fuel oil includes marine bunkers and crude oil used directly as fuel. Others consists of refinery gas, LPGs, solvents, petroleum coke, lubricants, bitumen, wax
and refinery fuel and loss.

Table 13: World Natural Gas Proved Reserves-2004

Proved reserves	At end 1984 Trillion cubic metres	At end 1994 Trillion cubic metres	At end 2003 Trillion cubic metres	At end 2004 Trillion cubic feet	At end 2004 Trillion cubic metres	Share of total	R/P ratio
USA	5.53	4.58	5.29	186.9	5.29	2.9%	9.6
Canada	2.81	1.90	1.60	56.6	1.60	0.9%	9.6
Mexico	2.17	1.94	0.42	14.9	0.42	0.2%	11.9
Total North America	**10.51**	**8.42**	**7.32**	**258.3**	**7.32**	**4.1%**	**9.6**
Argentina	0.67	0.54	0.61	21.4	0.61	0.3%	13.5
Bolivia	0.13	0.11	0.78	31.4	0.89	0.5%	*
Brazil	0.08	0.15	0.25	11.5	0.33	0.2%	29.5
Colombia	0.11	0.21	0.11	3.9	0.11	0.1%	17.0
Peru	†	0.34	0.25	8.7	0.25	0.1%	*
Trinidad & Tobago	0.31	0.29	0.53	18.8	0.53	0.3%	19.2
Venezuela	1.67	3.97	4.22	148.9	4.22	2.4%	*
Other S. & Cent. America	0.24	0.23	0.17	6.0	0.17	0.1%	*
Total S. & Cent. America	**3.23**	**5.83**	**6.98**	**250.6**	**7.10**	**4.0%**	**55.0**
Azerbaijan	n/a	n/a	1.37	48.4	1.37	0.8%	*
Denmark	0.10	0.12	0.09	3.1	0.09	*	9.9
Germany	0.21	0.22	0.21	7.0	0.20	0.1%	12.1
Italy	0.25	0.30	0.19	5.9	0.17	0.1%	12.8
Kazakhstan	n/a	n/a	3.00	106.9	3.00	1.7%	*
Netherlands	1.90	1.85	1.49	52.7	1.49	0.8%	21.1
Norway	0.56	1.73	2.46	84.2	2.39	1.3%	30.4
Poland	0.09	0.16	0.12	4.1	0.12	0.1%	26.4
Romania	0.21	0.43	0.31	10.4	0.30	0.2%	22.0
Russian Federation	n/a	n/a	48.00	1694.4	48.00	26.7%	81.5
Turkmenistan	n/a	n/a	2.90	102.4	2.90	1.6%	59.1
Ukraine	n/a	n/a	1.11	39.2	1.11	0.6%	60.6
United Kingdom	0.73	0.68	0.59	20.8	0.59	0.3%	6.1
Uzbekistan	n/a	n/a	1.86	65.7	1.86	1.0%	33.3
Other Europe & Eurasia	37.87	58.41	0.45	16.7	0.45	0.2%	40.9
Total Europe & Eurasia	**42.02**	**63.07**	**64.14**	**2259.7**	**64.02**	**35.7%**	**60.9**
Bahrain	0.21	0.15	0.09	3.2	0.09	0.1%	9.2
Iran	14.02	20.76	27.57	970.8	27.50	15.3%	*
Iraq	0.82	3.12	3.17	111.9	3.17	1.8%	*
Kuwait	1.04	1.50	1.57	55.5	1.57	0.9%	*
Oman	0.22	0.26	0.99	35.1	1.00	0.6%	56.5
Qatar	4.29	7.07	25.78	910.1	25.78	14.4%	*
Saudi Arabia	3.61	5.28	6.75	238.4	6.75	3.8%	*
Syria	0.10	0.24	0.25	13.1	0.37	0.2%	72.0
United Arab Emirates	3.11	6.78	6.06	213.9	6.06	3.4%	*
Yemen	-	0.43	0.48	16.9	0.48	0.3%	*
Other Middle East	†	†	0.05	1.9	0.05	*	31.7
Total Middle East	**27.40**	**45.56**	**72.77**	**2570.8**	**72.83**	**40.6%**	*
Algeria	3.44	2.96	4.55	160.4	4.55	2.5%	55.4
Egypt	0.24	0.63	1.72	65.5	1.85	1.0%	89.1
Libya	0.63	1.31	1.49	52.6	1.49	0.8%	*
Nigeria	1.36	3.45	5.00	176.4	5.00	2.8%	*
Other Africa	0.56	0.78	1.18	41.5	1.18	0.7%	*
Total Africa	**6.22**	**9.13**	**13.94**	**496.4**	**14.06**	**7.8%**	**96.9**
Australia	0.75	1.10	2.46	86.9	2.46	1.4%	69.9
Bangladesh	0.35	0.30	0.44	15.4	0.44	0.2%	33.0
Brunei	0.24	0.40	0.35	12.1	0.34	0.2%	28.3
China	0.89	1.67	2.23	78.7	2.23	1.2%	54.7
India	0.48	0.70	0.95	32.6	0.92	0.5%	31.1
Indonesia	1.70	1.82	2.56	90.3	2.56	1.4%	34.9
Malaysia	1.39	1.93	2.46	87.0	2.46	1.4%	45.1
Myanmar	0.26	0.27	0.45	18.5	0.53	0.3%	71.0
Pakistan	0.52	0.59	0.79	28.2	0.80	0.4%	34.4
Papua New Guinea	-	0.43	0.42	15.1	0.43	0.2%	*
Thailand	0.21	0.19	0.42	15.1	0.43	0.2%	21.1
Vietnam	-	0.13	0.24	8.3	0.24	0.1%	56.5
Other Asia Pacific	0.23	0.35	0.38	13.4	0.38	0.2%	38.4
Total Asia Pacific	**7.02**	**10.07**	**14.06**	**501.5**	**14.21**	**7.9%**	**43.9**
TOTAL WORLD	**96.30**	**142.10**	**179.21**	**6337.4**	**179.53**	**100.0%**	**66.7**
of which: European Union 25	3.62	3.44	2.80	97.1	2.75	1.5%	12.6
OECD	15.62	15.00	15.14	530.3	15.02	8.4%	13.7
Former Soviet Union	37.50	58.15	58.50	2066.2	58.51	32.6%	79.9

† Over 100 years.
† Less than 0.05.
* Less than 0.05%.
n/a not available

Notes: Proved reserves of natural gas – Generally taken to be those quantities that geological and engineering information indicates with reasonable certainty can be recovered in the future from known reservoirs under existing economic and operating conditions.

Reserves to production (R/P) ratio – If the reserves remaining at the end of any year are divided by the production in that year, the result is the length of time that those remaining reserves would last if production were to continue at that level.

Source of data – The estimates in this table have been compiled using a combination of primary official sources and third party data from Cedigaz and the OPEC Secretariat. The reserves figures shown do not necessarily meet the definitions, guidelines and practices used for determining proved reserves at the company level, for instance those published by the US Securities and Exchange Commission or recommended for the purposes of UK GAAP nor do they necessarily represent BP's view of proved reserves by country.

Table 14: World Natural Gas Production-2004

Natural gas

Production* Billion cubic metres	1994	1995	1996	1997	1998	1999	2000	2001	2002	2003	2004	Change 2004 over 2003	2004 share of total
USA	541.8	534.0	541.7	545.1	548.2	541.6	552.5	555.8	543.3	549.6	542.9	-1.2%	20.2%
Canada	149.1	158.7	163.6	165.8	171.0	177.4	183.2	186.8	187.8	182.7	182.8	●	6.8%
Mexico	25.9	28.6	28.0	31.7	34.3	37.2	35.8	35.3	35.3	36.4	37.1	2.0%	1.4%
Total North America	716.7	719.6	733.3	740.6	754.8	756.2	769.6	787.9	767.4	768.7	762.8	-0.8%	28.3%
Argentina	27.3	25.0	28.9	27.4	29.6	34.6	37.4	37.1	36.1	41.0	44.9	9.4%	1.7%
Bolivia	3.3	3.2	3.2	2.7	2.8	2.3	3.2	4.7	4.9	5.7	8.5	49.6%	0.3%
Brazil	4.5	4.8	5.5	6.0	6.3	8.7	7.2	7.6	9.2	10.1	11.1	9.6%	0.4%
Colombia	4.2	4.4	4.7	5.9	6.3	5.2	5.9	6.1	6.2	6.1	6.4	4.6%	0.2%
Trinidad & Tobago	6.2	6.1	7.1	7.4	8.6	11.7	14.1	15.2	17.3	24.7	27.7	12.0%	1.0%
Venezuela	24.7	27.0	29.7	30.8	32.3	27.4	27.9	29.6	28.4	25.2	28.1	11.5%	1.0%
Other S. & Cent. America	2.2	2.2	2.3	2.4	2.5	2.1	2.2	2.3	2.3	2.2	2.5	15.3%	0.1%
Total S. & Cent. America	67.4	73.2	81.4	82.5	88.5	90.9	97.9	102.6	104.4	115.0	129.1	12.2%	4.8%
Azerbaijan	6.0	6.2	5.9	5.6	5.2	5.6	5.3	5.2	4.9	4.8	4.6	-3.5%	0.2%
Denmark	4.9	5.3	6.4	7.9	7.6	7.8	8.1	8.4	8.4	8.0	9.4	16.4%	0.4%
Germany	16.6	18.1	17.4	17.1	16.7	17.9	16.9	17.0	17.6	17.7	16.4	-7.5%	0.6%
Italy	20.6	20.4	20.0	18.3	19.0	17.5	16.2	15.2	14.6	13.7	13.0	-5.5%	0.5%
Kazakhstan	4.2	5.5	6.1	7.6	7.4	9.3	10.8	10.8	10.6	12.9	18.5	42.9%	0.7%
Netherlands	66.4	67.0	75.9	67.1	63.6	59.3	57.3	61.9	59.9	58.4	68.8	17.9%	2.6%
Norway	26.8	27.8	37.4	43.0	44.2	48.5	49.7	53.9	65.5	73.1	78.5	7.3%	2.9%
Poland	3.4	3.5	3.6	3.6	3.6	3.4	3.7	3.9	4.0	4.0	4.4	8.7%	0.2%
Romania	18.7	18.0	17.2	15.0	14.0	14.0	13.8	13.6	13.2	13.0	13.2	1.6%	0.5%
Russian Federation	606.4	563.4	561.1	532.6	551.3	551.0	545.0	542.4	554.9	578.6	589.1	1.6%	21.9%
Turkmenistan	33.3	30.1	32.8	16.1	12.4	21.3	43.8	47.9	49.9	55.1	54.6	-0.9%	2.0%
Ukraine	17.0	17.0	17.2	17.4	16.9	16.9	16.7	17.1	17.4	17.7	18.3	3.4%	0.7%
United Kingdom	64.6	70.8	84.2	85.9	90.2	99.1	108.4	105.8	103.6	102.9	95.9	-6.7%	3.6%
Uzbekistan	44.0	45.3	45.7	47.8	51.1	51.8	52.6	53.5	53.8	59.6	55.8	4.1%	2.1%
Other Europe & Eurasia	16.8	15.9	14.6	13.4	12.4	11.5	11.2	11.0	11.2	10.7	10.9	2.0%	0.4%
Total Europe & Eurasia	907.7	904.2	945.4	899.1	915.5	934.9	959.5	967.7	989.4	1024.3	1051.5	2.7%	39.1%
Bahrain	7.1	7.2	7.4	8.0	8.4	9.7	8.8	9.1	9.5	8.6	9.8	1.4%	0.4%
Iran	31.8	35.3	39.0	47.0	50.0	58.4	60.2	66.0	75.0	81.5	85.5	4.9%	3.2%
Kuwait	6.0	9.3	9.3	9.3	9.5	9.6	9.6	8.5	8.0	9.1	9.7	6.6%	0.4%
Oman	2.9	4.1	4.4	5.0	5.2	5.5	9.7	14.0	15.0	16.5	17.6	6.7%	0.7%
Qatar	13.5	13.5	13.7	17.4	19.8	22.1	23.7	27.0	29.5	31.4	39.2	24.8%	1.5%
Saudi Arabia	42.8	42.9	44.4	45.3	46.8	46.2	49.8	53.7	56.7	60.1	64.0	6.6%	2.4%
Syria	1.5	1.9	2.5	3.8	4.3	4.5	4.2	4.1	5.0	5.2	5.2	–	0.2%
United Arab Emirates	25.8	31.3	33.8	36.3	37.1	28.5	38.4	39.4	43.4	44.8	45.8	2.2%	1.7%
Other Middle East	3.4	3.4	3.5	3.3	2.2	3.4	3.4	3.0	2.6	1.9	3.2	80.2%	0.1%
Total Middle East	134.8	148.9	158.0	175.4	184.0	193.8	206.8	224.8	244.7	259.9	279.9	7.7%	10.4%
Algeria	51.6	58.7	62.3	71.8	70.6	86.0	84.4	78.2	80.4	82.9	82.0	-1.0%	2.6%
Egypt	10.6	11.0	11.9	11.6	12.2	14.7	19.3	21.5	23.7	26.0	26.8	7.9%	1.0%
Libya	5.8	5.8	5.8	6.0	5.8	4.7	6.4	5.6	5.7	6.4	7.0	9.3%	0.3%
Nigeria	4.4	4.8	5.4	5.1	5.1	8.0	12.5	14.9	14.2	19.2	20.6	7.2%	0.9%
Other Africa	2.9	3.0	3.6	4.9	5.0	5.4	5.9	6.6	8.0	8.1	8.7	7.1%	0.3%
Total Africa	75.3	83.3	88.9	99.4	104.8	116.9	126.6	126.8	130.9	141.5	145.1	2.6%	5.4%
Australia	28.1	29.8	29.6	28.8	30.4	30.9	31.2	22.5	32.8	33.2	35.2	6.2%	1.3%
Bangladesh	6.6	7.4	7.8	7.6	7.8	8.3	10.0	10.7	11.4	12.3	13.2	7.0%	0.5%
Brunei	10.4	11.8	11.7	11.7	10.8	11.2	11.3	11.4	11.9	12.4	12.1	-2.0%	0.4%
China	16.6	17.6	19.9	22.2	22.3	24.9	27.2	30.3	31.9	34.4	40.8	18.5%	1.5%
India	16.6	19.4	20.5	23.0	24.7	25.9	28.9	27.2	28.7	29.9	29.4	-1.7%	1.1%
Indonesia	62.5	63.4	67.5	67.2	64.3	71.0	68.5	66.3	70.4	72.8	73.3	0.7%	2.7%
Malaysia	28.1	28.9	33.6	38.6	39.5	40.8	45.3	46.9	48.2	51.9	53.9	4.0%	2.0%
Myanmar	1.3	1.5	1.8	1.8	1.8	2.8	4.4	6.2	6.5	8.9	7.4	6.6%	0.3%
New Zealand	4.4	4.1	4.9	5.1	4.5	5.2	5.5	5.8	5.9	4.1	3.6	-13.6%	0.1%
Pakistan	13.3	14.6	15.4	15.6	16.0	17.3	18.9	19.9	20.6	21.1	23.2	10.0%	0.9%
Thailand	9.5	10.4	12.2	15.2	16.0	17.7	19.6	18.0	18.9	19.6	20.3	3.4%	0.8%
Vietnam	0.3	0.1	0.3	0.5	0.9	1.3	1.6	2.0	2.4	2.4	4.2	75.3%	0.2%
Other Asia Pacific	3.6	3.5	3.6	3.5	3.8	3.6	3.7	3.9	5.5	6.7	6.6	-1.2%	0.2%
Total Asia Pacific	199.4	212.4	224.4	241.8	241.6	260.9	272.9	281.1	294.2	307.7	323.2	5.0%	12.0%
TOTAL WORLD	2101.3	2141.7	2235.5	2230.9	2280.8	2351.7	2432.2	2480.9	2531.1	2517.1	2691.6	2.8%	100.0%
of which: European Union 25	188.0	195.4	219.0	211.1	209.8	213.1	219.4	220.1	215.4	211.9	215.2	1.6%	8.0%
OECD	866.7	879.1	925.8	932.1	1046.4	1056.7	1077.5	1103.0	1089.2	1094.4	1096.6	0.4%	40.8%
Former Soviet Union	671.2	669.8	669.0	627.4	644.6	666.3	674.5	677.3	692.2	722.1	741.3	2.5%	27.5%
Other EMEs	463.4	502.7	538.6	579.5	598.0	639.7	681.2	710.6	749.5	793.5	851.7	6.5%	31.6%

*Excluding gas flared or recycled
● Less than 0.05%

Note: As far as possible, the data above represents standard cubic metres (measured at 15°C and 1013 mbar), as it is derived directly from tonnes of oil equivalent using an average conversion factor. It does not necessarily equate with gas volumes expressed in specific national terms.
Because of rounding, some totals may not agree exactly with the sum of their component parts.
Natural gas production data expressed in billion feet per day is available at www.bp.com/statisticalreview.

Table 15 : World Natural Gas Consumption-2004

Consumption Billion cubic metres	1994	1995	1996	1997	1998	1999	2000	2001	2002	2003	2004	Change 2004 over 2003	2004 share of total
USA	611.6	628.0	649.6	633.2	642.2	643.3	658.7	641.4	661.0	649.3	646.7	0.2%	24.0%
Canada	78.8	80.2	85.9	82.8	85.0	83.1	93.0	82.8	86.6	93.2	89.5	-2.9%	3.3%
Mexico	27.0	28.1	28.6	32.3	35.4	37.4	39.5	39.0	42.7	45.6	48.2	5.1%	1.8%
Total North America	**717.4**	**746.3**	**763.4**	**769.3**	**762.6**	**764.8**	**791.2**	**763.2**	**789.9**	**783.3**	**784.3**	**0.1%**	**29.2%**
Argentina	24.3	27.0	31.9	28.6	30.5	32.4	33.2	31.2	30.3	34.6	37.9	9.5%	1.4%
Brazil	4.5	4.8	5.5	6.8	6.3	7.1	9.3	11.7	14.4	15.9	18.9	19.1%	0.7%
Chile	1.7	1.6	1.7	2.3	3.3	4.6	5.2	6.3	6.5	7.1	8.2	15.1%	0.3%
Colombia	4.2	4.4	4.7	5.9	6.2	5.2	5.9	6.1	6.1	6.0	6.3	4.6%	0.2%
Ecuador	0.1	0.1	6.1	0.1	0.1	0.1	0.1	0.2	0.1	0.1	0.1	∗	∗
Peru	0.4	0.4	0.4	0.2	0.4	0.4	0.3	0.4	0.4	0.5	0.9	84.3%	∗
Venezuela	24.7	27.5	29.7	30.9	32.3	27.4	27.9	29.6	28.4	25.2	28.1	11.5%	1.0%
Other S. & Cent. America	7.3	7.3	8.2	8.5	10.0	11.0	11.5	13.6	14.4	16.5	17.6	7.5%	0.7%
Total S. & Cent. America	**67.1**	**73.1**	**81.4**	**82.9**	**89.1**	**88.5**	**94.0**	**99.1**	**100.7**	**105.8**	**117.9**	**11.4%**	**4.4%**
Austria	7.2	7.9	8.4	6.1	8.3	8.5	8.1	8.6	8.5	9.4	9.5	0.9%	0.4%
Azerbaijan	8.1	8.0	6.9	5.6	5.2	5.6	5.4	7.8	7.8	8.0	8.5	6.9%	0.3%
Belarus	13.6	12.2	13.6	14.8	15.0	15.3	16.2	16.1	16.6	17.2	18.5	7.5%	0.7%
Belgium & Luxembourg	10.8	11.6	13.1	12.6	13.2	14.7	14.9	14.6	14.8	16.0	16.3	1.7%	0.6%
Bulgaria	4.1	5.0	5.2	4.1	3.5	3.0	3.3	3.0	2.7	2.6	3.1	21.3%	0.1%
Czech Republic	6.2	7.3	8.4	8.5	8.5	9.6	8.3	8.9	8.7	8.7	8.8	1.5%	0.3%
Denmark	3.5	3.5	4.1	4.4	4.9	5.0	4.9	5.1	5.1	5.4	5.4	∗	0.2%
Finland	3.1	3.2	3.3	3.2	3.7	3.7	3.7	4.1	4.0	4.5	4.4	-3.0%	0.2%
France	30.9	32.9	36.1	34.6	37.0	37.7	39.7	41.7	41.7	43.3	44.7	3.1%	1.7%
Germany	67.9	74.4	83.6	79.2	78.7	80.2	79.5	82.9	82.6	85.5	85.9	0.4%	3.2%
Greece	∗	∗	∗	0.2	0.9	1.4	1.9	1.9	2.0	2.3	2.4	7.5%	0.1%
Hungary	9.4	10.2	11.4	10.9	10.9	11.0	10.7	11.9	12.0	13.1	13.0	-0.8%	0.5%
Iceland	−	−	−	−	−	−	−	−	−	−	−	−	−
Republic of Ireland	2.4	2.8	3.0	2.1	3.1	3.3	3.6	4.0	4.1	4.1	4.1	-0.9%	0.2%
Italy	48.3	49.9	51.5	52.2	57.2	62.2	64.9	65.0	64.6	70.7	73.3	3.8%	2.7%
Kazakhstan	10.3	10.6	9.0	7.1	7.3	7.9	9.7	10.1	11.1	13.9	15.2	17.2%	0.6%
Lithuania	2.0	2.3	2.6	2.6	2.3	2.4	2.7	2.8	2.9	2.8	3.1	-0.3%	0.1%
Netherlands	38.9	37.6	41.7	39.7	39.7	37.9	39.2	39.1	39.5	40.3	43.5	8.0%	1.6%
Norway	2.9	2.9	3.2	3.7	3.9	3.6	4.0	3.6	4.0	4.3	4.6	5.6%	0.2%
Poland	9.2	9.8	10.5	10.5	10.8	10.9	11.1	11.5	11.2	11.2	13.2	17.7%	0.5%
Portugal	..	..	..	0.1	0.8	2.0	2.4	2.6	2.8	3.0	3.1	1.6%	0.1%
Romania	24.3	24.0	24.2	20.3	19.7	17.2	17.1	16.6	17.2	18.3	18.8	2.6%	0.7%
Russian Federation	390.9	377.6	378.9	350.4	364.7	363.0	377.2	372.7	388.9	392.9	402.1	2.3%	15.0%
Slovakia	5.0	5.7	6.2	6.3	6.4	6.4	6.5	6.9	7.2	7.0	6.8	-3.1%	0.3%
Spain	7.4	8.2	9.3	12.0	13.1	15.0	16.9	18.2	20.9	23.8	27.3	15.5%	1.0%
Sweden	0.8	0.8	0.9	0.9	0.9	0.8	0.7	0.7	0.9	0.9	0.8	-2.3%	∗
Switzerland	2.2	2.4	2.8	2.6	2.6	2.7	2.7	2.8	2.9	3.0	3.0	2.3%	0.1%
Turkey	6.5	6.8	9.3	9.4	9.3	12.0	14.1	16.0	17.4	20.9	22.1	5.7%	0.8%
Turkmenistan	10.2	9.0	10.0	10.1	10.3	11.3	12.6	12.9	13.2	14.8	15.5	5.7%	0.6%
Ukraine	81.3	76.2	82.5	74.3	68.8	73.0	73.1	70.9	66.0	71.2	70.7	-0.7%	2.6%
United Kingdom	66.1	70.5	82.1	84.5	87.9	92.5	96.6	96.3	95.1	96.4	98.0	2.7%	3.6%
Uzbekistan	41.3	42.4	43.3	45.4	47.0	49.3	47.7	51.1	52.4	47.2	48.3	4.5%	1.8%
Other Europe & Eurasia	10.9	13.0	13.5	14.7	14.6	12.9	12.4	15.1	14.2	14.3	13.7	-4.6%	0.5%
Total Europe & Eurasia	**929.0**	**929.4**	**977.5**	**936.1**	**959.9**	**981.3**	**1012.9**	**1025.7**	**1041.5**	**1074.9**	**1108.5**	**3.1%**	**41.2%**
Iran	31.8	35.2	36.9	47.1	51.8	58.4	62.9	70.2	79.2	82.9	87.1	5.1%	3.2%
Kuwait	8.0	9.2	8.5	9.7	9.3	8.8	9.6	8.5	8.0	8.9	9.7	8.6%	8.4%
Qatar	10.5	11.5	13.7	14.5	14.9	14.0	8.7	11.0	11.1	12.2	15.1	24.0%	0.6%
Saudi Arabia	42.9	42.9	44.4	46.3	46.8	48.2	49.8	53.7	56.7	60.1	64.0	6.5%	2.4%
United Arab Emirates	21.7	24.8	27.2	29.0	30.4	31.4	31.4	32.3	36.4	37.9	39.6	4.5%	1.5%
Other Middle East	14.9	16.1	17.3	19.8	20.5	21.5	22.1	22.8	23.6	20.9	26.6	11.4%	1.0%
Total Middle East	**130.6**	**141.8**	**150.7**	**164.9**	**173.7**	**180.1**	**186.4**	**199.4**	**215.1**	**226.1**	**242.2**	**7.2%**	**9.0%**
Algeria	19.6	21.0	21.6	20.2	20.9	21.3	19.8	20.5	20.2	21.2	21.2	-0.9%	0.8%
Egypt	10.4	11.0	11.3	11.8	12.0	14.3	18.2	21.5	22.7	24.6	25.7	4.5%	1.0%
South Africa	..	..	..	..	..	..	..	..	..	..	..	..	..
Other Africa	11.9	12.6	14.2	14.4	14.9	15.2	17.0	17.1	18.9	20.7	21.7	4.8%	0.9%
Total Africa	**41.9**	**44.6**	**47.2**	**46.1**	**47.7**	**50.9**	**55.2**	**59.1**	**61.7**	**66.7**	**68.6**	**2.9%**	**2.6%**
Australia	18.6	20.4	20.7	21.4	22.4	23.2	23.6	24.0	25.2	24.2	24.5	1.1%	0.9%
Bangladesh	6.0	7.4	7.6	7.6	7.8	9.3	10.0	10.7	11.4	11.3	13.2	7.0%	0.5%
China	16.6	17.7	17.7	19.5	19.3	21.4	24.5	27.8	29.6	32.9	39.0	19.0%	1.5%
China Hong Kong SAR	..	..	..	2.8	2.5	2.7	2.6	2.5	2.4	1.5	2.2	44.5%	0.1%
India	16.0	19.4	20.6	22.0	24.1	25.9	26.9	27.2	28.7	29.9	32.1	7.1%	1.2%
Indonesia	27.2	30.1	32.2	31.9	27.8	31.8	33.9	32.5	34.5	33.4	33.7	0.8%	1.3%
Japan	60.3	61.2	66.1	69.1	68.5	74.6	79.2	79.0	71.9	76.5	72.2	-5.7%	2.7%
Malaysia	13.6	13.7	13.9	16.7	17.4	18.1	24.3	25.9	26.8	31.8	33.2	4.4%	1.2%
New Zealand	4.4	4.2	4.7	5.1	4.5	5.2	5.5	5.7	5.5	4.1	3.6	-12.9%	0.1%
Pakistan	13.3	14.6	15.4	15.0	16.0	17.3	18.9	19.9	20.6	23.4	25.7	9.8%	1.0%
Philippines	−	−	−	−	−	−	−	1.6	1.8	2.2	2.5	-7.7%	0.1%
Singapore	1.5	1.5	1.5	1.5	1.5	1.7	1.7	4.5	4.9	6.3	7.8	45.7%	0.3%
South Korea	8.5	10.2	12.5	16.4	15.4	19.7	21.0	22.1	25.7	26.9	31.6	17.4%	1.2%
Taiwan	4.0	4.3	4.6	5.1	6.4	6.2	6.7	7.4	8.9	9.7	10.1	16.4%	0.4%
Thailand	9.5	10.0	11.9	14.8	15.9	17.4	20.5	22.5	24.4	27.5	28.7	4.7%	1.1%
Other Asia Pacific	3.4	3.5	3.8	4.3	4.7	5.0	5.9	6.4	6.8	7.8	8.0	38.1%	0.3%
Total Asia Pacific	**205.3**	**218.1**	**239.6**	**250.2**	**255.6**	**275.3**	**299.7**	**319.0**	**327.1**	**346.8**	**367.7**	**6.0%**	**13.7%**
TOTAL WORLD	**2061.2**	**2153.6**	**2259.8**	**2248.5**	**2288.6**	**2341.8**	**2439.3**	**2465.5**	**2535.8**	**2603.5**	**2689.3**	**3.3%**	**100.0%**
of which: European Union 25	315.7	341.5	378.9	376.0	391.4	400.6	419.9	430.2	431.8	450.3	466.9	2.5%	17.4%
OECD	1120.4	1161.7	1252.7	1264.1	1276.8	1308.2	1365.5	1341.7	1367.8	1387.6	1406.1	1.2%	52.3%
Former Soviet Union	587.0	547.0	553.9	519.1	529.4	538.2	551.9	553.1	565.5	574.9	590.0	2.6%	21.9%
Other EMEs	384.8	415.5	448.9	466.1	482.3	498.4	534.0	570.8	602.8	641.0	693.1	8.1%	25.8%

♦ Less than 0.05.
∗ Less than 0.05%.

Notes: The difference between these world consumption figures and the world production statistics on page 22 is due to variations in stocks at storage facilities and liquefaction plants, together with unavoidable disparities in the definition, measurement & conversion of gas supply and demand data.

As far as possible, the data above represents standard cubic metres (measured at 15°C and 1013 mbar), as it is derived directly from tonnes of oil equivalent using an average conversion factor. It does not necessarily equate with gas volumes expressed in specific natural terms.

Natural gas consumption data expressed in billion cubic feet per day is available at www.bp.com/statisticalreview.

Table-16 : World Coal Proven Resrves-2004

Proved reserves at end 2004 Million tonnes	Anthracite and bituminous	Sub bituminous and lignite	Total	Share of total	R/P ratio
USA	111338	135305	246643	27.1%	245
Canada	3471	3107	6578	0.7%	100
Mexico	860	351	1211	0.1%	135
Total North America	**115669**	**138763**	**254432**	**28.0%**	**235**
Brazil	–	10113	10113	1.1%	*
Colombia	6230	381	6611	0.7%	120
Venezuela	479	–	479	0.1%	53
Other S. & Cent. America	992	1898	2890	0.3%	*
Total S. & Cent. America	**7701**	**12192**	**19893**	**2.2%**	**290**
Bulgaria	4	2183	2187	0.2%	84
Czech Republic	2094	3458	5552	0.6%	90
France	15	–	15	*	17
Germany	183	6556	6739	0.7%	32
Greece	–	3900	3900	0.4%	55
Hungary	198	3159	3357	0.4%	240
Kazakhstan	28151	3128	31279	3.4%	360
Poland	14000	–	14000	1.5%	87
Romania	22	472	494	0.1%	16
Russian Federation	49088	107922	157010	17.3%	*
Spain	200	330	530	0.1%	26
Turkey	278	3908	4186	0.5%	67
Ukraine	16274	17879	34153	3.8%	424
United Kingdom	220	–	220	*	9
Other Europe & Eurasia	1529	21944	23473	2.6%	341
Total Europe & Eurasia	**112256**	**174839**	**287095**	**31.6%**	**242**
South Africa	48750	–	48750	5.4%	201
Zimbabwe	502	–	502	0.1%	154
Other Africa	910	174	1084	0.1%	420
Middle East	419	–	419	*	399
Total Africa & Middle East	**50581**	**174**	**50755**	**5.6%**	**264**
Australia	38600	39900	78500	8.6%	215
China	62200	52200	114500	12.6%	59
India	90085	2360	92445	10.2%	229
Indonesia	740	4228	4968	0.5%	38
Japan	359	–	359	*	268
New Zealand	33	538	571	0.1%	115
North Korea	300	300	600	0.1%	21
Pakistan	–	3050	3050	0.3%	*
South Korea	–	80	80	*	25
Thailand	–	1354	1354	0.1%	67
Vietnam	150	–	150	*	6
Other Asia Pacific	97	215	312	*	34
Total Asia Pacific	**192564**	**104325**	**296889**	**32.7%**	**101**
TOTAL WORLD	**478771**	**430293**	**909064**	**100.0%**	**164**
of which: OECD	172593	200687	373220	41.1%	190
Former Soviet Union	94613	132741	227354	25.0%	*
Other EMEs	211866	96695	308690	33.9%	162

More than 500 years.
* Less than 0.05%.

Source: World Energy Council

Notes: Proved reserves of coal - Generally taken to be those quantities that geological and engineering information indicates with reasonable certainty can be recovered in the future from known deposits under existing economic and operating conditions.
Reserves-to-production (R/P) ratio - If the reserves remaining at the end of the year are divided by the production in that year, the result is the length of time that those remaining reserves would last if production were to continue at that level.

Table-17: World Total Coal Production-2004

Production* Million tonnes oil equivalent	1994	1995	1996	1997	1998	1999	2000	2001	2002	2003	2004	Change 2004 over 2003	2004 share of total
USA	552.8	550.7	567.1	580.3	586.4	579.7	585.6	587.3	565.6	549.5	567.2	3.2%	20.8%
Canada	39.4	40.9	41.6	43.0	40.9	39.2	37.1	37.6	34.9	32.2	34.9	8.3%	1.3%
Mexico	4.3	4.1	4.6	4.5	4.8	4.9	5.4	5.4	5.2	4.6	4.3	-6.2%	0.2%
Total North America	**596.5**	**595.7**	**613.2**	**627.8**	**644.0**	**623.8**	**608.1**	**630.3**	**605.7**	**586.0**	**606.3**	**3.5%**	**22.2%**
Brazil	2.0	2.0	1.8	2.1	2.0	2.1	2.9	2.1	1.9	1.8	1.8	-6.5%	0.1%
Colombia	14.7	16.7	19.5	21.0	21.9	21.2	24.9	28.5	25.7	32.5	35.8	9.9%	1.5%
Venezuela	3.2	3.2	3.1	3.9	4.7	4.9	5.8	5.5	5.7	5.0	6.6	32.2%	0.2%
Other S. & Cent. America	1.3	1.2	1.2	1.1	0.4	0.5	0.5	0.5	0.4	0.3	0.2	-48.7%	*
Total S. & Cent. America	**21.3**	**23.1**	**25.6**	**28.1**	**29.1**	**28.7**	**33.9**	**36.7**	**33.7**	**39.6**	**44.1**	**11.5%**	**1.6%**
Bulgaria	4.8	5.2	5.2	4.9	5.0	4.2	4.4	4.4	4.4	4.4	4.4	0.1%	0.2%
Czech Republic	28.1	27.3	27.0	27.9	26.0	23.1	25.0	25.4	24.3	24.2	23.5	-3.1%	0.9%
France	5.7	5.3	5.2	4.3	2.6	3.3	2.3	1.5	1.1	1.3	0.5	-63.9%	*
Germany	77.8	74.6	70.0	66.9	61.3	59.4	56.5	54.1	55.0	54.1	54.7	1.1%	2.0%
Greece	7.4	7.5	7.2	7.7	8.1	8.0	8.2	8.5	9.1	9.6	9.5	-0.8%	0.3%
Hungary	2.9	2.6	2.2	3.3	2.0	3.1	2.9	2.9	2.7	2.9	2.9	4.1%	0.1%
Kazakhstan	53.5	42.6	39.3	37.2	36.0	30.0	38.5	40.7	37.8	43.2	44.4	2.5%	1.6%
Poland	89.3	91.1	94.5	92.1	79.6	77.0	71.3	71.7	71.3	71.4	69.8	-2.2%	2.6%
Romania	9.1	9.3	9.6	7.4	5.7	5.1	6.4	7.1	6.7	7.2	6.9	-4.4%	0.2%
Russian Federation	121.2	119.5	114.4	109.2	103.9	112.0	115.9	121.5	114.8	124.9	127.5	2.2%	4.7%
Spain	10.6	10.2	10.0	9.8	9.3	9.6	8.0	7.6	7.2	6.8	6.7	-2.0%	0.2%
Turkey	12.1	12.1	12.3	13.1	13.9	13.3	13.9	14.2	11.5	10.5	10.2	-3.0%	0.4%
Ukraine	48.5	44.2	39.1	39.9	39.9	41.3	42.2	43.8	43.0	41.5	41.9	1.0%	1.5%
United Kingdom	28.3	31.8	30.2	39.4	25.0	22.5	19.0	19.4	18.2	17.2	15.3	-11.2%	0.6%
Other Europe & Eurasia	13.9	14.0	13.4	15.9	16.7	13.4	14.2	14.4	15.3	15.9	16.4	2.8%	0.6%
Total Europe & Eurasia	**513.3**	**496.4**	**480.4**	**469.2**	**437.0**	**424.3**	**428.7**	**437.3**	**422.4**	**435.0**	**434.4**	**-0.1%**	**15.9%**
Total Middle East	**0.8**	**0.7**	**0.7**	**0.6**	**0.6**	**0.7**	**0.6**	**0.5**	**0.4**	**0.6**	**0.6**	**1.0%**	*
South Africa	111.1	116.9	118.9	124.6	127.1	125.6	126.6	126.0	124.1	133.9	136.9	2.2%	5.0%
Zimbabwe	3.5	3.6	3.3	3.4	3.5	3.2	2.9	2.9	2.6	2.0	2.1	6.9%	0.1%
Other Africa	1.4	1.4	1.3	1.2	1.4	1.3	1.2	1.2	1.4	1.3	1.4	6.2%	*
Total Africa	**116.0**	**121.9**	**123.5**	**129.2**	**132.0**	**130.1**	**130.7**	**130.1**	**128.1**	**137.1**	**140.3**	**2.3%**	**5.1%**
Australia	129.3	129.5	133.6	142.1	149.9	160.6	166.2	179.8	184.0	189.5	199.4	5.2%	7.3%
China	619.4	660.9	691.5	665.5	619.7	529.9	501.8	555.1	713.4	873.4	989.8	13.3%	36.2%
India	126.9	135.2	145.7	149.6	150.3	147.4	157.0	160.3	188.1	175.9	188.8	7.4%	6.9%
Indonesia	20.2	25.7	31.0	33.7	39.3	46.3	47.4	60.9	63.6	69.4	81.4	17.3%	2.0%
Japan	3.8	3.4	3.6	3.4	2.0	2.2	1.7	1.8	0.9	0.7	0.7	–	*
New Zealand	1.8	2.1	2.2	2.0	2.0	2.1	2.2	2.4	2.7	3.2	3.0	-4.2%	0.1%
Pakistan	1.4	1.4	1.5	1.4	1.5	1.5	1.4	1.5	1.6	1.5	1.3	-9.6%	*
South Korea	3.3	2.6	2.2	2.0	2.0	1.9	1.9	1.7	1.5	1.6	1.4	-2.3%	0.1%
Thailand	5.2	5.5	6.3	6.9	6.1	5.7	6.1	5.6	5.6	5.4	5.8	7.0%	0.2%
Vietnam	3.4	3.9	4.9	6.4	6.4	4.9	6.4	7.2	8.6	10.7	14.8	39.6%	0.5%
Other Asia Pacific	21.6	20.2	17.9	17.2	15.7	18.0	19.3	19.7	19.0	19.3	19.7	2.5%	0.7%
Total Asia Pacific	**930.2**	**980.5**	**1040.5**	**1035.1**	**993.7**	**913.5**	**919.5**	**992.1**	**1169.0**	**1350.4**	**1506.3**	**11.5%**	**55.1%**
TOTAL WORLD	**2178.1**	**2218.2**	**2218.9**	**2290.0**	**2236.5**	**2121.1**	**2112.4**	**2227.0**	**2359.2**	**2544.7**	**2732.1**	**7.2%**	**100.0%**
of which: OECD	992.1	997.0	1015.4	1038.6	1031.2	1010.4	993.1	1023.9	998.0	981.9	1006.9	2.5%	36.9%
Former Soviet Union	224.8	206.5	193.8	187.6	180.6	184.4	197.4	207.0	196.5	210.4	214.9	2.1%	7.9%
Other EMEs	961.2	1014.7	1072.7	1063.8	1024.4	926.2	920.9	996.1	1164.6	1356.4	1510.3	11.2%	55.3%

*Commercial solid fuels only, i.e. bituminous coal and anthracite (hard coal), and lignite and brown (sub-bituminous) coal.
♦ Less than 0.05%.
Notes: Because of rounding, some totals may not agree exactly with the sum of their component parts.
Coal production data expressed in million tonnes is available at www.bp.com/statisticalreview.

263

Table-18: World Total Coal Consumption-2004

Consumption* Million tonnes oil equivalent	1994	1995	1996	1997	1998	1999	2000	2001	2002	2003	2004	Change 2004 over 2003	2004 share of total
USA	501.7	506.2	529.3	540.4	545.3	544.9	569.1	552.3	552.0	562.1	564.3	0.3%	20.3%
Canada	24.5	26.2	25.7	26.8	28.1	27.8	28.4	32.0	31.0	30.6	30.5	-0.1%	1.1%
Mexico	4.5	5.5	5.7	5.7	5.9	6.0	6.2	8.8	7.6	9.6	9.0	4.3%	0.3%
Total North America	530.7	538.5	560.7	573.0	579.7	578.7	604.6	591.1	590.6	601.7	603.8	0.3%	21.7%
Argentina	1.0	0.9	0.9	0.8	0.8	0.9	0.8	0.6	0.5	0.7	0.7	7.4%	•
Brazil	10.3	10.8	11.3	11.5	11.4	11.9	12.5	12.2	11.5	11.4	11.4	—	0.4%
Chile	2.2	2.4	2.2	4.2	3.7	3.5	3.9	2.1	2.4	2.4	2.5	4.2%	0.1%
Colombia	3.6	3.4	3.2	2.1	2.8	2.1	2.2	3.3	2.0	2.6	2.7	4.0%	0.1%
Ecuador	–	–	–	–	–	–	–	–	–	–	–	–	–
Peru	0.4	0.4	0.3	0.4	0.4	0.5	0.5	0.4	0.4	0.4	0.4	1.2%	•
Venezuela	0.1	†	†	†	†	0.1	†	†	0.1	0.1	0.1	–	•
Other S. & Cent. America	0.4	0.4	0.5	0.4	0.5	0.6	0.6	0.7	0.9	0.9	1.0	4.5%	•
Total S. & Cent. America	18.0	18.3	19.4	20.4	19.7	19.6	20.6	19.4	17.7	18.4	18.7	1.6%	0.7%
Austria	2.5	2.4	2.7	3.1	3.0	3.2	3.2	2.9	3.0	3.5	3.5	•	0.1%
Azerbaijan	–	–	–	–	–	–	–	†	†	†	†	-33.2%	•
Belarus	0.7	0.2	0.6	0.6	0.4	0.1	0.1	0.1	0.1	0.1	0.1	28.9%	•
Belgium & Luxembourg	9.5	9.8	7.6	7.5	7.9	6.9	7.6	7.6	6.7	6.5	6.1	-5.6%	0.2%
Bulgaria	7.6	7.8	8.4	7.8	8.2	6.6	6.9	6.9	6.7	7.1	7.2	1.4%	0.3%
Czech Republic	23.7	22.5	23.6	22.8	20.5	19.0	21.0	21.2	20.6	20.3	20.4	-2.3%	0.7%
Denmark	7.6	6.6	9.0	6.7	5.6	4.7	4.0	4.2	4.2	5.7	4.4	-21.9%	0.2%
Finland	4.1	3.1	4.6	4.5	3.4	3.6	3.5	4.0	4.4	5.8	5.2	-10.6%	0.2%
France	13.7	14.5	15.4	13.4	13.1	14.3	13.9	11.6	12.4	13.0	12.5	-4.1%	0.4%
Germany	85.6	90.6	89.9	86.8	84.8	80.2	84.9	85.0	84.6	87.2	85.7	-1.8%	3.1%
Greece	8.4	8.2	7.8	7.6	8.8	9.1	9.2	9.3	9.8	9.4	9.3	-0.8%	0.3%
Hungary	3.6	3.6	3.7	3.7	3.4	3.4	3.2	3.4	3.1	3.4	3.0	-9.3%	0.1%
Iceland	0.1	0.1	0.1	0.1	0.1	0.1	0.1	0.1	0.1	0.1	0.1	-1.0%	•
Republic of Ireland	1.9	1.9	1.9	2.0	1.9	1.6	1.9	1.9	1.7	1.8	1.8	-0.2%	0.1%
Italy	15.7	12.5	11.2	11.0	11.6	11.6	13.0	13.7	14.2	15.3	17.1	11.8%	0.6%
Kazakhstan	34.5	27.5	25.9	22.4	22.9	18.8	23.2	22.5	22.8	25.2	27.5	9.2%	1.0%
Lithuania	0.1	0.1	0.1	0.1	0.1	0.1	0.1	0.1	0.1	0.2	0.1	-14.8%	•
Netherlands	9.5	9.8	9.3	9.5	9.4	7.7	8.6	8.5	8.9	9.1	9.1	-0.5%	0.3%
Norway	0.6	0.7	0.6	0.6	0.7	0.7	0.7	0.6	0.5	0.5	0.6	10.5%	•
Poland	72.3	71.7	73.2	70.1	63.8	61.0	57.6	58.0	56.7	57.7	57.7	•	2.1%
Portugal	3.4	4.2	2.9	3.6	3.6	3.6	4.5	3.7	4.1	3.8	3.9	3.0%	0.1%
Romania	9.4	9.7	9.5	8.4	7.6	6.7	7.0	7.2	7.6	7.6	7.2	-7.2%	0.3%
Russian Federation	126.4	119.4	115.7	106.3	100.0	104.1	106.8	110.0	102.9	109.4	105.9	-3.2%	3.8%
Slovakia	5.5	5.1	5.0	4.7	4.5	4.3	4.0	4.1	4.0	4.2	4.2	-0.7%	0.2%
Spain	18.0	18.5	15.5	17.7	17.7	20.5	21.6	19.5	21.9	20.5	21.1	3.0%	0.8%
Sweden	2.1	2.1	2.4	2.1	2.0	2.0	1.9	7.0	2.2	2.2	2.4	7.5%	0.1%
Switzerland	0.2	0.2	0.1	0.1	0.1	0.1	0.1	0.1	0.1	0.1	0.1	4.1%	•
Turkey	17.9	17.5	20.7	22.3	24.0	22.8	25.5	21.8	21.2	21.9	23.0	5.2%	0.8%
Turkmenistan	†	†	†	†	–	–	–	–	–	–	–	–	–
Ukraine	46.3	42.1	33.2	38.0	36.9	38.5	38.8	39.4	38.3	39.0	39.4	1.0%	1.4%
United Kingdom	48.7	47.5	44.4	39.6	39.7	35.6	36.9	40.0	36.7	39.2	38.1	-2.8%	1.4%
Uzbekistan	1.9	1.4	1.2	1.2	1.2	0.9	1.0	1.1	1.0	1.0	1.2	19.9%	•
Other Europe & Eurasia	16.6	18.2	18.3	21.3	21.7	17.0	18.0	17.2	18.2	19.2	19.5	1.9%	0.7%
Total Europe & Eurasia	600.8	580.3	564.9	548.3	530.3	509.6	527.5	526.7	520.9	540.5	537.2	-0.6%	19.3%
Iran	1.3	1.4	1.2	0.9	1.0	1.0	1.1	1.1	1.1	1.1	1.1	1.8%	•
Kuwait	–	–	–	–	–	–	–	–	–	–	–	–	–
Qatar	–	–	–	–	–	–	–	–	–	–	–	–	–
Saudi Arabia	–	–	–	–	–	–	–	–	–	–	–	–	–
United Arab Emirates	–	–	–	–	–	–	–	–	–	–	–	–	–
Other Middle East	3.8	4.1	5.0	5.4	5.8	5.7	6.2	7.2	7.6	7.9	8.0	1.0%	0.3%
Total Middle East	5.1	5.5	6.1	6.3	6.8	6.7	7.3	8.3	8.7	9.0	9.1	1.1%	0.3%
Algeria	0.6	0.6	0.5	0.5	0.5	0.5	0.5	0.6	0.6	0.8	0.8	7.1%	•
Egypt	1.0	0.7	0.9	0.8	0.8	0.6	0.7	0.7	0.7	0.7	0.7	–	•
South Africa	73.6	77.4	81.7	84.3	83.4	82.3	81.9	80.6	82.5	89.2	94.5	5.8%	3.4%
Other Africa	6.5	8.7	6.8	6.9	7.9	6.5	8.4	7.2	7.2	6.6	6.8	4.0%	0.2%
Total Africa	81.6	85.3	89.8	92.3	91.7	90.8	91.5	89.2	92.0	97.3	102.8	5.7%	3.7%
Australia	39.6	41.1	42.6	45.1	47.3	47.9	48.3	49.6	52.3	50.9	54.4	6.9%	2.0%
Bangladesh	†	0.2	0.2	0.3	0.1	•	0.2	0.4	0.4	0.4	0.4	—	•
China	608.4	671.9	691.6	691.7	608.3	492.3	415.0	517.7	692.4	834.7	956.9	14.6%	34.4%
China Hong Kong SAR	5.2	5.6	4.2	3.6	4.4	3.9	3.7	4.9	5.4	6.6	6.6	0.1%	0.2%
India	133.9	142.8	154.4	160.2	159.8	158.9	169.1	172.1	181.7	190.6	204.8	7.5%	7.4%
Indonesia	4.8	5.7	6.9	8.2	9.3	11.8	13.7	16.7	18.0	17.9	22.2	24.1%	0.8%
Japan	82.0	86.2	88.3	89.8	88.4	91.5	98.9	102.0	106.6	112.2	120.8	7.7%	4.3%
Malaysia	1.1	1.5	1.5	1.7	1.8	1.8	1.9	2.6	2.6	4.2	5.7	37.3%	0.2%
New Zealand	1.3	1.2	1.2	1.2	1.1	1.2	1.1	1.3	1.3	1.9	1.8	-3.7%	0.1%
Pakistan	2.2	2.2	2.2	2.1	2.1	2.1	2.0	2.1	2.4	2.9	3.2	9.0%	0.1%
Philippines	1.3	1.4	2.0	2.4	2.7	2.9	4.2	4.5	4.7	4.7	5.0	5.7%	0.2%
Singapore	–	–	–	–	–	–	–	–	–	–	–	–	–
South Korea	26.7	28.1	32.2	34.8	36.1	38.2	43.0	45.7	49.1	51.1	53.1	3.9%	1.9%
Taiwan	16.6	17.1	19.4	21.9	23.8	24.8	28.9	30.8	32.9	35.3	36.4	4.1%	1.3%
Thailand	6.1	7.1	8.7	8.7	7.3	7.9	7.8	8.8	9.2	9.4	10.2	8.9%	0.4%
Other Asia Pacific	22.2	21.3	19.1	19.9	19.4	19.1	20.7	22.4	23.2	23.9	24.8	3.8%	0.9%
Total Asia Pacific	948.4	1032.5	1064.7	1081.5	1010.7	904.3	898.7	982.8	1184.0	1346.6	1506.6	11.9%	54.2%
TOTAL WORLD	**2185.5**	**2259.2**	**2305.6**	**2319.4**	**2238.3**	**2109.7**	**2149.1**	**2217.3**	**2413.1**	**2613.5**	**2778.2**	**6.3%**	**100.0%**
of which: European Union 25	341.4	337.5	332.4	318.5	309.6	294.1	302.3	302.0	300.8	310.8	307.0	-1.2%	11.0%
OECD	1036.1	1047.0	1077.2	1092.6	1095.1	1073.2	1122.9	1114.0	1121.2	1149.5	1163.2	1.2%	41.9%
Former Soviet Union	211.5	192.4	178.6	171.2	163.2	164.4	169.9	172.7	166.9	175.6	175.0	-0.4%	6.3%
Other EMEs	935.9	1019.8	1049.7	1064.7	991.0	871.2	855.3	930.6	1124.9	1288.4	1440.1	11.8%	51.8%

*Commercial solid fuels only, i.e. bituminous coal and anthracite (hard coal), and lignite and brown (sub bituminous) coal
†Less than 0.05
• Less than 0.05%

Table-19: World Nuclear Energy Total Consumption-2004

Consumption* Million tonnes oil equivalent	1994	1995	1996	1997	1998	1999	2000	2001	2002	2003	2004	change 2004 over 2003	2004 share of total
USA	152.6	160.4	160.7	149.8	160.5	173.5	175.6	180.2	185.6	181.9	187.9	3.2%	30.1%
Canada	24.4	22.1	21.6	18.7	16.2	16.6	16.5	17.4	17.1	16.9	20.5	21.3%	3.3%
Mexico	1.0	1.9	1.8	2.4	2.1	2.3	1.9	2.0	2.2	2.4	2.1	-11.9%	0.3%
Total North America	177.9	184.5	185.5	170.8	178.8	192.4	197.9	202.5	205.1	201.2	210.4	4.6%	33.7%
Argentina	1.9	1.6	1.7	1.8	1.7	1.6	1.4	1.6	1.3	1.7	1.8	4.1%	0.3%
Brazil	†	0.6	0.5	0.7	0.7	0.9	1.4	3.2	3.1	3.0	2.6	-13.1%	0.4%
Chile	..	..	..	..	..	..	..	..	..	..	..	..	..
Colombia	..	..	..	..	..	..	..	..	..	..	..	..	..
Ecuador	..	..	..	..	..	..	..	..	..	..	..	..	..
Peru	..	..	..	..	..	..	..	..	..	..	..	..	..
Venezuela	..	..	..	..	..	..	..	..	..	..	..	..	..
Other S. & Cent. America	..	..	..	..	..	..	..	..	..	..	..	..	..
Total S. & Cent. America	1.9	2.2	2.2	2.5	2.4	2.5	2.8	4.8	4.4	4.7	4.4	-6.9%	0.7%
Austria	..	..	..	..	..	..	..	..	..	..	..	..	..
Azerbaijan	..	..	..	..	..	..	..	..	..	..	..	..	..
Belarus	..	..	..	..	..	..	..	..	..	..	..	..	..
Belgium & Luxembourg	9.2	9.4	9.8	10.7	10.5	11.1	10.9	10.5	10.7	10.9	10.9	1.4%	1.8%
Bulgaria	3.5	3.9	4.1	4.0	2.8	2.6	4.1	4.4	4.6	3.9	3.8	-2.7%	0.6%
Czech Republic	2.9	2.8	2.9	2.9	3.0	3.0	3.1	3.3	4.2	5.3	6.0	1.8%	1.0%
Denmark	..	..	..	..	..	..	..	..	..	..	..	..	..
Finland	4.4	4.3	4.4	4.8	5.0	5.3	5.1	5.2	5.4	5.5	5.5	-0.2%	0.9%
France	81.5	85.4	89.9	89.5	87.8	89.2	84.0	95.0	98.6	98.5	101.4	1.6%	16.2%
Germany	34.2	34.9	36.6	38.5	36.6	38.5	38.4	38.7	37.3	37.4	37.8	1.2%	6.1%
Greece	..	..	..	..	..	..	..	..	..	..	..	..	..
Hungary	3.2	3.2	3.2	3.2	3.2	3.2	3.2	3.2	3.2	2.6	2.7	6.2%	0.4%
Iceland	..	..	..	..	..	..	..	..	..	..	..	..	..
Republic of Ireland	..	..	..	..	..	..	..	..	..	..	..	..	..
Italy	..	..	..	..	..	..	..	..	..	..	..	..	..
Kazakhstan	0.1	†	†	0.1	†	..	..	..	..	..	..	..	..
Lithuania	1.7	2.7	3.5	2.7	2.1	2.2	1.9	2.6	3.2	3.5	3.4	-2.5%	0.5%
Netherlands	0.9	0.9	0.9	0.5	0.9	0.9	0.9	0.9	0.9	0.9	0.9	-4.8%	0.1%
Norway	..	..	..	..	..	..	..	..	..	..	..	..	..
Poland	..	..	..	..	..	..	..	..	..	..	..	..	..
Portugal	..	..	..	..	..	..	..	..	..	..	..	..	..
Romania	..	..	0.3	1.2	1.2	1.2	1.2	1.2	1.2	1.1	1.3	10.2%	0.2%
Russian Federation	22.1	22.5	24.7	24.5	23.8	27.1	29.5	31.0	32.1	33.0	32.4	-3.8%	5.2%
Slovakia	2.7	2.6	2.6	2.4	2.6	3.0	3.7	3.9	4.1	4.0	3.9	-4.7%	0.6%
Spain	12.5	12.5	12.7	12.5	13.4	13.3	14.1	14.4	14.3	14.0	14.3	2.1%	2.3%
Sweden	18.8	15.8	16.6	15.8	15.9	16.6	13.0	18.3	15.4	15.5	17.3	13.7%	2.8%
Switzerland	5.5	5.6	5.7	5.8	5.8	6.6	6.0	6.1	6.2	6.2	6.1	-1.9%	1.0%
Turkey	..	..	..	..	..	..	..	..	..	..	..	..	..
Turkmenistan	..	..	..	..	..	..	..	..	..	..	..	..	..
Ukraine	16.6	16.0	18.0	18.0	17.0	18.3	17.5	17.3	17.7	18.4	19.7	6.9%	3.2%
United Kingdom	20.0	20.1	21.4	22.2	22.6	21.5	19.3	20.4	19.9	20.1	18.1	-10.9%	2.9%
Uzbekistan	..	..	..	..	..	..	..	..	..	..	..	..	..
Other Europe & Eurasia	1.0	1.7	1.6	1.5	1.5	1.6	1.5	1.6	1.8	1.6	1.8	9.1%	0.3%
Total Europe & Eurasia	237.8	243.7	258.6	260.8	257.3	263.2	267.4	276.3	280.9	245.5	287.2	0.9%	46.0%
Iran	..	..	..	..	..	..	..	..	..	..	..	..	..
Kuwait	..	..	..	..	..	..	..	..	..	..	..	..	..
Qatar	..	..	..	..	..	..	..	..	..	..	..	..	..
Saudi Arabia	..	..	..	..	..	..	..	..	..	..	..	..	..
United Arab Emirates	..	..	..	..	..	..	..	..	..	..	..	..	..
Other Middle East	..	..	..	..	..	..	..	..	..	..	..	..	..
Total Middle East	..	..	..	..	..	..	..	..	..	..	..	..	..
Algeria	..	..	..	..	..	..	..	..	..	..	..	..	..
Egypt	..	..	..	..	..	..	..	..	..	..	..	..	..
South Africa	2.3	2.7	2.8	3.0	3.2	3.1	3.1	2.6	2.9	3.0	3.4	12.7%	0.5%
Other Africa	..	..	..	..	..	..	..	..	..	..	..	..	..
Total Africa	2.3	2.7	2.8	3.0	3.2	3.1	3.1	2.6	2.9	3.0	3.4	12.7%	0.5%
Australia	..	..	..	..	..	..	..	..	..	..	..	..	..
Bangladesh	..	..	..	..	..	..	..	..	..	..	..	..	..
China	3.1	2.9	3.2	3.3	3.4	3.4	3.8	4.0	5.7	9.9	11.3	14.1%	1.8%
China Hong Kong SAR	..	..	..	..	..	..	..	..	..	..	..	..	..
India	1.1	1.7	1.9	2.3	2.6	2.3	3.6	4.3	4.4	4.1	3.8	-7.7%	0.6%
Indonesia	..	..	..	..	..	..	..	..	..	..	..	..	..
Japan	58.7	65.1	67.3	72.6	74.0	71.9	72.3	72.7	71.3	52.1	64.8	24.5%	10.4%
Malaysia	..	..	..	..	..	..	..	..	..	..	..	..	..
New Zealand	..	..	..	..	..	..	..	..	..	..	..	..	..
Pakistan	0.1	0.1	0.1	0.1	0.1	†	0.2	0.5	0.4	0.4	0.5	7.0%	0.1%
Philippines	..	..	..	..	..	..	..	..	..	..	..	..	..
Singapore	..	..	..	..	..	..	..	..	..	..	..	..	..
South Korea	13.3	15.2	16.7	17.4	20.3	23.3	24.7	25.4	27.0	29.3	29.6	0.9%	4.7%
Taiwan	7.9	9.0	9.6	9.2	8.3	9.7	8.7	8.0	9.0	9.8	8.9	1.5%	1.4%
Thailand	..	..	..	..	..	..	..	..	..	..	..	..	..
Other Asia Pacific	..	..	..	..	..	..	..	..	..	..	..	..	..
Total Asia Pacific	84.3	93.0	97.8	104.1	108.8	110.2	113.3	114.8	117.7	104.8	118.9	13.5%	19.9%
TOTAL WORLD	504.1	526.1	546.9	541.3	550.5	571.8	584.5	604.3	611.8	559.2	620.2	4.4%	100.0%
of which: European Union 25	190.8	195.6	205.2	206.9	206.4	208.9	208.6	215.9	216.7	220.9	223.4	1.2%	35.8%
OECD	443.5	462.0	474.4	469.9	480.2	498.8	506.5	518.7	525.7	506.0	529.6	4.9%	84.8%
Former Soviet Union	39.6	41.2	46.4	45.6	44.0	46.2	49.4	51.2	53.4	56.0	56.0	♦	9.0%
Other EMEs	21.0	22.6	24.2	25.8	26.3	26.3	28.6	31.0	33.9	37.2	38.6	3.9%	6.2%

*Converted on the basis of thermal equivalence assuming 38% conversion efficiency in a modern thermal power station
†Less than 0.05
♦Less than 0.05%
Note: Nuclear energy data expressed in terawatt-hours is available at www.bp.com/statisticalreview

Table-20 : World Total Hydroelectricity Consumption-2004

Consumption*
Million tonnes oil equivalent

	1994	1995	1996	1997	1998	1999	2000	2001	2002	2003	2004	Change 2004 over 2003	2004 share of total
USA	58.7	70.4	78.7	80.6	72.3	71.5	61.7	47.6	59.4	61.1	59.8	-2.2%	9.4%
Canada	74.2	75.9	90.2	79.4	75.1	77.8	81.1	75.5	79.4	78.0	78.4	0.5%	12.0%
Mexico	4.6	6.2	7.1	6.0	5.6	7.4	7.5	6.4	5.6	4.5	5.7	27.2%	0.9%
Total North America	**137.5**	**152.6**	**166.0**	**166.0**	**153.6**	**156.9**	**150.3**	**129.5**	**143.4**	**141.6**	**141.9**	**0.2%**	**22.4%**
Argentina	6.2	8.1	5.2	6.4	6.0	4.9	6.5	8.4	9.1	7.6	6.8	-10.4%	1.1%
Brazil	54.9	57.5	69.1	63.1	66.0	68.3	68.9	60.6	64.7	69.2	72.4	4.6%	11.4%
Chile	3.9	4.2	3.8	4.9	3.6	5.1	4.3	4.9	5.2	5.1	4.9	-4.4%	0.9%
Colombia	7.3	7.3	8.0	7.1	6.9	7.6	6.9	7.1	7.6	8.1	8.6	5.9%	1.4%
Ecuador	1.5	1.2	1.4	1.6	1.5	1.6	1.7	1.6	1.7	1.7	1.7	–	0.3%
Peru	2.9	2.9	3.0	3.0	2.1	3.3	3.7	4.0	4.1	4.2	4.0	-5.7%	0.6%
Venezuela	11.6	11.6	12.2	13.0	13.1	13.7	14.2	13.7	13.5	13.7	16.0	16.7%	2.5%
Other S. & Cent. America	13.4	14.2	18.3	17.2	17.3	17.7	18.4	16.9	17.0	16.4	17.8	-3.5%	2.8%
Total S. & Cent. America	**101.7**	**105.1**	**116.2**	**115.6**	**117.5**	**118.2**	**124.7**	**117.1**	**122.6**	**126.0**	**132.1**	**3.2%**	**20.8%**
Austria	8.4	8.7	9.1	8.4	8.8	9.4	9.8	9.8	8.6	7.3	7.3	•	1.1%
Azerbaijan	0.4	0.4	0.3	0.4	0.4	0.3	0.3	0.5	0.5	0.6	0.6	11.8%	0.1%
Belarus	†	†	†	†	†	†	†	†	†	†	†	•	•
Belgium & Luxembourg	0.4	0.5	0.5	0.5	0.6	0.5	0.6	0.6	0.6	0.5	0.5	-4.9%	0.1%
Bulgaria	0.2	0.5	0.7	0.7	0.8	0.7	0.6	0.4	0.5	0.5	0.5	–	0.1%
Czech Republic	0.4	0.5	0.5	0.5	0.4	0.5	0.5	0.6	0.6	0.4	0.6	42.9%	0.1%
Denmark	†	†	†	†	†	†	†	†	†	.1	.1	20.0%	•
Finland	2.7	2.9	2.7	2.7	3.3	2.9	3.3	2.1	3.4	2.1	3.4	38.4%	0.5%
France	18.3	17.2	15.9	15.3	14.9	17.6	16.4	18.0	15.1	14.7	14.8	0.8%	2.3%
Germany	5.1	5.5	4.9	4.7	4.6	5.3	5.9	5.8	6.2	6.5	6.1	12.0%	1.0%
Greece	0.7	0.9	1.0	0.9	0.9	1.1	0.9	0.6	0.6	1.2	1.1	-7.1%	0.2%
Hungary	†	†	†	0.1	†	†	†	†	†	†	†	17.9%	•
Ireland	1.0	1.1	1.1	1.2	1.3	1.4	1.4	1.5	1.6	1.6	1.6	0.7%	0.3%
Republic of Ireland	0.3	0.2	0.2	0.2	0.3	0.2	0.3	0.3	0.3	0.2	0.2	-5.1%	•
Italy	10.8	9.5	10.7	10.6	10.7	11.7	11.5	12.2	10.7	10.0	11.0	10.0%	1.7%
Kazakhstan	2.1	1.9	1.7	1.5	1.4	1.4	1.7	1.8	2.0	2.0	2.0	2.5%	0.3%
Lithuania	0.2	0.2	0.3	0.2	0.2	0.2	0.1	0.2	0.2	0.2	0.2	-1.6%	•
Netherlands	†	†	†	†	†	†	†	†	†	†	.1	31.3%	•
Norway	25.5	27.7	23.5	25.1	26.0	27.6	22.2	27.4	29.4	24.0	24.7	3.0%	3.9%
Poland	0.9	0.9	0.9	0.9	1.0	1.0	0.9	1.0	0.9	0.7	0.8	12.1%	0.1%
Portugal	2.4	1.9	3.4	3.0	3.0	1.7	2.7	3.3	1.6	3.6	2.8	-24.3%	0.4%
Romania	3.0	3.6	3.6	4.0	4.3	4.1	3.3	3.4	3.6	3.0	3.8	26.2%	0.6%
Russian Federation	39.8	40.1	34.9	35.0	35.3	38.4	37.4	39.8	37.2	35.6	40.0	12.6%	6.3%
Slovakia	1.0	1.2	1.0	1.0	1.0	1.1	1.1	1.2	1.2	0.9	0.9	13.4%	0.1%
Spain	8.5	5.5	3.4	8.5	8.8	7.0	8.3	9.9	6.0	9.3	7.9	-20.0%	1.5%
Sweden	13.4	15.2	11.7	15.6	16.7	16.2	17.8	17.9	15.0	12.1	12.7	4.8%	2.0%
Switzerland	9.0	8.1	6.7	8.0	7.8	9.3	8.7	9.7	8.3	6.3	8.9	-3.6%	1.3%
Turkey	6.9	8.0	9.2	8.8	9.6	7.8	7.0	5.4	7.6	8.8	10.4	18.2%	1.6%
Turkmenistan	..	..	..	..	..	..	..	..	..	..	..	..	..
Ukraine	2.6	2.2	2.0	1.9	3.6	3.2	2.6	2.6	2.2	2.1	2.7	27.6%	0.4%
United Kingdom	1.5	1.4	1.1	1.3	1.5	1.6	1.8	1.5	1.3	1.3	1.7	26.2%	0.3%
Uzbekistan	1.6	1.4	1.5	1.2	1.3	1.5	1.5	1.2	1.6	1.7	1.7	-1.4%	0.3%
Other Europe & Eurasia	15.3	15.1	16.9	16.2	16.6	16.9	15.9	15.4	15.3	15.7	16.3	3.9%	2.6%
Total Europe & Eurasia	**180.8**	**182.7**	**174.0**	**176.3**	**185.2**	**186.7**	**191.5**	**194.4**	**181.9**	**174.7**	**184.7**	**5.7%**	**29.1%**
Iran	1.9	1.9	1.9	1.2	1.7	1.2	0.9	0.9	1.6	2.2	2.7	24.5%	0.4%
Kuwait	..	..	..	..	..	..	..	..	..	..	..	..	..
Qatar	..	..	..	..	..	..	..	..	..	..	..	..	..
Saudi Arabia	..	..	..	..	..	..	..	..	..	..	..	..	..
United Arab Emirates	..	..	..	..	..	..	..	..	..	..	..	..	..
Other Middle East	0.8	0.9	1.1	1.1	1.1	0.7	0.8	0.7	1.1	1.3	1.2	-1.4%	0.2%
Total Middle East	**2.6**	**2.8**	**2.9**	**2.4**	**2.8**	**1.9**	**1.7**	**1.6**	**2.9**	**3.4**	**4.9**	**14.9%**	**0.6%**
Algeria	†	†	†	†	†	†	†	†	†	†	0.1	-5.0%	•
Egypt	2.5	2.6	2.7	†	3.1	3.4	3.2	3.3	3.2	2.2	3.3	3.1%	0.5%
South Africa	0.6	0.4	0.9	1.1	0.9	0.8	0.9	0.8	0.9	0.8	0.8	5.5%	0.1%
Other Africa	10.5	11.1	11.2	11.6	12.2	13.7	14.0	14.6	15.2	15.4	15.6	0.9%	2.5%
Total Africa	**13.6**	**14.2**	**14.7**	**15.5**	**16.2**	**17.9**	**18.1**	**18.7**	**19.3**	**19.5**	**19.8**	**1.4%**	**3.1%**
Australia	3.7	3.7	3.8	3.8	3.7	3.7	3.7	3.7	3.6	2.7	3.8	3.0%	0.6%
Bangladesh	0.2	0.1	0.2	0.2	0.2	0.2	0.2	0.2	0.3	0.3	0.3	3.8%	•
China	27.8	42.2	42.2	42.5	44.9	49.2	55.0	59.1	62.2	63.7	74.2	16.6%	11.7%
China Hong Kong SAR	..	..	..	..	..	..	..	..	..	..	..	..	..
India	19.2	17.2	15.6	15.9	18.9	18.6	17.4	16.3	15.5	15.7	19.9	21.0%	3.0%
Indonesia	1.6	1.7	1.9	1.2	2.2	2.1	2.3	2.6	2.3	2.4	2.5	4.3%	0.4%
Japan	17.4	19.9	19.7	21.2	23.6	21.0	20.7	20.4	20.6	22.9	22.6	-0.5%	3.6%
Malaysia	1.5	1.4	1.2	0.9	1.1	1.7	1.6	1.6	1.2	1.3	1.4	7.7%	0.2%
New Zealand	6.8	6.2	5.9	5.2	5.7	5.3	5.6	5.1	5.7	5.4	6.3	16.6%	1.0%
Pakistan	4.9	5.1	5.6	4.2	5.5	4.9	4.0	4.1	4.6	5.8	6.1	5.0%	1.0%
Philippines	1.3	1.4	1.6	1.4	1.1	1.8	1.9	1.6	1.6	1.8	1.9	6.5%	0.3%
Singapore	..	..	..	..	..	..	..	..	..	..	..	..	..
South Korea	0.9	1.2	1.2	1.2	1.4	1.4	1.2	0.9	1.2	1.6	1.3	-14.9%	0.2%
Taiwan	2.0	2.0	2.0	2.2	2.4	2.0	2.0	2.1	1.4	1.6	1.5	-4.9%	0.2%
Thailand	1.0	1.5	1.7	1.6	1.2	0.8	1.4	1.4	1.7	1.7	1.8	10.9%	0.3%
Other Asia Pacific	7.1	7.7	7.4	7.0	6.9	7.7	9.1	8.9	9.6	8.4	9.3	-0.8%	1.5%
Total Asia Pacific	**103.3**	**111.3**	**109.9**	**104.4**	**118.7**	**119.3**	**124.8**	**128.1**	**130.7**	**136.8**	**152.0**	**11.1%**	**24.0%**
TOTAL WORLD	**539.5**	**569.7**	**577.5**	**548.9**	**594.6**	**602.8**	**674.0**	**689.1**	**601.0**	**601.1**	**634.4**	**5.6%**	**100.0%**
of which: European Union 25	74.5	73.8	73.5	75.6	78.7	79.8	80.5	87.3	73.6	72.1	73.7	2.2%	11.6%
OECD	290.7	300.7	308.9	314.6	308.6	312.4	312.6	299.2	290.5	288.3	292.7	1.5%	46.1%
Former Soviet Union	56.0	54.6	48.9	48.3	51.1	51.5	52.1	54.2	52.0	51.4	56.3	9.5%	8.9%
Other EMEs	202.9	213.4	219.9	222.2	232.3	238.3	249.4	246.5	255.5	264.4	285.5	8.0%	45.0%

Converted on the basis of thermal equivalence assuming 38% conversion efficiency in a modern thermal power station
† Less than 0.05
.. Less than 0.05%
Note: Hydroelectricity data expressed in terawatt-hours is available at www.bp.com/statisticalreview

Appendix-3

(Source: Accessed on 25 June 2005 at: http://www.fas.org/irp/congress/1996)
IRAN AND LIBYA SANCTIONS ACT OF 1996 (House of Representatives - June 18, 1996)
[Page: H6469]

Mr. GILMAN. Mr. Speaker, I move to suspend the rules and pass the bill (H.R. 3107) to impose sanctions on persons exporting certain goods or technology that would enhance Iran's ability to explore for, extract, refine, or transport by pipeline petroleum resources, and for other purposes, as amended.

The Clerk read as follows:

H.R. 3107

Be it enacted by the Senate and House of Representatives of the United States of America in Congress assembled,

SECTION-1 SHORT TITLE.

This Act may be cited as the 'Iran and Libya Sanctions Act of 1996'.

SEC-2.FINDINGS.

The Congress makes the following findings:

(1) The efforts of the Government of Iran to acquire weapons of mass destruction and the means to deliver them and its support of acts of international terrorism endanger the national security and foreign policy interests of the United States and those countries with which the United States shares common strategic and foreign policy objectives.

(2) The objective of preventing the proliferation of weapons of mass destruction and acts of international terrorism through existing multilateral and bilateral initiatives requires additional efforts to deny Iran the

268

financial means to sustain its nuclear, chemical, biological, and missile weapons programs.

(3) The Government of Iran uses its diplomatic facilities and quasi-governmental institutions outside of Iran to promote acts of international terrorism and assist its nuclear, chemical, biological, and missile weapons programs.

(4) The failure of the Government of Libya to comply with Resolutions 731, 748, and 883 of the Security Council of the United Nations, its support of international terrorism, and its efforts to acquire weapons of mass destruction constitute a threat to international peace and security that endangers the national security and foreign policy interests of the United States and those countries with which it shares common strategic and foreign policy objectives.

SEC. 3. DECLARATION OF POLICY.

(a) **Policy With Respect to Iran**: The Congress declares that it is the policy of the United States to deny Iran the ability to support acts of international terrorism and to fund the development and acquisition of weapons of mass destruction and the means to deliver them by limiting the development of Iran's ability to explore for, extract, refine, or transport by pipeline petroleum resources of Iran.

(b) **Policy With Respect to Libya**: The Congress further declares that it is the policy of the United States to seek full compliance by Libya with its obligations under Resolutions 731, 748, and 883 of the Security Council of the United Nations, including ending all support for acts of international terrorism and efforts to develop or acquire weapons of mass destruction.

SEC. 4. MULTILATERAL REGIME.

(a) **Multilateral Negotiations**: In order to further the objectives of section 3, the Congress urges the President to commence immediately diplomatic efforts, both in appropriate international fora such as the United Nations, and bilaterally with allies of the United States, to establish a multilateral sanctions regime against Iran, including provisions limiting the development of petroleum resources, that will inhibit Iran's efforts to carry out activities described in section 2.

(b) **Reports to Congress**: The President shall report to the appropriate congressional committees, not later than 1 year after the date of the enactment of this Act, and periodically thereafter, on the extent that diplomatic efforts described in subsection (a) have been successful. Each report shall include--

(1) the countries that have agreed to undertake measures to further the objectives of section 3 with respect to Iran, and a description of those measures; and

(2) the countries that have not agreed to measures described in paragraph (1), and, with respect to those countries, other measures (in addition to that provided in subsection (d)) the President recommends that the United States take to further the objectives of section 3 with respect to Iran.

(c) **Waiver**: The President may waive the application of section 5(a) with respect to nationals of a country if--

(1) that country has agreed to undertake substantial measures, including economic sanctions, that will inhibit Iran's efforts to carry out activities described in section 2 and information required by subsection (b)(1) has been included in a report submitted under subsection (b); and

(2) the President, at least 30 days before the waiver takes effect, notifies the appropriate congressional committees of his intention to exercise the waiver.

(d) **Enhanced Sanction**:

(1) **Sanction**: With respect to nationals of countries except those with respect to which the President has exercised the waiver authority of subsection (c), at any time after the first report is required to be submitted under subsection (b), section 5(a) shall be applied by substituting `$20,000,000' for `$40,000,000' each place it appears, and by substituting `$5,000,000' for `$10,000,000'.

(2) **Report to congress**: The President shall report to the appropriate congressional committees any country with respect to which paragraph (1) applies.

(e) **Interim Report on Multilateral Sanctions; Monitoring**: The President, not later than 90 days after the date of the enactment of this Act, shall report to the appropriate congressional committees on--

(1) whether the member states of the European Union, the Republic of Korea, Australia, Israel, or Japan have legislative or administrative standards providing for the imposition of trade sanctions on persons or their affiliates doing business or having investments in Iran or Libya;

(2) the extent and duration of each instance of the application of such sanctions; and

(3) the disposition of any decision with respect to such sanctions by the World Trade Organization or its predecessor organization.

SEC. 5. IMPOSITION OF SANCTIONS.

(a) **Sanctions With Respect to Iran**: Except as provided in subsection (f), the President shall impose 2 or more of the sanctions described in paragraphs (1) through (6) of section 6 if the President determines that a person has, with actual knowledge, on or after the date of the enactment of this Act, made an investment of $40,000,000 or more (or any combination of investments of at least $10,000,000 each, which in the aggregate equals or exceeds $40,000,000 in any 12-month period), that directly and significantly contributed to the enhancement of Iran's ability to develop petroleum resources of Iran.

(b) **Sanctions With Respect to Libya**:

(1) **Trigger of Mandatory sanctions**: Except as provided in subsection (f), the President shall impose 2 or more of the sanctions described in paragraphs (1) through (6) of section 6 if the President determines that a person has, with actual knowledge, on or after the date of the enactment of this Act, exported, transferred, or otherwise provided to Libya any goods, services, technology, or other items the provision of which is prohibited under paragraph 4(b) or 5 of Resolution 748 of the Security Council of the United Nations, adopted March 31, 1992, or under paragraph 5 or 6 of Resolution 883 of the Security Council of the United Nations, adopted November 11, 1993, if the provision of such items significantly and materially--

(A) Contributed to Libya's ability to acquire chemical, biological, or nuclear weapons or destabilizing numbers and types of advanced conventional weapons or enhanced Libya's military or paramilitary capabilities;

(B) Contributed to Libya's ability to develop its petroleum resources; or

(C) Contributed to Libya's ability to maintain its aviation capabilities.

(2) **Trigger of discretionary sanctions**: Except as provided in subsection (f), the President may impose 1 or more of the sanctions described in paragraphs (1) through (6) of section 6 if the President determines that a person has, with actual knowledge, on or after the date of the enactment of this Act, made an investment of $40,000,000 or more (or any combination of investments of at least $10,000,000 each, which in the aggregate equals or exceeds $40,000,000 in any 12-month period), that directly and significantly contributed to the enhancement of Libya's ability to develop its petroleum resources.

(c) **Persons against Which the Sanctions Are To Be Imposed**: The sanctions described in subsections (a) and (b) shall be imposed on--

(1) Any person the President determines has carried out the activities described in subsection (a) or (b); and

(2) Any person the President determines--

(A) Is a successor entity to the person referred to in paragraph (1),

(B) is a parent or subsidiary of the person referred to in paragraph (1) if that parent or subsidiary, with actual knowledge, engaged in the activities referred to in paragraph (1); or

(C) Is an affiliate of the person referred to in paragraph (1) if that affiliate, with actual knowledge, engaged in the activities referred to in paragraph (1) and if that affiliate is controlled in fact by the person referred to in paragraph (1).

For purposes of this Act, any person or entity described in this subsection shall be referred to as a `sanctioned person'.

(d) **Publication in Federal Register**: The President shall cause to be published in the Federal Register a current list of persons and entities on whom sanctions have been imposed under this Act. The removal of persons or entities from, and the addition of persons and entities to, the list, shall also be so published.

(e) **Publication of Projects**: The President shall cause to be published in the Federal Register a list of all significant projects which have been publicly tendered in the oil and gas sector in Iran.

(f) **Exceptions**: The President shall not be required to apply or maintain the sanctions under subsection (a) or (b)--

(1) in the case of procurement of defense articles or defense services--

(A) under existing contracts or subcontracts, including the exercise of options for production quantities to satisfy requirements essential to the national security of the United States;

(B) if the President determines in writing that the person to which the sanctions would otherwise be applied is a sole source supplier of the defense articles or services, that the defense articles or services are essential, and that alternative sources are not readily or reasonably available; or

(C) if the President determines in writing that such articles or services are essential to the national security under defense co production agreements;

(2) in the case of procurement, to eligible products, as defined in section 308(4) of the Trade Agreements Act of 1979 (19 U.S.C. 2518(4)), of any foreign country or instrumentality designated under section 301(b)(1) of that Act (19 U.S.C. 2511(b)(1));

(3) to products, technology, or services provided under contracts entered into before the date on which the President publishes in the Federal Register the name of the person on whom the sanctions are to be imposed;

(4) to--

(A) spare parts which are essential to United States products or production;

(B) component parts, but not finished products, essential to United States products or production; or

(C) routine servicing and maintenance of products, to the extent that alternative sources are not readily or reasonably available;

(6) to information and technology essential to United States products or production; or

(7) to medicines, medical supplies, or other humanitarian items.

[Page: H6470]

SEC. 6. DESCRIPTION OF SANCTIONS.

The sanctions to be imposed on a sanctioned person under section 5 are as follows:

(1) **Export-import bank assistance for exports to sanctioned persons**: The President may direct the Export-Import Bank of the United States not to give approval to the issuance of any guarantee, insurance, extension of credit, or participation in the extension of credit in connection with the export of any goods or services to any sanctioned person.

(2) **Export sanction**: The President may order the United States Government not to issue any specific license and not to grant any other specific permission or authority to export any goods or technology to a sanctioned person under--

(i) the Export Administration Act of 1979;

(ii) the Arms Export Control Act;

(iii) the Atomic Energy Act of 1954; or

(iv) any other statute that requires the prior review and approval of the United States Government as a condition for the export or re-export of goods or services.

(3) **Loans from United States financial institutions**: The United States Government may prohibit any United States financial institution from making loans or providing credits to any sanctioned person totaling more than $10,000,000 in any 12-month period unless such person is engaged in activities to relieve human suffering and the loans or credits are provided for such activities.

(4) **Prohibitions on financial institutions**: The following prohibitions may be imposed against a sanctioned person that is a financial institution:

(A) **Prohibition on designation as primary dealer**: Neither the Board of Governors of the Federal Reserve System nor the Federal Reserve Bank of New York may designate, or permit the continuation of any prior designation of, such financial institution as a primary dealer in United States Government debt instruments.

(B) **Prohibition on service as a repository of government funds**: Such financial institution may not serve as agent of the United States Government or serve as repository for United States Government funds.

The imposition of either sanction under subparagraph (A) or (B) shall be treated as 1 sanction for purposes of section 5, and the imposition of both such sanctions shall be treated as 2 sanctions for purposes of section 5.

(5) **Procurement sanction**: The United States Government may not procure, or enter into any contract for the procurement of, any goods or services from a sanctioned person.

(6) **Additional sanctions**: The President may impose sanctions, as appropriate, to restrict imports with respect to a sanctioned person, in accordance with the International Emergency Economic Powers Act (50 U.S.C. 1701 and following).

SEC. 7. ADVISORY OPINIONS.

The Secretary of State may, upon the request of any person, issue an advisory opinion to that person as to whether a proposed activity by that person would subject that person to sanctions under this Act. Any person who relies in good faith on such an advisory opinion which states that the proposed activity would not subject a person to such sanctions, and any person who thereafter engages in such activity, will not be made subject to such sanctions on account of such activity.

SEC. 8. TERMINATION OF SANCTIONS.

(a) **Iran**: The requirement under section 5(a) to impose sanctions shall no longer have force or effect with respect to Iran if the President determines and certifies to the appropriate congressional committees that Iran--

(1) has ceased its efforts to design, develop, manufacture, or acquire--

(A) a nuclear explosive device or related materials and technology;

(B) chemical and biological weapons; and

(C) ballistic missiles and ballistic missile launch technology; and

(2) has been removed from the list of countries the governments of which have been determined, for purposes of section 6(j) of the Export Administration Act of 1979, to have repeatedly provided support for acts of international terrorism.

(b) **Libya**: The requirement under section 5(b) to impose sanctions shall no longer have force or effect with respect to Libya if the President determines and certifies to the appropriate congressional committees that Libya has fulfilled the requirements of United Nations Security Council Resolution 731, adopted January 21, 1992, United Nations Security Council Resolution 748, adopted March 31, 1992, and United Nations Security Council Resolution 883, adopted November 11, 1993.

SEC. 9. DURATION OF SANCTIONS; PRESIDENTIAL WAIVER.

(a) Delay of Sanctions:

(1) **Consultations**: If the President makes a determination described in section 5(a) or 5(b) with respect to a foreign person, the Congress urges the President to initiate consultations immediately with the government with primary jurisdiction over that foreign person with respect to the imposition of sanctions under this Act.

(2) **Actions by government of jurisdiction**: In order to pursue consultations under paragraph (1) with the government concerned, the President may delay imposition of sanctions under this Act for up to 90 days. Following such consultations, the President shall immediately impose sanctions unless the President determines and certifies to the Congress that the government has taken specific and effective actions, including, as appropriate, the imposition of appropriate penalties, to terminate the involvement of

the foreign person in the activities that resulted in the determination by the President under section 5(a) or 5(b) concerning such person.

(3) **Additional delay in imposition of sanctions**: The President may delay the imposition of sanctions for up to an additional 90 days if the President determines and certifies to the Congress that the government with primary jurisdiction over the person concerned is in the process of taking the actions described in paragraph (2).

(4) **Report to congress**: Not later than 90 days after making a determination under section 5(a) or 5(b), the President shall submit to the appropriate congressional committees a report on the status of consultations with the appropriate foreign government under this subsection, and the basis for any determination under paragraph (3).

(b) **Duration of Sanctions**: A sanction imposed under section 5 shall remain in effect--

(1) for a period of not less than 2 years from the date on which it is imposed; or

(2) until such time as the President determines and certifies to the Congress that the person whose activities were the basis for imposing the sanction is no longer engaging in such activities and that the President has received reliable assurances that such person will not knowingly engage in such activities in the future, except that such sanction shall remain in effect for a period of at least 1 year.

(c) Presidential Waiver:

(1) **Authority**: The President may waive the requirement in section 5 to impose a sanction or sanctions on a person described in section 5(c), and may waive the continued imposition of a sanction or sanctions under subsection (b) of this section, 30 days or more after the President determines and so reports to the appropriate congressional committees that it is important to the national interest of the United States to exercise such waiver authority.

(2) **Contents of report**: Any report under paragraph (1) shall provide a specific and detailed rationale for the determination under paragraph (1), including--

(A) a description of the conduct that resulted in the determination under section 5(a) or (b), as the case may be;

(B) in the case of a foreign person, an explanation of the efforts to secure the cooperation of the government with primary jurisdiction over the sanctioned person to terminate or, as appropriate, penalize the activities that resulted in the determination under section 5(a) or (b), as the case may be;

(C) an estimate as to the significance--

(i) of the provision of the items described in section 5(a) to Iran's ability to develop its petroleum resources, or

(ii) of the provision of the items described in section 5(b)(1) to the abilities of Libya described in subparagraph (A), (B), or (C) of section 5(b)(1), or of the investment described in section 5(b)(2) on Libya's ability to develop its petroleum resources, as the case may be; and

(D) a statement as to the response of the United States in the event that the person concerned engages in other activities that would be subject to section 5(a) or (b).

(3) **Effect of report on waiver**: If the President makes a report under paragraph (1) with respect to a waiver of sanctions on a person described in section 5(c), sanctions need not be imposed under section 5(a) or (b) on that person during the 30-day period referred to in paragraph (1).

[Page: H6471]

SEC. 10. REPORTS REQUIRED.

(a) **Report on Certain International Initiatives**: Not later than 6 months after the date of the enactment of this Act, and every 6 months thereafter, the President shall transmit a report to the appropriate congressional committees describing--

(1) the efforts of the President to mount a multilateral campaign to persuade all countries to pressure Iran to cease its nuclear, chemical, biological, and missile weapons programs and its support of acts of international terrorism;

(2) the efforts of the President to persuade other governments to ask Iran to reduce the presence of Iranian diplomats and representatives of other government and military or quasi-governmental institutions of Iran and to

278

withdraw any such diplomats or representatives who participated in the takeover of the United States embassy in Tehran on November 4, 1979, or the subsequent holding of United States hostages for 444 days;

(3) the extent to which the International Atomic Energy Agency has established regular inspections of all nuclear facilities in Iran, including those presently under construction; and

(4) Iran's use of Iranian diplomats and representatives of other government and military or quasi-governmental institutions of Iran to promote acts of international terrorism or to develop or sustain Iran's nuclear, chemical, biological, and missile weapons programs.

(b) **Other Reports**: The President shall ensure the continued transmittal to the Congress of reports describing--

(1) the nuclear and other military capabilities of Iran, as required by section 601(a) of the Nuclear Non-Proliferation Act of 1978 and section 1607 of the National Defense Authorization Act for Fiscal Year 1993; and

(2) the support provided by Iran for acts of international terrorism, as part of the Department of State's annual report on international terrorism.

SEC. 11. DETERMINATIONS NOT REVIEWABLE.

A determination to impose sanctions under this Act shall not be review able in any court.

SEC. 12. EXCLUSION OF CERTAIN ACTIVITIES.

Nothing in this Act shall apply to any activities subject to the reporting requirements of title V of the National Security Act of 1947.

SEC. 13. EFFECTIVE DATE; SUNSET.

(a) **Effective Date**: This Act shall take effect on the date of the enactment of this Act.

(b) **Sunset**: This Act shall cease to be effective on the date that is 5 years after the date of the enactment of this Act.

SEC. 14. DEFINITIONS.

As used in this Act:

(1) **Act of international terrorism**: The term `act of international terrorism' means an act--

(A) which is violent or dangerous to human life and that is a violation of the criminal laws of the United States or of any State or that would be a criminal violation if committed within the jurisdiction of the United States or any State; and

(B) which appears to be intended--

(i) to intimidate or coerce a civilian population;

(ii) to influence the policy of a government by intimidation or coercion; or

(iii) to affect the conduct of a government by assassination or kidnapping.

(2) **Appropriate congressional committees**: The term `appropriate congressional committees' means the Committee on Finance, the Committee on Banking, Housing, and Urban Affairs, and the Committee on Foreign Relations of the Senate and the Committee on Ways and Means, the Committee on Banking and Financial Services, and the Committee on International Relations of the House of Representatives.

(3) **Component part**: The term `component part' has the meaning given that term in section 11A(e)(1) of the Export Administration Act of 1979 (50 U.S.C. App. 2410a(e)(1)).

(4) **Develop and development**: To `develop', or the `development' of, petroleum resources means the exploration for, or the extraction, refining, or transportation by pipeline of, petroleum resources.

(5) **Financial institution**: The term `financial institution' includes--

(A) a depository institution (as defined in section 3(c)(1) of the Federal Deposit Insurance Act), including a branch or agency of a foreign bank (as defined in section 1(b)(7) of the International Banking Act of 1978);

(B) a credit union;

(C) a securities firm, including a broker or dealer;

(D) an insurance company, including an agency or underwriter; and

(E) any other company that provides financial services.

(6) **Finished product**: The term `finished product' has the meaning given that term in section 11A(e)(2) of the Export Administration Act of 1979 (50 U.S.C. App. 2410a(e)(2)).

(7) **Foreign person**: The term `foreign person' means--

(A) an individual who is not a United States person or an alien lawfully admitted for permanent residence into the United States; or

(B) a corporation, partnership, or other nongovernmental entity which is not a United States person.

(8) **Goods and technology**: The terms `goods' and `technology' have the meanings given those terms in section 16 of the Export Administration Act of 1979 (50 U.S.C. app. 2415).

(9) **Investment**: The term `investment' means any of the following activities if such activity is undertaken pursuant to an agreement, or pursuant to the exercise of rights under such an agreement, that is entered into with the Government of Iran or a nongovenmental entity in Iran, or with the Government of Libya or a nongovernmental entity in Libya, on or after the date of the enactment of this Act:

(A) The entry into a contract that includes responsibility for the development of petroleum resources located in Iran or Libya (as the case may be), or the entry into a contract providing for the general supervision and guarantee of another person's performance of such a contract.

(B) The purchase of a share of ownership, including an equity interest, in that development.

(C) The entry into a contract providing for the participation in royalties, earnings, or profits in that development, without regard to the form of the participation.

The term `investment' does not include the entry into, performance, or financing of a contract to sell or purchase goods, services, or technology.

(10) **Iran**: The term `Iran' includes any agency or instrumentality of Iran.

(11) **Iranian diplomats and representatives of other government and military or quasi-governmental institutions of Iran**: The term `Iranian diplomats and representatives of other government and military or quasi-governmental institutions of Iran' includes employees, representatives, or affiliates of Iran's--

(A) Foreign Ministry;

(B) Ministry of **Intelligence** and Security;

(C) Revolutionary Guard Corps;

(D) Crusade for Reconstruction;

(E) Qods (Jerusalem) Forces;

(F) Interior Ministry;

(G) Foundation for the Oppressed and Disabled;

(H) Prophet's Foundation;

(I) June 5th Foundation;

(J) Martyr's Foundation;

(K) Islamic Propagation Organization; and

(L) Ministry of Islamic Guidance.

(12) **Libya**: The term `Libya' includes any agency or instrumentality of Libya.

(13) **Nuclear explosive device**: The term `nuclear explosive device' means any device, whether assembled or disassembled, that is designed to produce an instantaneous release of an amount of nuclear energy from special nuclear material (as defined in section 11aa. of the Atomic Energy Act of 1954) that is greater than the amount of energy that would be released from the detonation of one pound of trinitrotoluene (TNT).

(14) **Person**: The term `person' means--

(A) a natural person;

(B) a corporation, business association, partnership, society, trust, any other nongovernmental entity, organization, or group, and any governmental entity operating as a business enterprise; and

(C) any successor to any entity described in subparagraph (B).

(15) **Petroleum resources**: The term `petroleum resources' includes petroleum and natural gas resources.

(16) **United States or State**: The term `United States' or `State' means the several States, the District of Columbia, the Commonwealth of Puerto Rico, the Commonwealth of the Northern Mariana Islands, American Samoa, Guam, the United States Virgin Islands, and any other territory or possession of the United States.

(17) **United States person**: The term `United States person' means--

(A) a natural person who is a citizen of the United States or who owes permanent allegiance to the United States; and
(B) a corporation or other legal entity which is organized under the laws of the United States, any State or territory thereof, or the District of Columbia, if natural persons described in subparagraph (A) own, directly or indirectly, more than 50 percent of the outstanding capital stock or other beneficial interest in such legal entity.

Appendix-4
World Geostrategic Places: Geographic features of enduring strategic value

Straits	Passes	Islands	Regions
• Bering Strait	• Bolan Pass	› Antilles	› Caspian Sea
• Cape of Good Hope	• Brenner Pass	› Balearic Islands	› Caucasus
• Dardanelles	• Cumberland Gap	› Crete	› Fergana Valley
• Florida Strait	• Fulda Gap	› Cuba	› Flanders
• Gulf of Aden	• Great St. Bernard Pass	› Cyprus	› Hindu Kush
• Kattegat	• Iron Gate	› Great Britain	› Iraq
• Panama Canal	• Jelepla Pass	› Guam	› Kashmir
• Straits of Dover	• Khunjerab Pass	› Hawaiian Islands	› Kuwait
• Straits of Gibraltar	• Khyber Pass	› Iceland	› Mississippi Delta
• Strait of Hormuz	• Nathula Pass	› Japan	› Mitteleuropa
• Suez Canal	• St. Gotthard Pass	› Malta	› Moldavia
• Straits of Malacca	• Torugart Pass	› Ryukyu Islands	› Morocco
• Taiwan Strait		› Sicily	› Nile Delta
	• Wakhan Corridor	› Singapore	› Nova Scotia
• Tsushima Strait		› Taiwan	› Palestine
			› Provence
		› Philippine Islands	› RhineRiver Valley
			› Ruhr Valley
			› Steppe
			› Transoxiana

Source: http://en.wikipedia.org/wiki/Geostrategy

END NOTES

1. Daniel Yergin; "The Prize: The Epic Quest For Oil, Money and Power;" (Free Press, New York, London, Toronto, Sydney, 2003) p.177

2. Ibid

3. Ibid. p.183

4. Ibid

5. George Monbiot, "A Pro- Western Regime in Kabul Should Give the US an Afghan Route for the Caspian Oil", The Guardian, 23 October 2001.

6. J D Henry, "Baku: An Eventful History"; (Archibald Constable & Co, London, 1986) p.30

7. Pepe Escobar, "Pipelinistan, Part 1: The Rule of the Game," Asia Times, (www.atimes.com) 24 August 2004.

8. Dr W.H Ziegler, "Reflection on the Political Implications of Oil Depletion," News Letter NO.13, January 2002 (ASP. OADC London, UK) p.3

9. Senator Sam Brownback, "US Economic and Strategic Interests in the Caspian Sea Region," Caspian Crossroads (US) Vol 3, Issue No. 2, Fall 1997 (accessed at www.ourworld.compuserve.com.homepage.) 14 January 2004.

Chapter I: Historic Perspective, Geography and Significance of Central Eurasia

10. S. Jagchid and P. Hayer; Mongolia's Culture and Society, (Boulder Westview Press, 1979) p.10

11. David Christian, A History of Russia, Central Asia and Mongolia, Vol-I (Blackwell Publishers, 1998) p.16

12. H J Mackinder, "The Geographical Pivots of History", Geographical Journal Vol 23, 1904, p.27

13. Christian, op cit, p.18

14   H A R Gibbs, The Arabs Conquests in Central Asia; (New Press London, 1970), p.14

15   Dr Muhammad Anwar Khan, Central Asia; Introductory Booklet; (Area Study Center University of Peshawar, n.d). p.1

16   See, CIS Map 1995/96 Edition' 1:7000, 000 Hallwag Stuttgart

17   Ahmed Rashid: Jihad: The Rise of Militant Islam in Central Asia; (Vanguard, Lahore/Karachi/Islamabad, 2002), p.17

18   Gibbs, op cit, pp.53-54

19   Dr Muhammad Anwar Khan, "The land of Central Asia", Central Asia, Journal No.45 (Area Study Center, University of Peshawar), pp.14-18.

20   Christian, op cit, p.311

21   Ibn Battuta: Travels in Asia and Africa, (Routledge & Kegan Paul, London, 1929), p. 169

22   Anwar op cit, p.30

23   Nicholas V Riasonovsky: A History Of Russia; (Oxford University Press, New York, 1976) pp.220-223 and 225.

24   Dr Azmat Hayat Khan, "Ethnic Factor in Central Asian Republics", Central Asia, Journal No.47 (Area Study Center, University of Peshawar) pp.113-114

25   Scott B. MacDonald, "Central Asia Back on Frontline," KWR International Advisor No: 12; Dec 2001 p.5 (KWR.Advisor@kwrintl.com) accessed in November 2003.

26   Azmat, op cit, pp 77-80

27   Giampaolo Capisani, The Hand Book of Central Asia, (IB Taurus Publishers, London, New York, 2000) pp.20-22

28   Ibid, pp39-43

29   Ibid, pp.57-59

30   Ibid, pp 60-62. Also, see for example, Dr Muhammad Anwar Khan: Central Asia (booklet); (Area Study Center University of Peshawar n.d) p.17

31   Capisani, op cit pp.110-112

32   Ibid, pp.130-135

33   Chiara Betta, "Xingjian or Eastern Turkistan: The Conundrum of Chinese Central Asia"

Central Asia Journal No.50 (Area Study Center, University of Peshawar, 2002) p.213

3   4   John F R Wright, Suzanne Goldenberg and Richard Schofield- (Eds): Trans- Caucasian Boundaries; (UCL Press Ltd, 1996) p.1

3   5   Shirin Akiner: Islamic People Of Soviet Union: 2nd (London: Kegan Paul International, 1986), p.17

3   6   George Joffe, "Nationalities and Borders in Transcaucasia and the Northern Caucasus" in John F R Wright, Suzanne Goldenberg & Richard Schofield (Eds): Transcaucasian Boundaries, (UCL Press, 1996), p.14

3   7   Ibid, pp 16-18

3   8   'Caspian Sea Region' Country Analysis Brief, (US Energy Information Administration: www.eia.doe.gov) January 2004.

3   9   Mohammad Ajam, "Names of the Caspian", Payam-e-Darya No.131, October 2004 (CNetiranArticlesCultureIranologyNamesoftheCaspianSea. htm) September 2004

4   0   Shirin Akiner, "Caspian Intersection: Contextual Introduction; Politics, Energy and Security," The Caspian, (Routledge Curzon, Taylor and Francis Group, London & New York-2004) p.3

4   1   "Caspian Sea Region": Country Analysis Brief (US Energy Information Administration: www.eia.doe.gov) August 2003.

4   2   R.J Forbes: Studies in Early Petroleum History :(Lei den, EJ Brills, 1958) p.154

4   3   Professor Khawaja Masud, " The Promethean Savant", The News, 8 August 2005, p.6. Also note that taking inspiration from these 'fires' to the extent of obsession in a rather primitive era saw a monumental follower during 20th Century. The discoverer of earth shaking equation was no longer impressed by his achievement while he spent rest of his life postulating to understand 'light'. In Zoroastrian era light and fire were almost synonymous. The great poet of the EAST (Iqbal) rightly remarked in 'Pyam-e-Mashriq' (Message of the East) that a Zoroastrian was born in the family of Moses. He meant Einstein.

4   4   Times Atlas, (www.infoplease.com/ipa), 17 January 2004.

4 5   Erich Ludendroff: <u>The Nation at War</u>; trans, A S Rappopart (London: Hutchinson, 1936) p.79

4 6   "Azerbaijan" <u>Country Analysis Brief</u>, (US Energy Information Administration: <u>www.eia.doe.gov)</u> <u>August</u> 2004. Also see Sulejman Alijarly, "The Republic of Azerbaijan: Notes on the State Borders in the Past and Present", in Wright, Goldenberg and Schofield, op cit pp 113-120

4 7   Ibid, (See under 'Iran')

4 8   Farid A Khawari: <u>Oil and Islam</u> (Roundtable Publishing Inc, Malibu CA, 1990) pp98-101

4 9   'Iran' :<u>Times Almanacs</u> (<u>www.infoplease.com/ipa</u>) August 2004.

5 0   See for example, 'Turkmenistan' <u>Country Analysis Brief</u> (<u>www.eia.doe.gov</u>) September 2003 and figure taken from, 'Turkmenistan' <u>Time Almanacs</u> (<u>www.infoplease.com</u>) July 2004.

5 1   See under 'Kazakhstan', Time Almanacs (<u>www.infoplease.com</u>) July 2004.

5 2   'Kazakhstan', <u>Country Analysis Brief</u>, (US Energy Information Administration <u>www.eia.doe.gov</u>) December 2004.

5 3   Information on Russia is largely drawn from Riasonovsky, op cit p.220-230

'Russia' <u>Country Analysis Brief</u> (<u>www.eia.doe.gov</u>) December 2004.

'Russia' <u>Time Almanacs</u> (<u>www.infoplease.com</u>) January 2005

5 4   Ibid.

5 5   Eric Herring, "Berlin Blockade" and "Cuban Missile Crisis", <u>Danger and Opportunity</u>; (Manchester University Press, Manchester and New York 1995) pp. 89 and 149.

5 6   Christopher J Walker, "The Armenian Presence in Mountainous Karabakh" in Wright, Goldenberg & Schofield, op cit, pp 89-112 and 'Armenia' <u>Times Almanacs</u>, (www.infoplease.com) February 2005.

5   7   'Georgia' <u>Times Almanacs</u> (www.infoplease.com) July 2004.

5   8   Julian Birch, "The Georgian/South Ossetian Territorial and Boundary Dispute, in Wright, Goldenberg & Schofield, op cit, pp 151-160

5   9   'William Hale, "Turkey, the Black Sea and Transcaucasia", in Wright, Goldenberg & Schofield, op cit, pp 54-60 and 'Turkey' <u>Times Almanacs</u> (www.infoplease.com) March 2005.

Chapter II: Oil and Gas Statistics

60   Henry op cit pp12-13

61   Yergin, op cit p.796.

6   2   Yergin, op cit, p.499-500.

6   3   M.A Abrams and A.A Narimanov; "Geochemical Evaluation of Hydrocarbons and Their Potential Sources in the Western, South Caspian Depression, Republic of Azerbaijan," <u>Maritime and Petroleum Geology</u>: 14(4), 1997 pp. 451-458

6   4   In parlance of oil companies, large oil field is called 'elephant'.

6   5   Manik Talwani, Andrei Belopolsky, Dianne L.Berry' "Geology and Petroleum Potential of Central Asia," (Presentation; Rice University, accessed at worldoil.com) 23 June 2003.

6   6   Ibid, p.5. Also for the wider perception about the usefulness of geological survey, see for example, Thomas Ahlbrandt and Christopher Schenk, "Digital Geological Maps Support USGS World Energy Assessment" <u>American Oil and Gas Reporter,</u> Vol. 39, No. 5, May 1996, accessed at http://greenwood.cr.usgs.gov/World Energy/GSmaps on 8 August 2004.

6   7   J W Clark, "Observation on the Geology of Azerbaijan" <u>International Geology Review-35</u>; 1993, pp.230-231.

6   8   Ibid, p.32.

6   9   Energy Information Administration; <u>Annual Energy Review;</u> 1995(US Department of Energy) p.10

7   0   Talwani & Belopolsky, op cit p.15

7   1   Ibid, pp 16-17

7   2   Ibid, p.23

7   3   Modern 'Mary'. In the course of history, Merv had different names. Some called it Marw-al-Rud. Arabs and Armenians called it 'Mervirot' and Mrot respectively. In some accounts its names also appear as Margh and Marw-al-Shahidjan

(see Encyclopedia of Islam, New Edition, under 'Marw' p.614 and Encyclopedia Britannica, Vol vii, p.44)

7   4   "Amu Darya Liquid Potentials Indicated": <u>Oil and Gas Journal</u>, June 1991, pp106-108 and Talwani & Belopolsky, op cit p.25

7   5   Statistics taken from Wood Mackenzie's: <u>Oil and Gas Journal</u>; 1998 and Talwani & Belopolsky, op cit, pp. 27-28

7   6   See later that other current studies place the Caspian Region oil reserves at 4-5% of the world total.

7   7   Ziegler, op cit, p 4.

7   8   "The Caspian Sea Region",. <u>Country Analysis Brief</u>, EIA, US Energy Department, (eia.doe.gov) December2004

7   9   Ibid

8   0   The argument is based on the projected Tables and Figures in the Text.

8   1   Carol R. Saivetz, "Caspian Geopolitics: The View from Moscow: <u>The Brown Journal of World Affairs</u>; Summer/Fall 2000-Vol. VII, Issue 2, p.56 and also see 'Turkmenistan' <u>Country Analysis Brief</u>, (US Department of Energy: www.eia.doe.gov) December 2004

8   2   'Uzbekistan' <u>Country Analysis Brief</u>, (US Department of Energy: www.eia.doe.gov) December 2004

8   3   The argument is based on the projected Tables and Figures in the Text. Tables and Figures Sources have been indicated on them or in the text if their sponsor did not permit any addition or deletion on them.

8   4   Ibid.

8   5   Ibid

8   6   "Statistical Review of World Energy 2005'; Annual Report; (British Petroleum Company) June 2005.(www.bp.com/statisticalreview).

8   7   The argument is based on the projected Tables and Figures in the Text. Tables and Figures Sources have been indicated on them or in the text if their sponsor does not permit any addition or deletion on them. Tables9-20, Appendix-2 are based on BP Review, ibid.

8   8   Ibid. See that the 'World Oil' and 'Oil and Gas Journal' figures as on Table 8 have been brought in discussion where necessary.

8   9   Ibid.

9   0   Ibid.

9   1   Ibid.

289

Chapter III: Hydrocarbon and Pipeline Politics

9   2   Dieter Farwick, "Globalized Geopolitics in 21st Century" WSN
News Letter, (World Security Foundation, New York: www.worldsecuritynetwork.com)
24 August 2005.

9   3   Yergin, op cit p.554

9   4   Randolph S. Churchill: Winston S. Churchill; Vol 2 (London
Heinemann, 1968), p.529

9   5   Yergin, op cit, p.13

9   6   Ibid, p.484

9   7   Ibid, p.772

9   8   Ross McCluney, "Population Energy and Economic Growth: The
Moral Dilemma" in Andrew Mckillop & Shiela Newman (Eds): The Final Energy Crisis;
(Pluto Press, London-2005), p.177

9   9   Nicholas Awde, "Introduction", in Wright, Goldenberg &
Schofield (Eds): Transcaucasus Boundaries; (UCL Press Ltd, London-1996) p. 5-6

1   01   Martha Brill Olcott, Central Asia's Second Chance, (Carnegie
Endowment for International Peace, Washington DC, 2005), pp. 57-58.

1   02   Gregory Gleason, "Upstream Downstream: The Difficulties of
Central Asian Water and Energy Swaps," Eurasianet.org February 6, 2003

1   03   Frank Vivian, "Perilous Lifelines to West: Conflict-Ridden
Caspian Basin is the World's Next Persian Gulf," San Francisco Chronicle, August 10,
1998. P.11

1   04   Arundhati Roy. "Most Cowardly War in History," The Nation
(Pakistan), 9 July 2005, p.10

1   05   Theodore Jonas, "Caspian Sea Legal Status", Azerbaijan Oil and
Gas; 2001(United States-Azerbaijan Chamber of Commerce,
http://users.javanet.com/users/azerbaijan)

1   06   Christopher Pala, "Russian Caspian View Violates Law in Eyes of
Kazakhstan's Minister", Platt's Oil gram News, 22 November 1994, P. 5.

1   07   'Turkmenistan' Country Analysis Brief, (US Energy Information
Administration www.eia.doe.gov) December 2004.

1   08   Paola Ceragioli and Maurizio Martellini, "The Geopolitics of
Pipelines," Asian Times: (www.atimes.com) 29 May 2003

1   09   Charles Coe, "Sea's Legal Status Remains beyond Grasp of
Caspian Leaders," News and Trends Central Asia; Vol. 7. No: 10, 16 May 2002.

1   10   Andrew Mckillop, "Oh Kyoto", The Final Energy Crisis; (UCL
Press Ltd London, 2005) p.139

1   11   'Caspian Sea Region: <u>Country Analysis Brief</u>, (US Energy Information Administration) **www.eia.doe.gov**^{) December 2004.}

1   12   Ibid

1   13   Dick Cheney, "Defending Liberty in Global Economy," (Speech) Cato Institute, 23 June 1998

1   14   Rosemarie Forsythe, "<u>The Politics of Oil in Caucasus and Central Asia</u>", (Oxford University Press Inc, New York, 1996), p.6

1   15   Dr. Svante Cornell, "The Caucasian Conundrum and the Geopolitics of Conflict," <u>Marco Polo Magazine</u>, No. 4. May 2000, p.27

1   16   Brig (Retd) Dr. Muhammad Aslam Khan, "NATO's Expansion: Prospects and Pitfalls", <u>Central Asia</u>, No.55 Winter 2004(Area Study Center, University of Peshawar) p.205

1   17   Olcott, op cit, p.94

1   18   Timothy L. Thomas, "Russian National Interest and the Caspian Sea," <u>Perceptions</u>; December 1999-February 2000, Vol. IV, No. 4, pp. 75-96.

1   19   "Links-Oil Companies Links A-Z", <u>Energy 365</u>, 22 August 2004.

1   20   Willy Olsen, "The Role of Oil in the Development of Azerbaijan", in Shirin Akiner (Ed): <u>The Caspian: Politics, Energy and Security</u>; (Routledge Curzon, London, New York, 2004) p.128-130

1   21   Vice President Chevron Petroleum Inc. Mr. E.P. Price's speech to World Affairs Council of Orange City, County Irvine, California, 9 August 1994.

1   22   Table 9 and Table 10 refer.

1   23   'Caspian Region Pipelines' <u>Country Analysis Brief</u>, (US Energy Information Administration: **www.eia.doe.gov**^{) December 2004.}

1   24   These are mainly BP 30.1%, SOCAR 25%, Chevron Texaco 8,9%Statoi l8.7%, TPAO 6.5%, Eni/Agip 5%, Itochu 3.4%, ConocoPhillips 2.5%, Inpex 2.5% and Amerada Hess/Delta 2.4%

1   25   'Azerbaijan' <u>Country Analysis Brief</u>, (US Energy Information Administration: **www.eia.doe.gov**^{) December 2004.}

1   26   'Kazakhstan' <u>Country Analysis Brief</u>, (US Energy Information Administration: **www.eia.doe.gov**^{) December 2004.}

1   27   Full Text of ILSA available as Appendix-3.

1   28   Paola Ceragioli and Maurizio Martellini, "The Geopolitics of Pipelines," <u>Asia Times</u>: 29 May 2003 (www.atimes.com), p.4

1   29   In an exclusive query raised to Michael Cohen of Energy Information Administration, US Department Of Energy, on 8 October 2005, as to why US maps were still showing BTC as projected/ incomplete after its inauguration on 25 May 2005, he asserted that BTC status to 'completed' would take effect from December

2005 when it starts operating commercially. It also points to certain apprehensions that BTC consortium is finding it difficult to fully charge the BTC to its operational capacity.

1   30   He is chairperson of the Central Asia-Caucasus Institute and Silk Road Studies programme ex Joint Transatlantic Research and Policy Center. Also a professor at John Hopkins University, Washington DC

1   31   S. Fredrick Starr and Svante E Cornell, (eds), "The Baku-Tbilisi–Ceyhan Pipeline: Oil Window to the West"; (John Hopkins University, Washington DC – 2005) pp 9-13.

1   32   "Pipeline Poker", The Economist, 7 February 1998 p.8

1   33   The argument is based on pipelines orientation, their capacities and oil and gas table.

1   34   Hugh Pope, "US Plays High Stakes War Game in Kazakhstan", The Wall Street Journal, 16 September 1997, p. A16

1   35   James P. Dorian, "China and Central Asia's Volatile Mix: Energy, Trade and Ethnic Relations," East-West Center No. 31 May 1997, p.5

1   36   Previous oil and gas statistics, pipelines orientation and regional geopolitics in the preceding pages/chapters make the basis of the argument.

1   37   Jyoti Malhotra, "From Border Conflict to Oil Rivalry", The News (Pakistan), 10 September 2005, p.7

1   38   Dr Azmat Hayat Khan, "The Game of Oil and Security in Central Eurasia", Central Asia. No. 52, Summer 2003(Area Study Center, University of Peshawar) p.83

Chapter IV: Geo-Strategic Dimensions of the New Great Game

1   39   Wikipedia: The Free Encyclopedia (http://en.wikipedia.org/wiki/Geostrategy), 24 September 2004

1   40   "Spectrum of Strategy", Handbook of 1992 Armed Forces War Course; (National Defense College, Rawalpindi) pp.17-18

1   41   Mackinder's famous dictum, which he read out in his lecture, "Who rules East Europe, commands the heartland. Who rules heartland, commands the world island. Who rules the world island, commands the world." See H.J. Mackinder, "The Geographical Pivots of History" Geographical Journal Vol. 23 No. 4, 1904, pp 421-444

1   42   List of strategic places is at Appendix 4.

1   43   Dr. Muhammad Anwar Khan, "Age of Imperialism", <u>Central</u>
<u>Asia</u>. No.52, Summer 2003, Journal of Area Study Center (University of Peshawar,
2003), p.1. For his reference to 'Masterly Inactivity' please see his: <u>England, Russia and</u>
<u>Central Asia (A Study in Diplomacy), 1857-1878,</u> (University Book Agency Khyber
Bazaar Peshawar, 1962) p.64 and p.23 for 'Great Game' acronym.

1   44   Lynn Montross, "<u>War Through the Ages,</u>" (Happer & Row: New
York, Evanston, and London, 1986), p.407

1   45   Dr Jennifer Siegel,: <u>End Game: Britain, Russia and the Final</u>
<u>Struggle for Central Asia;</u> (IB Taurus Publishers, London, New York, 2002), pp.15, 20.

1   46   Wikipedia, op cit

1   47   Patrick O' Sullivan and Jesse W. Miller, "<u>The Geography of</u>
<u>Warfare,</u>" (Croom Helm Ltd London, Canberra, 1983), p.10

1   48   Amy Myers Jaffe and Robert A Manning, "The Myth of Caspian
Great Game: The Real Geopolitics of Energy," <u>Survival,</u> Winter1998-1999(Council of
Foreign Relations, US: (www.treemedia.com/cfrlibrary/library), 25
September 2003.

1   49   Henry Kissinger, "<u>Diplomacy</u>", (Simon & Schuster Ltd, London
1994), pp.810-813.

1   50   Noam Chomsky, "<u>Towards a New Cold War</u>', (The New Press,
New York, 2003), p.xiv

1   51   Zbigniew Brzezinski: <u>The Grand Chessboard: American Primacy</u>
<u>and its Geo-Strategic Imperatives,</u> (New York Basic Books: 1997) p.53

1   52   Ibid, P.125

1   53   Lutz Kleveman, "<u>The New Great Game: Blood and Oil in Central</u>
<u>Asia"</u> (Grove Press, New York, 2003); p.3

1   54   Brzezinski, op cit, p.40

1   55   Ibid; p.55

1   56   Michael C.Ruppert,"<u>A War in the Planning for Four Years: How</u>
<u>Stupid They Think We Are"</u> (From the Wilderness Publications,
www.fromthewilderness.com) 23 August 2003.

1   57   Chomsky, op cit, p.203.

1   58   Colin J. Campbell, "The Caspian Chimera" in Mckillop & Sheila
(Eds); <u>The Final Energy Crisis;</u> (Pluto Press London. 2005) p.98

1   59   Ahmad Rashid, "<u>Jihad: Rise of Militant Islam in Central Asia,</u>"
(Vanguard Books Pvt Ltd Pakistan and Yale University Press USA-2002), p.189

1   60   Eric Herring, "<u>Danger and Opportunity: Explaining International</u>
<u>Crisis Outcomes,</u>" (Manchester University Press, Manchester and New York, 1995), p.37

1   61   The issue about Israel is extremely controversial, out of the book purview and hence would not be dilated upon.

1   62   Paul Roberts, "The End of Oil: The Decline of Petroleum Economy and the Rise of New Energy Order," (Bloomsbury London-2004), p.10

1   63   Jay Hanson, "The End of Fossil Fuels," (Die off. Org) 8 March 2003

1   64   Though Thomas Hardy was stalked by social worries while he lived in era (1840-1928) when oil market could be a problem but never the oil, which was in abundance. In his masterpiece novel, Tess of the D, Urbervilles, there is usually a mention about galloping horse carriages and the hydrocarbon based twinkling lamps. Nowhere the gasoline guzzlers were in sight as of today. The life then was simple and environments scenic while Thomas Hardy never fell short of some beautiful expressions to confine them in his touchingly romantic prose.

1   65   Roberts, op cit, p.54

1   66   Richard C Duncan and Walter Youngquist, "OPEC Oil Pricing and Independent Oil Producers," (Presentation at PTTC Workshop, Petroleum Technology Transfer Council, Petroleum Engineering Programme, University of South California, Los Angeles, California-1998), p.5

1   67   Some abbreviations used in the table mean following: -

Petroleum and oil are used synonymously
NGL means Natural Gas Liquids
EUR denotes Expected Ultimate Recovery.
FSU means Former Soviet Union
QI means cumulative production of year
RR stands for Remaining Reserve
G means billions = (10) 9 and 'bbl' means barrel.

1   68   Neela Banerjee, "For Exxon Mobil Size is a Strength and a Weakness", New York Times, March 4, 2003.

1   69   James Picerno, "If We Really Have the Oil", Wealth Manager Magazine, (www.wealth.bloomburg.com) September 2002.

1   70   The depletion and sustainability through substitutes (a remote option) is a vast study that could stretch to several volumes and hence only crucial aspects would be highlighted to stay on the track.

1   71   Albert A.Barlett, "An Analysis of US and World Oil Production in Patterns Using Hubert Style Curves," Mathematical Geology, Vol.32. No.1, 2000(Department of Physics, University of Colorado, Boulder, Colorado, USA), pp 1-16.

1   72   Howard T Odum," Energy and Environmental Decision Making," Wiley; 1996

294

| 1 | 73 | Hanson op cit p.17 |

1   74   "International Energy Outlook 2005", US Department of Energy Report, July 2005 (eia.doe.gov.com)

1   75   Van Dyke, "Oil Production: West Africa May Overtake Saudi Arabia", Vanguard, Lagos, 23 November 2002. Mr. Van Dyke is the president of Van Co. Energy Corporation.

1   76   Roberts, op cit, p.96

1   77   The ensuing argument is based on the statistics, figures and sources projected in the preceding pages/chapters.

1   78   During his visit to Israel, Richard Nixon virtually gestured to gun down Israeli cabinet in June 1974 with imaginary machine-gun in hand, making Chicago style 'burr' sound. At another occasion, he told Hafiz-al-Asad (Syria) that Israelis should be pushed back until they fell off the cliff, making chopping actions with hand: (see for example Yergin op cit p.632)

1   79   Roberts, op cit, p.2566

1   80   Mckillop and Newman; op cit, p.106

1   81   Brzezinski, op cit, p.96. Earlier in 1973, Joachim C. Fest used the term 'phantasmagoria' in his book 'Hitler'.

1   82   Ibid, op cit. p.90

1   83   Michael T Klare, "Blood and Oil: The Dangers and Consequences of America's Growing Dependency on Imported Petroleum," (Henry Holt and Company New York-2004), pp 126-127

1   84   Richard Skolosky and Tanya Paley: NATO and Caspian Security: A Mission too Far" (The Rand Corporation, Santa Monica California-USA, 1999) p.9

1   85   White House Press Office Statement on 1 August 1997; on the eve of visit of the President of Azerbaijan (library.whitehouse.gov/archive)

1   86   Roberts, op cit, pp 251-252.

1   87   US Department of State, "Congressional Budget Justification; Foreign Operation, Fiscal Year-2005 (report) pp.322-370

1   88   Defense Secretary, Donald Rumsfeld remarks during joint press conference with Kazakhstan Defense Minister on 25 February 2004. (www.defenselink.gov) 10 April 2004.

1   89   Skolosky and Paley, op cit, p.7

1   90   Dr. Azmat Hayat Khan, "Oil and Security in Central Asia and the Caspian Region," Central Asia Journal No.50." Summer 2002 (Area Study Center, University of Peshawar); p.10

1   91   Yergeny Bendersky, "Russia in SCO," Power and Interest News Report; PINR."(www.pinr.com), 3 November 2005

1   92   Adam Wolfe, "The Great Game Heats up in Central Asia, "Power and Interest News Report: PINR; (www.pinr.com) 3 August 2005

Chapter V: Actors Roles and Ambitions

1   93   Stephen Sestanovich's Testimony before House International Relations Committee, 30 April 1998. Stephen Sestanovich was ambassador to CIS.

1   94   Douglas Blum, "The Sustainable Development and the New Oil Boom: Comparative
and Competitive Outcome in the Caspian Sea", Working Paper Series No. 4, (Harvard University), 1997" p.21.

1   95   Steve Levine, "High Stakes"; Newsweek, 17 April 1995, p.10

1   96   Carter Page, "US Involvement in the Business and Politics of the Caspian Sea Region", in Shirin Akiner(ed): The Caspian: Politics, Energy and Security, (Routledge Curzon, Taylor & Francis Group, Oxford shire-London, 2004) p.274

1   97   Kaleem Omar, "Concerning America's Deadly Role as Global Oil Police", The News (Pakistan), 4 September 2005, p.7

1   98   William Blum is the author of a book 'Rogue State' who claims to cover US covert crimes against humanity.

1   99   Stephen J Blank, "The United States: Washington's New Frontier in the TransCaspian," in Michael p. Croissant and Bulent Aras (eds), "Oil and Geopolitics in Caspian Sea Region; (Pager, Westport, Connecticut, London-1999) p. 255

2   00   Ibid, p.258.

2   01   Michael Mandelbaum, "The Caspian Region in Twenty First Century" in Robert Ebel, Rajan Menon (Eds): Energy and Conflicts in Central Asia and Caucasus: (Rowman & Littlefield Publishers, Inc, 2000). P.27

2   02   Kleveman, op cit, p.259. Also see William Endghal comments in his essay, "Central Asia, Washington and Beijing Energy Goe-politics," Open Caucasus Forum, www.globalresearch.ca/index, December19 2005. The author has reported the inauguration of KCP on 15 December 2005 with capacity to pump 200,000 bbl/d to China. Since Kazakhstan can only muster 100,000 bbl/d, Russia is likely to export 100,000 bbl/d through this pipeline. According to the author it presents a serious set back to the Western camp, particularly the USA.

2   03   "Caspian Oil: Not the Great Game Revisited," Strategic Survey 1997/98 (International Institute for Strategic Studies; London 1998) p p.22-29.

2   04   John W R Leppingwell, "The Russian Military and Security Policy in the Near Abroad," Survival. Vol.36 No.3 Autumn 1994, p.77.

2   05   Akiner, op cit. p.244

2   06   Jean Christopher Peuch, "Private and National Interests in Caspian Region," in Bulent Gokay (Ed): The Politics of Caspian Oil: (Pal grave Publishers Ltd.2001), p.170

2   07   Skolosky and Paley, op cit, p.31

2   08   Mehdi Parvizi Amineh: Towards the Control of Oil Resources in the Caspian Region; (St. Martin's Press, New York-1999), p.87

2   09   Andrei Shoumikhin, "Russia Developing Cooperation on the Caspian", in Michael P Croissant & Bulent Aras: Oil and Geopolitics in Caspian Sea Region' (Praeger, Westport, Connecticut-London-1999), pp.136-137

2   10   Brzezinski, op cit, p.148

2   11   The argument is based on the statistics and sources of geopolitics covered in the preceding text.

2   12   Kleveman, op cit, p. 114

2   13   Klare, op cit, p.168

2   14   Skolosky and Paley, op cit, p.37.

2   15   Amineh, op cit, p.127

2   16   Brzezinski, op cit, pp.138-139.

2   17   A Khodakov, "Legal Framework for Cooperation in the Caspian Sea," CACR, Vol. 4 No.10, Summer 1995, p.150.

2   18   Suha Bolukbasi, "Jockeying For Power in the Caspian Basin," in Shirin Akiner (ed) The Caspian Politics, Energy and Security: (Routledge Curzon, Taylor& Francis Group: London and Newyork-2004), p.220

2   19   Amineh, op cit, p.113

2   20   Kleveman, op cit, p. 121

2   21   Skolosky and Paley, op cit, p.47

2   22   Fred Halliday, "Condemned to React, Unable to Influence" in John F. R. Wright, Suzanne Goldenberg & Richard Schofield (Eds); Transcaucasian Boundaries, (UCL Press-1996), p.71

2   23   Brzezinski, op cit, P.140

2   24   These are Syria, Iran, Iraq, Greece, Armenia, Azerbaijan, Georgia and Bulgaria .Turkey's relations remain strained with first five for one reason or another.

2   25   William Hale," Turkey, the Black Sea and Transcaucasia," in John FR Wright, Suzanne Goldenberg and Richard Schofield (eds): Transcaucasian Boundaries, (UCL press -1996) P.55

2   26   Skolosky and Paley, op cit, PP. 42 - 43

2   27   Zeyno Baran, "The Baku –Tbillisi-Ceyhan Pipeline: Implication for Turkey "in S. Frederick Starr and Svante Cornell (Eds): Baku-Tbilisi-Ceyhan Pipeline, Oil Window to the West, (Uppsala University Press, Sweden, 2005) p.108

2   28   Jyoti Malhotra, "From Border Conflict to Oil Rivalry", The News (Pakistan), 10 September 2005, p.7

2   29   The discussion is based on the statistics and sources of geopolitics covered so far.

2   30   Skolosky and Paley, op cit, P.48

2   31   Akiner, op cit, p.391

2   32   These are Australia, Brunei, China, India, Indonesia, Malaysia, Thailand and Vietnam

2   33   Tariq Usman Haider," Central Asia and Pakistan" in K M Asaf and Abdul Barakat: Central Asia: Internal and External Dynamics (Pan Graphics (pvt) ltd Islamabad, 1997) p.117

2   34   Skolosky and Paley, op cit, P.49

2   35   Amineh, op cit, P.131

2   36   Chomsky, op cit, p. 21

2   37   'Treaty Establishing a Constitution for Europe": EUR-LEX; Official Journal of the European Union, Vol. 47, 16 December 2004.

2   38   European Council Presidency Conclusion on Energy, Brussels: European Neighborhood Watch, Issue No. 17, June 2006, pp. 11-16

2   39   The argument is based on the sources of previous text.

2   40   Jane Mayer, "Contract Sports," New Yorker, 16 and 23 February 2004, Pp.80-91

Chapter-VI: Conclusions

2   41   Sheila N Heslin,"Key Constraints to Caspian Pipeline Development: Status, Significance and Outlook," (James A Baker- Public Policy Paper: Caspian Sea Library, www.eia.doe.gov) 8 February 2004, P.1

2   42   Marcin Kaczmarski, "Russia Creates a New Security System to Replace CIS," PINR, www.pinr.com, 21 December 2005

2   43   Cited in Genrikh A. Tofimenko, "The Central Asian Region: US Problem with Oil and Gas Exports," Moscow, Ssha (in Russian) No. 11, November 1998

2   44   A legendary Roman General who is believed to have never lost any battle.

2   45   Akiner, op cit, P. 370

298

2   46   'Blat' has no proper equivalent in English to describe its essence. It denotes the tradition of exchanging 'gifts' as a part of culture, which was not considered shameful even in lower hierarchy of the Soviets. (See for example, Ibid, p.375)

2   47   Alec Rasizade, "Azerbaijan and the Oil Trade: Prospects and Pitfalls," Brown Review of World Affairs, Vol IV, No.2, Fall 1997. Pp 277-278

2   48   Zhao Huasheng, "China, Russia and the United States: Prospects for Cooperation in Central Asia," CEF (Quarterly), The Journal of the China-Eurasia Forum, February 2003, p.35

2   49   Ibid, p.37

2   50   Klare, op cit, P.156

2   51   Energy Information Administration, US Department of Energy (www.eia.doe.gov) 10 Dec 2003

2   52   Klare, Op cit, P.205

2   53   See for example, some book titles of eminent writers on this subject like Lutz Kleveman and Michael Klare have not missed the word 'blood' along with 'oil'.

Chapter VII: Recommending A Synopsized Way-Out Strategy

2   54   Anthony Mcgrew, "Globalization and Global Politics", in John Baylis and Steve Smith (Eds): The Globalization of World Politics; (Oxford University Press Inc, New York, 2006), p.19

2   55   Smith and Baylis, op cit, pp12-13

2   56   Robert M. Cutler, "Comparative Energy Security in the Caspian Region: A New Paradigm for Sustainable Development?" Global Governance, 15 no. 2 (April-June, 1999), pp.251-252

2   57   Klare, op cit, p.183

2   58   Mckillop, op cit, p.148

LIST OF ILLUSTRATIONS

Figure

Map

ABBREVIATIONS

ACG: Azeri, Chiragh, Guneshli (oil fields)

AIOC: Azerbaijan International Operating Company or Consortium

ASP: Atyrau-Samara Pipeline

ASSR: Autonomous Soviet Socialist Republic

bbl: barrels

Bcm or bcm: billion cubic meters

Bcf/bcf: billion cubic feet

BTC: Baku-Tbillisi-Ceyhan

BTE: Baku-Tbillisi-Erzurum (a substitute name for SCP)

CARs: Central Asian Republics

Cent Gas: Central Asian Gas (Pipeline)

CENTCOM: Central Command

CIS: Common Wealth of Independent States

CNPC: China National Petroleum Corporation

CPC: Caspian Pipeline Consortium (Project)

CSTO: Collective Security Treaty Organization

DOE: Department of Energy

ECO: Economic Cooperation Organization

EEZ: Exclusive Economic Zone

EIA: Energy Information Administration.

EUCOM: European Command

EUR: Expected Ultimate Recovery

FDI: Foreign Direct Investment

FSU: Former Soviet Union

Gb: billion barrels

GUUAM: Georgia, Ukraine, Uzbekistan, Azerbaijan and
Moldova (Alliance)

IAEA: International Atomic Energy Agency.

IEA: International Energy Agency.

ILSA: Iran-Libya Sanctions Act

INOGATE: Interstate Oil and Gas Transport to Europe

KCGP: Kazakhstan China Gas Pipeline

KCP: Kazakhstan China Pipeline

KKK: Kurpezhe-Kurt Kui (pipeline)

Km or km: Kilometer(s)

Makni: Muhammad Aslam Khan Niazi

M or m: meter(s)

Mt: Million Tonne(s)

NATO: North Atlantic Treaty Organization

NGOs: Non-Governmental Organizations

NM: Nautical Mile(s).

OKIOC: Off- Shore Kazakhstan International Operating
Company

ONGC: Oil and Natural Gas Corporation (India)

OPEC: Organization of Petroleum Exporting Countries

OSCE: Organization of Security and Cooperation in
Europe

p or pp: page or pages

PFP: Partnership for Peace

P-A: Platform-Alpha

PSA: Production Sharing Agreement

Q: Cumulative Production of a Year

RR: Remaining Reserves

SCO: Shanghai Cooperation Organization

SCP: South Caucasus Pipeline

SOCAR: State Oil Company of Azerbaijan Republic

Sq km: square kilometer(s)

SSR: Soviet Socialist Republic

TAP: Turkmenistan-Afghanistan-Pakistan (Pipeline)

Tcf or tcf: trillion cubic feet

TCGP: Trans-Caspian Gas Pipeline

Tcm or tcm: trillion cubic meters

TCOP: Trans-Caspian Oil Pipeline

TNCs: Transnational Corporations

TNOCs: Trans National Oil Companies

TPAO: Turkish National Oil Company

TRACECA: Transport Corridor Europe-Caucasus-Asia

UAE: United Arab Emirates

UNCLOS: UN Convention on Law of Seas

USCENTCOM: US Central Command

USDOE: United States Department of Energy

USEUCOM: US European Command

USG: United States Government

WMDs: Weapons of Mass Destruction

WTC: World Trade Center

WW- I or WW-II: World War-I or World War-II

ACKNOWLEDGEMENTS

Research is an arduous job and needs vast reservoir of patience that I undertook in June 2002, adding and deleting the contents until modifying my PhD dissertation to a book form that generally reflects the time frame up to year 2005.

I am grateful to Dr. Azmat Hayat Khan, Director Area Study Center, University of Peshawar, for his wholehearted cooperation and ever willingness to even import latest books on the subject. My sincere thanks are due to Dr. Muhammad Anwar Khan, ex Vice Chancellor, University of Peshawar, for his guidance and Professor Albert A. Bartlett, University of Colorado, USA, who, in response to my queries, sent me a pack of relevant material by post that lent additional clarity to my thoughts. Extraordinarily updated maps and statistics inclusion became possible through tremendous cooperation extended to me by Michael Cohen of Energy Information Administration of US Department of Energy. I am extremely indebted to him. Invaluably objective comments rendered by Dr. Artem Rudnitsky, Deputy Rector Diplomatic Academy, Moscow and Natalia Melekhina, State Institute of International Relations, Moscow were a source of tremendous help.

My script emerged presentable due to meticulous typing effort pooled in by my wife, daughters, Hirra Khan, Sara Khan and son, Abdul Mujeeb Khan. All of them, over and above their own taxing academic schedule, kept me in good pace by converting my scribbled material promptly to a neat and accurate draft. My other sons and daughter; Captain Abdul Muqeet Khan, Dr. Abdul Haseeb Khan and Dr. Javyria Khan remained a great source of strength who maintained keen watch on my progress while monitoring from distant locations. Their joyful encouraging expressions let my hope glimmer even brightly.

My gratitude offering would remain deficient if I do not acknowledge the professional effort put in by my publisher, Mr. Adam Salviani. I owe him sincere compliments.

Finally, inadequacies in style, expression and contents that are obviously exclusively mine, if encroaching upon sensibilities of any person, organization or state may be forgiven for the sake of my quest for truthful approach to the book substance. I acknowledge that being a human being, I am likely to err.

May God bless us all.

Dr. Makni

December 2007

Pakistan

ABOUT THE AUTHOR

Dr. Muhammad Aslam Khan Niazi has about thirty two years of military experience and is from the Regiment of Artillery. A recipient of 'sitara-e-imtiaz', he has served on various command, staff, instructional, administration, operational, research and evaluation appointments during his long career in the Pakistan Army. He holds a first class Master's Degree in International Relations as well as a doctorate in "Central Asian Studies" from the University of Peshawar, Pakistan. He frequently writes for the National and International Media. He is also a member of the WSN International Advisory Board, a project that networks for 'global peace'.

Printed in the United States
R4077700001B/R40777PG115232LVX1B/1}/P